IN SEARCH
OF PARADISE

IN SEARCH
OF PARADISE

*Middle-Class Living
in a Chinese Metropolis*

Li Zhang

CORNELL UNIVERSITY PRESS

Ithaca and London

First published 2010 by Cornell University Press
First printing, Cornell Paperbacks, 2010

Printed in the United States of America

Library of Congress Cataloging-in-Publication Data

Zhang, Li, 1965 May–
   In search of paradise : middle-class living in a Chinese metropolis /
Li Zhang.
      p. cm.
   Includes bibliographical references and index.
   ISBN 978-0-8014-4833-1 (cloth : alk. paper) —
   ISBN 978-0-8014-7562-7 (pbk. : alk. paper)
   1. Housing—China—Kunming Shi.   2. Real estate business—
China—Kunming Shi.   3. Middle class—China—Kunming Shi.
4. Privatization—China—Kunming Shi.   5. Land use—China—
Kunming Shi.   6. City planning—China—Kunming Shi.   7. Kunming
Shi (China)—Geography.   I. Title.
   HD7368.K86Z43   2010
   305.5'5095135—dc22   2009041332

Cornell University Press strives to use environmentally responsible suppliers and materials to the fullest extent possible in the publishing of its books. Such materials include vegetable-based, low-VOC inks and acid-free papers that are recycled, totally chlorine-free, or partly composed of nonwood fibers. For further information, visit our website at www.cornellpress.cornell.edu.

Cloth printing   10 9 8 7 6 5 4 3 2 1
Paperback printing   10 9 8 7 6 5 4

For Emily, Mark, and my father

Contents

Figures

Acknowledgments

This book is the culmination of seven years' research and several field trips to southwest China. Returning to Kunming—my hometown—to study the profound impact of the privatization of home ownership on urban space, class-making, and community governing offered a rare opportunity for me to re-experience the city where I grew up. This book represents my long-term struggle to make sense of the changes and emerging social landscapes brought by post-Mao marketization and commercialization. Overall, it was a rewarding and enlightening process that allowed me to delve deeper into Kunming's social world, a world to which I am still closely connected. At the same time, I was also saddened to see the old cityscape vanishing rapidly and a new uneven geography of urban living transforming the city into a hierarchical space visibly marked by money, power, and consumer desires.

Throughout this process I have accumulated many intellectual and personal debts. Above all, I wish to extend my deepest gratitude and appreciation to the people in Kunming—homeowners, developers, property management staff, migrant home-remodeling workers, domestic workers, and security guards—who welcomed me into their world and generously shared with me their aspirations, fears, longings, and sorrows in their search for a better life. Some of them became long-term friends and let me probe some difficult issues in their private lives. Without their help and cooperation, the ethnographic research this book draws from would not be possible. I thank them for their time, patience, and hospitality from the bottom of my heart.

My fieldwork, research, and writing were made possible by a number of grants, awards, and fellowships: the Wenner-Grenn Foundation for

Anthropological Research, the University of California President's Research Fellowship in the Humanities, UC Davis Chancellor's Fellow Program, and the Faculty Research Grants, the Institute of Governmental Affairs, and the Davis Humanities Institute at the University of California at Davis. I thank them all for the generous financial support. My sabbatical leave also provided a block of precious time during which the main body of the book was drafted.

I have benefited greatly from numerous productive discussions and conversations with the following colleagues, friends, and students: David Bray, Teresa Caldeira, Rob Culp, Deborah Davis, Marisol de la Cadenas, Michael Dutton, James Ferguson, Sara Friedman, Susan Greenhalgh, Erik Harms, Michael Herzfeld, James Holston, You-Tien Hsing, Jennifer Hubbert, Sandra Hyde, Andrew Jones, Suad Joseph, Alan Klima, Matthew Kohrman, Ching Kwan Lee, Xin Liu, Susan Mann, Shannon May, Elizabeth Perry, Rima Praspaliauskiene, Benjamin Read, Roger Rouse, Suzana Sawyer, Bill Skinner, Alan Smart, Carol Smith, Luigi Tomba, James Watson, Rubie Watson, Mayfair Yang, Fulong Wu, Alexei Yurchak, and Yongming Zhou. Their insights, suggestions, critical reading, and provocative questions have challenged me to sharpen my analytical lens at different stages of the writing. In particular, I would like to thank Aihwa Ong, Ann Anagnost, Joe Dumit, and Ralph Litzinger for their careful and astute reading of my introduction and for encouraging me to situate the project in a larger comparative scope beyond China. I enjoyed immensely the many stimulating informal conversations I had with Aihwa and Joe over lunch and coffee, which made the writing process much more pleasant. I am fortunate to have Aihwa as an informal mentor as well as a kind friend. She is never afraid of offering candid and sharp critiques of my work yet at the same time she always believes in my project, offers most engaging comments, and encourages me to ask bold questions. I also wish to thank my student Bascom Guffin for his very helpful reading of and thoughtful editorial assistance for the first draft of this manuscript.

Various parts of the research were presented at the annual meetings of the American Anthropological Association, the Association for Asian Studies, and the Royal Geographic Society Annual Conference. I was also invited to present my work at seminars, workshops, and conferences hosted by Columbia University, College of the Holy Cross, Harvard University, MIT, Princeton University, the University of California at Berkeley, the University of Chicago, the University of Sydney, the University of Wisconsin—Madison, Yale University, and Yunnan University. I very much enjoyed the intellectual exchange with the audiences at these occasions. My initial editor, Peter Wissoker, was extremely attentive, warm, and supportive. I am grateful for his sensible suggestions and unflagging enthusiasm for this project. After Peter left Cornell University Press, I was fortunate to work with another fine editor, Roger Haydon, who patiently guided me through the later phases of the publishing process with confidence. At the press, I also wish to thank Candace Akins for her skillful help in the production stage, and John Raymond for his careful copyediting work. Special thanks also go to the anonymous reviewer, and to Jeff Maskovsky and Hilary Cunningham, who read the manuscript carefully, challenged me with tough questions, and offered most engaging and detailed comments. My revision benefited greatly from their insights and critique, which helped strengthen the manuscript.

EARLIER, slightly different versions of the following chapters were published in these works: a small part of Chapter 1, in 2006, as "Contesting Spatial Modernity in Late Socialist China," *Current Anthropology* 47 (3): 461–84. Chapter 4, in 2008, as "Private Homes, Distinct Lifestyles: Performing a New Middle Class," in *Privatizing China: Socialism from Afar,* edited by Li Zhang and Aihwa Ong, Cornell University Press. Chapter 5, in 2004, as "Forced from Home: Property Rights, Civic Activism, and the Politics of Relocation in China," *Urban Anthropology* 33 (2–4): 247–81.

Calligraphy on page ii courtesy of Professor Zhang Wenxun. All photos were taken by the author.

MY family across the Pacific is an oasis of love, security, and support. While in Kunming my parents nourished me and my daughter with countless wonderful home-prepared meals—a typical way for Chinese parents to express their love. My father, a retired university professor, already in his early eighties, has been keenly interested in my project from the very beginning and played a key role in the initial stage of formulating the research focus. He is a true role model for me. His love, integrity, serenity toward life, and unceasing intellectual vigor will always inspire me to become a better and more complete human being. I also am grateful to my parents and my sister for sharing their *guanxi* networks with me and for introducing me to several friends of theirs who became key informants for this research. My father insisted on accompanying me to two potentially dangerous residential sites where intense conflict between homeowners and the management was taking place.

Finally and most important, I owe a great emotional debt to my husband, Mark Miller, for being always there for me and for his unflagging confidence in me and in every project I have undertaken. His love, kindness, and passion for discovery have sustained me through the years. Our daughter, Emily, who was conceived at the same time this project was first conceived, is a constant source of delight. She has been with me on every field trip I have taken for this research. I cherish her company and especially her bright smiles that have made all the journeys magically enjoyable.

IN SEARCH
OF PARADISE

Introduction

A new revolution in homeownership and living is sweeping through the booming Chinese metropolises. This time the main actors on the social stage are not peasants, migrants, or working-class proletarians but middle-class professionals and entrepreneurs in search of their private paradise in a society dominated by consumerism. No longer seeking happiness and fulfillment through collective sacrifice and socialist ideals, they now hope to create a good life of material comfort and social distinction in the newly constructed gated communities. In less than two decades, China has changed from a predominantly public housing regime to a country with one of the highest private homeownership rates in the world. This is partly reflected in the startling growth of commercialized housing since 1990 as the national sale of new residential buildings has doubled from about twenty-seven million square meters in 1991, during the early stage of housing and real estate reform, to fifty-five million square meters in 2006. The expansion of the real estate industry is striking, with the average number of people employed by the real estate enterprises nearly tripling in just ten years, from 683,000 in 1997 to 1.6 million in 2006.[1]

Spurred on by the real estate boom, the quest for the good life and social distinction by the rising middle classes is profoundly transforming the physical and social landscapes of urban China.[2] This is a paradigm shift in the way urban Chinese live their lives and think about themselves, a dramatic move away from yearning for a social utopia under Maoist socialism and toward building a private paradise in postsocialist times. Yet the privatization of property and urban living has engendered a simultaneous movement of public engagement among homeowners to confront the encroaching power of the developers. This double movement of privatized living and public sphere activism is a distinct feature of the cultural politics of the middle classes in contemporary China.

The expression "private paradise" (*geren de tiantang*) first caught my attention during an informal tour of a private home in Kunming. Xiao Bai, a close friend from high school, knew I was working on a project on housing reform and invited me to visit her friend's family who had just moved into a new gated community. The couple, who lived there with their daughter, ran a successful private travel agency and had recently purchased a four-bedroom condominium in a suburban area where new real estate developments were flourishing. By American standards their home and the residential compound were by no means extraordinary, yet in local people's eyes they were spacious, luxurious, and modern. The gated compound was landscaped with lush trees and colorful flowers. We walked by a meticulously tended lawn and a water fountain in the central garden. As soon as we entered the house Xiao Bai became engrossed in the interior design and the furnishings. The crystal chandelier hanging from the living room ceiling, the soft sofas with creamy colored fabric, the shining marble tiled floor, and other carefully chosen furniture transformed the place into a warm, inviting, and comfortable personal space that was beyond the reach of ordinary Chinese citizens. As we toured each room and praised how wonderful the home was, Xiao Bai surprised me by saying, "this home is just like a private paradise! This is my dream too. Someday I hope I will be able to build and decorate my own miniature paradise—a place that belongs to me and nourishes me." The Chinese phrase *tiantang* ("paradise" or "heaven") does not necessarily carry a religious connotation. It can simply refer to a perfect place of ultimate comfort and satisfaction. Throughout my fieldwork people have also used other words, such as "oasis" (*lüzhou*) and "small palace" (*xiao huanggong*), to describe their ideal living place. Yet the image of private paradise best captures the desires, sentiments, and aspirations of the Chinese new middle classes in their pursuit of the good life and distinction after socialism.

This book is an ethnographic account of the profound spatial, cultural, and political effects of privatizing homeownership and living in Kunming, the capital of Yunnan Province and a thriving metropolis in southwest China. It primarily draws on a total of fifteen months of fieldwork between 2000 and 2007. It is a tale of how the rise of private homeownership is reconfiguring urban space, class subjects, gender, and ways of living in the reform era. This emerging regime of urban living is built on a radical remaking of the spatial, social, and moral order and encompasses several key aspects of the way life is reorganized and made meaningful in postsocialist China—the spatial and architectural form of residence, domestic configuration, the cultural milieu of community, forms of sociality, and the management of these privatized spaces.[3] My account focuses on the transformative role of homeownership, new residential space, and lifestyle practices in shaping middle-class subjects and activism as well as urban governing strategies.

My ethnography addresses a major concern in urban studies from a unique angle. Much has been written about the spread of gated communities and the gentrification of the inner city, and the implications for understanding the politics of race, class, citizenship, and the built environment (see Blakely and Snyder 1997; Caldeira 2000; Davila 2004; Davis 1992; Ley 1996; Low 2004). These writers have explored the intrinsic link between spatial configurations and class dynamics, and demonstrated the detrimental impact of declining public space on the democratic polity and the rights of the poor. Although these studies acknowledge the fragmented and mutating nature of class dynamics, class composition in the societies examined (mostly capitalist) is relatively established. By contrast, my study looks at the *emergent* moment of class-making in a formerly socialist society that had passionately denied the existence of social class in its recent history. It highlights the amorphous, disjointed, and unstable nature of the new Chinese middle classes shaped by this specific historical juncture.

Why focus on housing and regimes of living? Private homeownership is a significant driving force in myriad social changes that are turning China into a global economic and political power. Its effects goes far beyond the economic and material realm because it has altered the way many Chinese live and think about class, status, social space, and selfhood. To grasp how China is evolving, it is essential to understand the mutually constitutive and transformative relationship among three key aspects of the emerging urban regimes of living: spatial form, class-specific subjects, and modes of community governing. The aim of this book is to unravel this complex, dialogic relationship through examining everyday situated practices. A key concept I develop in this book is "the spatialization of class," by which I mean that the production of commodity housing (as it is known in China), gated communities, and private living provides the physical and social ground on which the making of the new middle classes becomes possible. Once spatially dispersed under the *danwei* (work unit) and public housing system, urban Chinese could not easily be identified as different social classes. But today, under the new commercialized housing regime, individuals who have acquired wealth are able to converge in stratified, private residential communities. Such emerging places offer a tangible location for a new class to materialize itself through spatial exclusion, cultural differentiation, and lifestyle practices. The new spatial and social formation has also compelled novel modes of governing that are distinctly different from those of the socialist era. The new approach to community management, which relies heavily on private authorities and modern surveillance technologies, rather than on state agencies or work units, is an integral part of the shift in China's urban governing strategies.

This book is also an exploration of the fraught experiences of urban middle classes shaped by a hybrid form of political economy, which combines market forces, socialist state rule, and neoliberal techniques. This is a process full of tension, contradiction, and fragmentation. On the one hand, Chinese middle-class urbanites desire status recognition, engage in conspicuous consumption, and yearn for privacy, comfort, and exclusivity. They use gates, walls, and other security devices to shield them from the outside world and keep unwanted others away. They invest a considerable amount of money and energy in home remodeling and interior decoration in order to create a private domestic paradise. In so doing, families are turning inward and neighbors remain strangers to one another. On the other hand, facing the encroachments of real estate developers and managers, middle-class homeowners are increasingly compelled to engage in civic activism that pushes them outside of their private oasis into the public sphere. Some take their protests to the streets and public spaces, some seek legal action against the developers (sometimes even local officials) in court, and others utilize the media and the Internet to spread their discontent and organize grassroots collective action. The widespread struggle against what they perceive as exploitative property management companies inevitably disrupts their pursuit of a comfortable life and social harmony. My research sheds light on this double movement (the search for paradise-like living and the search for rights and justice) in order to understand how Chinese middle-class urbanites negotiate the deep-seated tension between their desires for privacy, tranquility, and domestic comfort, and their struggle over property and protection of their rights (*weiquan*). In March 2007, a new national property law, which recognizes the legal status and protection of private property, was enacted for the first time in the history of the People's Republic of China. This historical change enables urban homeowners to become more audacious in fighting for their entitlements and in defending their private paradise.

Locating the "New Middle Classes"

Much attention has been given to the rise of the new middle classes and mass consumer cultures in Asia over the past decade (see Fernandes 2006; Goodman 1999, 2008; Lett 1998; Liechty 2003; Robi 1996). The fascination with the new middle classes is closely tied to the Asian economic miracle (crystallized in the rise of Asia's so-called Four Little Dragons—Hong Kong, Taiwan, South Korea, and Singapore), the subsequent regional financial crisis in the late 1990s, and the incredible growth of the gross domestic product that China and India have sustained. These stunning economic transformations have created the conditions in which a distinct form of social life and culture is taking shape and disrupting the old existing social order. The rise of the new middle classes epitomizes this historical change in the region.

In C. Wright Mills's pioneer study of the new middle classes, *White Collar: The American Middle Classes,* he delineates the conditions and styles of America's new middle classes shaped by the growth of corporations and rapid bureaucratization. For Mills, the white collar worker symbolizes a distinct, expanding social stratum that is "characteristic of twentieth-century existence" (1951, ix). Ezra Vogel was the first scholar to pay close attention to the emerging middle classes in modernizing Asia. In *Japan's New Middle Class: The Salary Man and His Family in a Tokyo Suburb* (1963), he uses occupation as the primary criterion to define an emerging social stratum in a society that has reached a high level of industrialization and urbanization: "The 'old middle-class' (the small independent businessman and landowner) has been declining in power and influence and is gradually being replaced by this 'new middle-class,' the white-collar employees of the large business corporations and government bureaucracies" (1963, 5). Although this clear-cut conceptualization of the new middle class might be appropriate to the unique situation of Japan at that time, it is too limiting for understanding the emerging middle classes in other Asian societies today. In South Korea, China, and India, for example, the so-called new middle class is a complex and unstable social formation consisting of people with diverse occupations and social backgrounds. The historical conditions that produce them also vary. For example, the extent of the rural-urban transition and the way capital and labor move from one place to another are not the same in these different locations. Thus, what links them together is not necessarily a shared structural position—that is, an occupation or relationship to the means of production—or historical condition, but a similar orientation in lifestyles expressed in homeownership, consumerism, and economic liberalism (see Chua 2000; Fernandes 2006; Robi 1996). For this reason, I believe that a practice-centered approach will allow us to better examine how an amorphous social group takes shape despite its internal structural differentiation.

The emergence of the new middle classes in China is fundamentally linked to the post-Mao market reforms and economic liberalization that set the condition for the growth of private businesses and the accumulation of private wealth. The privatization of existing public housing and the rise of "commodity housing" (*shangpin fang*) play a critical role in the expansion of private property ownership. In this context, homeownership has become a decisive factor in the formation of a new propertied social group and a popular indicator of one's economic status. Similar to the situation of South Korea (Lett 1998), China's new middle classes are also largely an urban phenomenon and consist of a relatively small and privileged segment in relation to the total population.[4] Even if we take the high-end estimation of two hundred million people, the middle classes account for less than 16 percent of the total Chinese population, which in 2007 was about 1.3 billion.[5] Yet, the popular image we get from the international media is of a much larger, rapidly growing middle class that will and should expand further through economic development. This problematic representation is driven by a teleological thinking rooted in modernization theory that assumes all nation-states will pass through several stages of production and eventually generate a large, stabilizing middle class as have capitalist societies in the West (see Anagnost 2008).

An Emerging, Fragmented, and Precarious *Jieceng*

The new middle classes in China are referred to as *xinzhongchan jieceng*, which translates as the "new middle propertied strata." Since the end of the Maoist regime, Chinese people have largely avoided the term "class" (*jieji*) in talking about social stratification because this concept was highly politicized and closely related to brutal and violent class struggle that caused much suffering under Mao. It is another term, *jieceng*, that is commonly used to refer to socioeconomic differentiation as it allows one to speak about different socioeconomic locations without resorting to such preformulated, politically charged categories as "capitalists," "proletarians," or "working class." Replacing the language of *jieji* with that of *jieceng* is itself a political act because it is a conscious effort to disengage from the Maoist form of politics that is seen by many as destructive. Yet, some caution that the use of jieceng runs the risk of presenting fundamental socioeconomic inequality as merely a form of cultural difference displayed in tastes and lifestyles (Anagnost 2008). To avoid this pitfall, we must pay attention to the two different aspects of jieceng making: social and cultural positioning, and capital accumulation. Throughout the book, I use the term *jieceng* frequently because it is commonly invoked by the people I studied. My intention is not to displace "class" and "status" altogether, but rather to take advantage of the ambiguity inherent in this notion to challenge the conceptual divide between class and status, production and consumption, the economic and cultural spheres.[6] Recent anthropological studies have demonstrated the centrality of consumption, not just production, in understanding the formation and transformation of class identity in the era of globalization and capitalist restructuring (see Freeman 2000; Miller 1987; Mills 1999; Yao 2006).[7] Building on these insights, my analysis is an attempt to highlight how a new jieceng is formed through the production of private housing as well as the consumption of new residential spaces.

Pierre Bourdieu's treatment of class as a multidimensional space is useful in thinking about *zhongchan jieceng* as shaped by not only the volume but also the composition of economic capital, cultural capital, and social capital (1991). This multifaceted approach allows me to treat the Chinese new middle classes as a dynamic and complex formation. But Bourdieu tended to focus on how social and cultural capital is accumulated and deployed and says little about how economic capital is accumulated. I propose to look at both processes: how people acquire money through entrepreneurial activities and employment and how people strive to accumulate and make sense of what is considered "suitable" cultural and symbolic capital in China.

The new middle classes in China are marked by three distinct characteristics: their moment of emergence, their highly heterogeneous composition, and their heightened sense of insecurity. First, it has long been recognized that class is not a fixed thing but an ongoing process of "happening." As E. P. Thompson succinctly put it, "I do not see class as a 'structure,' nor even as a 'category,' but as something which in fact happens (and can be shown to have happened) in human relationships" (1964, 9). Although one can claim that all class-making is in fact a process of happening, I suggest that what we are witnessing in China today represents a unique moment of *emerging* accompanied by a higher degree of flux and fragmentation due to the absence of a relatively established, identifiable middle class, a situation created by thirty years of socialist rule. As a real estate developer in Kunming points out, "One may be able to see the emergence of social stratification based on people's incomes, but it is still very difficult to speak of any *zhongchan jieceng* because there has not emerged a distinct class culture shared by those who have accumulated material wealth. Class-making after Mao is still in its very early, amorphous stage; this is going to be a very long and confusing process." To grasp this initial moment of emerging, flux, and disorientation, one must take a closer look at everyday processes of class-making and happening in which individuals come to rearticulate their interests and reshape their identity through certain common idioms.

Second, China's *zhongchan jieceng* consists of a highly heterogeneous and fragmented group of people (expressed in the Chinese word *za*). Because of the difficulty in defining it, some Chinese scholars consider this category more of a cultural construct that serves as an aspiration for society.

> In Chinese people's minds, "*zhongchan jieceng*" is more of a cultural concept than a stratification measure of social class....Chinese people have a difficult time defining it, but vaguely see it as consisting of "those who own houses and cars." Youth are particularly envious of the respectable jobs, tasteful lifestyles, and fashionable clothing these people have. They have become the aspiration for many people today. (Shen 2005, 36)

Although I agree that *zhongchan jieceng* lacks a shared structural position and social identity, I do not think that it should be treated merely as a discursive construct. Rather, it is an emerging social stratum that can be identified at this time through homeownership status, consumer practices, and property-based activism. As Luigi Tomba notes, "Although these groups might appear amorphous and lack the cohesiveness required by the traditional definitions of class, they appear increasingly to shape their status around a new set of collective interests, especially in their modes of consumption and access to resources" (2004, 3).[8]

Third, *zhongchan jieceng* is developing a class trajectory yet it remains a precarious social stratum. As Bourdieu points out, "Individuals do not move about in social space in a random way, partly because they are subject to the forces which structure this space. (1984, 110). Although the "field of the possibles" sets the relatively stable social trajectory of a class, the shift from one trajectory to another can take place as a result of collective and individual events. There is a great deal of instability associated with the formation of class trajectories, especially with respect to new social configurations.[9] Barbara Ehrenreich's (1989) and Katherine Newman's (1999) studies of class mobility in the United States demonstrate that the middle classes often occupy an unstable position and are highly sensitive to economic changes. They have a constant fear of falling behind on the social and economic ladder. This sense of insecurity has been exacerbated under global neoliberal marketization in advanced capitalist societies where restructuring has led to the loss of many middle-class jobs and a Keynesian welfare state is no longer the norm. In emergent economies, the fear of falling is even more intensified because the socialist safety nets have been eroded rapidly while the new social welfare system is not yet in place. Economically, private wealth generated by urban professionals, entrepreneurs, and merchants in China often comes from unconventional channels and thus lacks legal protection. Although the national economy has been growing at a fast pace, there is a profound sense of uncertainty about how long the economic miracle will last and where one can put his or her newfound wealth in safekeeping. Yet, this fear can also drive individuals to take bigger risks, such as venturing into the "gray" economy, in order to accumulate more wealth and secure their privileged position. Thus, the fear of falling may serve as a crucial element in creating new risk-taking middle-class subjects in China.

Socially and culturally, the new middle classes also inhabit a highly ambivalent space. In his study of middle-class culture in Nepal, Mark Liechty attributes its contested and fragmented character to what he calls "cultural betweenness"—between high and low, global and local, new and old, "tradition" and "modernity" (2003, 25). Middle-class subjects in Kathmandu must negotiate these diverging forces to produce a social life that is considered "suitably modern." Among American white collar classes, Mills (1951) observed a "status panic" caused by the ambivalence and instability embedded in their claims for prestige. The new middle classes I studied in Kunming are often associated with those who are perceived as economically well-to-do but lacking symbolic capital (such as higher education, manners, and tastes). Their social insecurity is thus partially derived from their hyperawareness of such negative public perceptions. This sense of insecurity drives many of them to seek not only conspicuous material consumption but also excessive investments in cultivating their children's talents and abilities in order to prepare them to become the cultured elites. They hope such cultural capital will eventually lead to the acquisition of a better reputation and respectability. Consumption thus becomes the main conduit to gain cultural and symbolic capital, and the key for claiming and authenticating social status.

Another reason why consumption is particularly important in cultivating and performing jieceng in the reform era is the difficulty in pinpointing the exact sources of personal wealth or gauging one's income by simply looking at his or her occupation during the reform era. During my fieldwork, one of the most difficult issues I encountered was that relatively wealthy people were reluctant to talk about the source of their income or the nature of their businesses. In fact, it is a social taboo among the upper and middle classes to ask how one generates income because many business transactions take place outside the parameters of the law and official rules.[10] If the production of wealth has to be kept secret and intentionally made opaque, then conspicuous material consumption serves as a viable way to assert and maintain one's class status.[11] Yet, what constitutes desirable and suitable capital is a contingent and contested matter. In critiquing Bourdieu's treatment of symbolic capital as largely homogeneous and stable, Anthony Free argues that "the criteria according to which status is recognized are vulnerable to change, rather than a durable capital" (1996, 402). There is the question of social recognition that challenges the objectivity of symbolic capital. As Mills puts it, "Prestige involves at least two persons: one to claim it and another to honor the claim" (1951, 239). This insight is pertinent to the cultural politics of the middle classes in China. As an emergent group without preestablished cultural norms, the recognition of symbolic and cultural capital is highly contested. My ethnography highlights this unsettled and sometimes confusing cultural process of class-making at its budding time.

The "Double Movement" Revisited

A distinctive form of activism among China's new middle classes, which can be termed the "double movement," is emerging: the search for a private paradise and seclusion, and the engagement in public activism to defend their paradise. This dual process is articulated with a broader, inherent tension within an emerging market economy. In his seminal book *The Great Transformation*, Karl Polanyi argues that in modern capitalist societies there exists "a double movement," which is generated by two different organizing principles, namely economic liberalism and social protection: "The market expanded continuously but this movement was met by a countermovement checking the expansion in definite directions. Vital though such a countermovement was for the protection of society, in the last analysis it was incompatible with the self-regulation of the market, and thus with the market system itself" (1944, 136). For him, the commodification of land, labor, and natural resources will inevitably trigger various kinds of societal mobilization to protect the social fabric.

Even though the Chinese reform regime has never formally adopted free market liberalism and the state remains a salient player in orchestrating social and economy life, a similar process of commodification and marketization is taking place. During late and postsocialist primitive accumulation, the miraculous economic growth or capital accumulation is largely made possible by two crucial simultaneous processes: *dispossession* and *devaluation*. The first one involves the dispossession of state and public assets and natural resources through corruption and illegal transfers, the dispossession of factory workers through massive layoffs, and the dispossession of countless working-class families through forced relocation during urban redevelopment. The second one, as Ann Anagnost (forthcoming) demonstrates, involves the devaluation of manual labor in order to subsidize highly skilled labor through the deployment of a value-coding mechanism known as *suzhi,* which denotes the quality of a subject or a population. These acts have engendered several prominent oppositional movements: the rising labor activism among urban workers and migrant laborers (Lee 2007), protests and legal actions of suburban villagers whose farmland is taken by real estate developers (Cai Yongshun 2003; Hsing 2009a), and environmental activism led by nongovernmental organizations (Litzinger 2004; Yang 2005). Most noticeably, sociologist C. K. Lee has offered an insightful analysis of two different forms of labor activism in China's rust-belt and sunbelt as a result of the commodification of labor and changing state legislation (2007). These insurgent forces do not necessarily reject market liberalism altogether, however, nor do they want to restore Maoist collectivism. Rather, they seek to keep market expansion and commodification in check by calling for state legislation, legal protection, and other forms of intervention.

The urban middle classes I studied in Kunming inhabit a highly ambivalent position. On the one hand, they are the very products and beneficiaries of economic liberalization. As such, their consuming power, lifestyles, and dreams of the good life are deeply intertwined with the rise of the market economy and a mass consumer culture. On the other hand, many of them are becoming increasingly vulnerable in a highly unbalanced power relationship vis-à-vis the property developers who now act as a new form of authority beyond the scope of market activities. Their embrace of private property and bourgeois lifestyles thus does not automatically lead them to a total endorsement of neoliberal governance that shifts the responsibility and power to private developers and other commercial entities. Indeed, Kunming homeowners in the new residential developments are frequently locked in battles over communal land use and property management. At the same time, a massive displacement of long-term inner-city residents has taken place since the 1990s due to a new master city plan that prioritizes real estate development in modernizing Kunming. In this context, powerful property developers and management companies have become a new kind of authority in governing and reordering social life. Affected residents have responded with individual and collective actions to confront the unbridled power of corporate developers and called for government intervention or legal protection. In March 2007 a woman in Sichuan Province became a national symbol for such battles against developers. She rejected what she considered to be inadequate compensation from a developer and defied a court order to move. Her small home standing among a vast construction site was both vulnerable and powerful. It was one of the most widely circulated images in the international media that year.

As I will demonstrate in this book, these fragmented countermovements should not be seen as "natural" responses to market expansion or an abstract critique of commodification altogether. Rather, these are situated practices that are produced under specific social and economic conditions with different aims. For example, the self-protection activism among Kunming middle-class homeowners is very different from the resistance to relocation generated among dispossessed inner-city residents. Although both groups make use of the language of property rights, their specific aims are different. The former, involving mostly entrepreneurs, professionals, and cadres, is primarily concerned with problems related to the use of privatized communal space, fees levied on them, and the quality of the services promised by the management. The latter, consisting of mostly lower-income families, fight to secure their place in the city. Although there is a class dimension to their actions, they cannot be reduced to class-driven mobilizations. The nature of their activism is different from that of NIMBYism (not in my backyard) and gentrification conflicts found in most postindustrial capitalist cities of North America and Europe.[12] Kunming homeowners do not oppose public projects that are considered a benefit to the common good yet might affect the character of their community and quality of life; they oppose commercial projects that would simply erase their own community, infringements on collective space by exploitative developers to profit twice over, or property managers who do not deliver promised services. Their activism is derived primarily from a strong sense shared by middle-class homeowners of entitlement to private property, a better neighborhood environment, quality services, and privacy (Read 2008). Researchers have debated the nature of grassroots urban activism associated with gentrification, NIMBYism, and the like. Some tend to characterize such activism as a form of class struggle inscribed on the level of space (for example, Blakely and Snyder 1997; Davis 1992; Neil Smith 1996). Others argue that such neighborhood mobilizations cannot be reduced to class-based movements even though it is important to recognize the impact of class structure on the city (Castells 1984; Ley 1996). My account heeds how local political-economic interests shape the cellular-based community activists in Kunming while showing how such activism can in practice contribute to the emerging class differentiation.

Another contradiction of the new *zhongchan jieceng* I elaborate in this book consists of two parallel processes of middle-class making, namely the politics of exclusion and the politics of aspiration. The new middle classes in China, as in India and Nepal, are seen as a social group that is aspirational. Their privileged lifestyles and distinctive images, produced through the mass media, are portrayed as something attainable because "the heart of the construction of this social group rests on the assumption that other segments of the middle-class and upwardly mobile working class can potentially join it" (Fernandes 2006, xviii). Part of the appeal of the new middle classes is precisely the projected openness and inclusiveness, which allows others to envision themselves living such a life one day. The advertising industry contributes to and profits from such popular aspirations by producing images that appeal to a broad spectrum of consumers. Yet, paradoxically, the social distinction the middle classes enjoy is often produced through exclusionary practices in everyday life. In chapter 3, I provide a detailed account of how spatial exclusion and security systems are implemented and justified in the name of public order and crime prevention in Kunming. These practices reinforce and exacerbate the inequality and tension between social groups. The spatial segregation promoted by protected, private property compounds is becoming a pronounced feature of postreform Chinese cities.

The Spatialization of Class

Postsocialist studies has examined a wide range of important changes in formerly socialist societies that have been reconfigured by capitalism and globalization.[13] Scholars have explored shifting state power and its articulation with society (Humphrey 1991, 2002; Verdery 1996), changing market and property relations (Mandel and Humphrey 2002; Verdery 2004), expanding consumer culture (Barker 1999), labor and gender politics (Dunn 2004; Gal and Kligman 2000), and the politics of popular culture (Ries 1997; Rofel 2007; Yurchak 2006). Few, however, have focused on the making of the middle classes and its relationship to new urban spatial configurations in postsocialist metropolises.[14] I maintain that the politics of class, through the lens of homeownership and spatial reordering, lies at the heart of postsocialist transformations because it brings many critical cultural, political, and social issues together. As scholars have suggested, postsocialist changes are not simply about the privatization of the economy or market liberalization but also about the making of new kinds of persons and class subjects (see Dunn 2004, 5; Rivkin-Fish 2009; Verdery 1996, 135). In her study of the remaking of labor in postsocialist Poland, Elizabeth Dunn shows that the reconfiguration of personhood is deeply embedded in the privatization process, during which Polish workers have been transformed into "privatized individuals" (2004). Michele Rivkin-Fish's recent work provides insights into the critical role of popular memory in the making of new class subjectivities in post-Soviet Russia (2009). While Dunn is largely concerned with the remaking of postsocialist workers and Rivkin-Fish with memory practices, my inquiry explores the making of the Chinese new middle classes through urban professionals and entrepreneurs in search of "the good life" in private paradises. This is a process involving not only the political economy of housing and community production but also the cultivation of new lifestyles, mentalities, dispositions, and aspirations among those who come to inhabit these places.

My approach aims to integrate culture and economy, production and consumption through an analytical notion that I call the "spatialization of class." Today most scholars would agree that class-making takes place not only within the domain of relations of production but also outside of it. Yet, it is still useful to revisit E. P. Thompson's seminal work, *The Making of the English Working Class,* in which he convincingly demonstrates the importance of integrating cultural and economic accounts of class formation. Although his analysis is rooted in the Marxist notion of class conflict, his detailed account of the everyday life of the English working class clearly shows that class is as much cultural as economic and that it occurs in both economic production and social production. Since the 1970s, Marxist feminists and scholars have criticized the way the workplace is treated as the only or primary arena for constituting working-class politics. They have called our attention to other social and cultural domains in which class-making takes place. Building on this strand of analysis, I suggest that one way to illuminate *how* culture and economy, production and consumption are articulated in the course of middle-class making in China is to unravel the complex process of spatial production. Here I conceptualize *production* broadly to include the physical production of housing, community, and cityscape by the real estate industry, as well as the social production by those who come to inhabit such spaces and endow them with meanings. Thus, the "spatialization of class" is at once an economic and cultural process because not only is urban space radically reorganized into a visibly hierarchical and segregated form by recent real estate developments but also new social groups and class subjects are created and made discernible through this spatial production.

My attempt to theorize the connection between spatial politics and class in Kunming draws from Henri Lefebvre's insightful elaboration on the mutually constitutive relationship between spatial production and new social formations in capitalist and socialist societies:

Any "social existence" aspiring or claiming to be "real," but failing to produce its own space, would be a strange entity, a very peculiar kind of abstraction unable to escape from the ideological or even the "cultural" realm. It would fall to the level of folklore and sooner or later disappear altogether, thereby immediately losing its identity, its denomination and its feeble degree of reality. (1991, 53)

As for the class struggle, its role in the production of space is a cardinal one in that this production is performed solely by classes, fractions of classes and groups representative of classes. Today more than ever, the class struggle is inscribed in space. (1991, 55)

The above quotations from *The Production of Space* represent a core argument of Lefebvre that the production of space constitutes a central problem for new social formations. For him, the production of a concrete social and physical space is the realization of a "social existence" that otherwise would remain ideological or cultural. Lefebvre's attention to the critical role of the production of space in class-making broadens our conception of what constitutes "production" beyond narrowly defined economic production. In a similar spirit, David Harvey writes: "We must relate social behaviour to the way in which the city assumes a certain geography, a certain spatial form. We must recognize that once a particular spatial form is created it tends to institutionalize and, in some respects, to determine the future development of social process" (1973, 27). Building on such insights, my research highlights a specific form of spatial production—new housing and community developments, and analyzes its place in the making of the new middle classes in Chinese society.[15] This spatial production affects the political economy of urban restructuring, capital accumulation, new ways of living, and social identification. In this ongoing process, the meaning of being middle class is constantly defined and redefined by a variety of social actors including real estate developers, advertisers, homeowners, and those who are excluded from such spaces.

Another aspect of the spatialization of class is the cultivation of a distinct, localized middle-class "cultural milieu" made possible by the new geography of living.[16] This cultural milieu in China is expressed through two notions: *jieceng wenhua* and *suzhi*. The former consists of taste, judgment, and the acquisition of cultural capital by a social group through housing choices and lifestyle practices. Taste, as reflected in residential choices, has a productive role here in that "it classifies the classifier" (Bourdieu 1984, 6). The latter refers to the quality of a subject or a population. Like habitus (Bourdieu 1977), suzhi is neither idiosyncratic nor completely predetermined by the socioeconomic position of a social group; rather, both suzhi and habitus mediate between the conditions of existence and subjective experiences. They are articulated through specific spatial practices and the embodied practices of individuals while mediating between social practices and the conditions of existence. Ann Anagnost (forthcoming) and Andrew Kipnis (2007) have convincingly shown that the obsession with suzhi in post-Mao public discourses is deeply intertwined with the cultural politics of class and the neoliberal techniques of the self (see also Hsu 2007). My task is to demonstrate how private homeownership and the new regimes of living enable the cultivation of a legible *jieceng wenhua* and suzhi central to middle-class making.

Experiments in Postsocialist Governing

Astonished by the remarkable postsocialist changes, some Western observers and scholars in the early 1990s hastily celebrated newfound personal freedoms and the triumph of free markets. Later scholarship on postsocialist conditions has critiqued this simplistic view by providing more sophisticated accounts of how the state refashions and reinserts itself in social and economic life and how citizens are subject to new forms of disciplinary power and control by private authorities.[17] The situation of China is more complex because it clearly does not fit any teleological narratives of regime change. According to the official discourse, China is still a socialist country, yet enormous transformations centered on privatization and commercialization have deeply reconfigured its economic, social, and cultural practices. There have been important shifts in governing practices despite the continued domination of one-party rule and the official commitment to socialist ideology. Given this unique situation, how can we best conceptualize the current state of being without resorting to rigid periodization or being bogged down by the problem of labeling? In this book, I use the term "late socialism" to loosely refer to the earlier phase of the Chinese reform, and "postsocialism" to signify the later phase of the reform since the shift to the Jiang Zemin leadership in 1993, during which the privatization of state-owned enterprises and property speeded up and deepened. Many China scholars including myself see the 1989 Tiananmen movement and aftermath as a turning point for reform because a number of major policy changes took place around that time.[18] Later, in January 1992, Deng Xiaoping's historic tour of south China and a series of speeches he delivered on the tour firmly secured the path for bolder reform and opening. This juncture should not be treated too rigidly, however, as there have been both continuities and changes taking place over this same period.

During the postsocialist period, the influence of neoliberal strategies in economic, social, and political practices became more obvious even though neoliberalism is never openly acknowledged in the official state ideology. In this study, neoliberalism is not treated as a universal structural arrangement or set of global/national economic policies as Harvey (2005) and Stiglitz (2002) do, but as a "set of calculative practices that articulate diverse political environments in a contingent manner" (Ong and Zhang 2007, 9). Recent anthropological inquiries have drawn our attention to the limits of neoliberalism. Most noticeably, Catherine Kingfisher and Jeff Maskovsky have called for "the need to move beyond abstract and totalizing approaches that treat neoliberalism as a thing that acts in the world" (2008, 115). They urge that scholars focus on the instabilities, partialities, and practices of neoliberalism as a fraught process and how it articulates with other cultural and political-economic formations (see also Clarke 2004). Elsewhere, I have argued (Ong and Zhang 2007) that if we treat neoliberalism as a set of malleable governing technologies and economic practices, then any political regime can adopt and reconfigure such strategies according to its specific social conditions without radically altering its overall state apparatus (see also Ong 2006). In this book, I show how the incorporation of practices relying on the devolution of power, governing from afar, and self-governing has made possible a kind of flexible postsocialism. Thus, Chinese postsocialism, or "socialism with Chinese characteristics" as the Chinese state insists on calling it, is a seemingly bizarre incarnation of socialist authoritarian rule mixed with new governing practices influenced by neoliberal thinking yet reconfigured by local conditions. Giovanni Arrighi has argued that this innovative, hybrid path of gradual change, rather than a full embrace of Western neoliberal doctrines or "shock therapy," is crucial for the "Chinese ascent" in the twenty-first century (2007).

Meanwhile, there is a growing scholarship on the effects of privatization and social change in reform-era China. Most studies, however, focus on the reform of state-owned enterprises, its troubling effects on the urban working class, and the spread of entrepreneurialism and the market sphere. Few studies have provided an in-depth ethnographic account of the transformative role of homeownership in the reconfiguration of urban governing and the formation of new class subjects in contemporary China.[19] This study is the first book-length ethnography to focus on the multilayered effects of the housing revolution in the post-Tiananmen experiments in urban governing. As I will show, the experiments in governing and the shifting power dynamics in Kunming are best articulated in two ways: the privatization of urban authorities, and the shift to governing through community and self.

First, market-driven developers and property management agencies have taken on the role of the government in administering local affairs, keeping social order, and recasting citizens into new kinds of subjects. These agencies are a bricolage of diverse elements: some are still considered state-owned enterprises; some are subsidiaries of district governments within cities; some are wholly private firms with no direct connection to the government. Yet, they all operate very much like private firms or are run according to the private "enterprise model." Because these entities often act as commercial enterprises or service providers, their proxy role in governing is often glossed over by a depoliticized discourse that depicts them as merely profit-making agents.[20] Yet, as I will show, these entities have become a new, vital source of authority in the remaking of Chinese urban subjects and spatial order. In chapter 7, I explore in greater detail from whence these commercialized authorities derive their power, how they attempt to govern, and what problems are entailed in this process. I suggest that it is increasingly difficult or less meaningful to draw a clear distinction between "the state" and "private entities" in thinking about governing. We need to question the conventional binary opposition of the state to the private (or the market), a conceptual formulation derived from the nineteenth-century liberal discourse on political economy in the context of Europe. I thus call for a historically and culturally contingent understanding of the articulation between state and nonstate authorities.

Second, another key experiment in managing new residential spaces is the notion of governing through community and self.[21] This shift does not mean that government is removed from or less concerned with regulating local communities; rather, it suggests a new way of thinking about what counts as effective and practical governing given emerging social conditions under privatization. As Nikolas Rose notes, "In the institution of community, a sector is brought into existence whose vectors and forces can be mobilized, enrolled, deployed in novel programmes and techniques which encourage and harness active practices of self-management and identity construction, of personal ethics and collective allegiances" (1999, 176). As such, communities (*shequ*), new and old, commercially developed and danwei-based, are mobilized by the state to collaborate with developers and commercial property management agencies to maintain order, implement government policies, and solve socioeconomic problems in Chinese cities today (see also Bray 2006; Cho n.d.). But governing through community in the Chinese context takes place in a much narrower sense than what Rose broadly sees as communities of collective allegiance. Here it is the residential community that is the focus of mobilization, during which a dominant form of private real estate authority is thriving.

Governing through community also requires a new kind of desirable citizen who acts as a self-responsible and self-governing subject (Ong and

Zhang 2008; Rose 1999). This involves a fundamental shift in how people think about themselves and how they shape their conduct. Without the recognition of self-possession and self-animation on the part of the subjects, the strategy of governing through community and self would not work. The capability to govern one's conduct in contemporary China is premised on the notion of civility, *wenming,* which was initially promoted by the reform state but is now widespread among the public (see Anagnost 1997). Nikolas Rose calls this new kind of power dynamic the "community-civility game" as "it puts new questions into play about the kinds of people we are, the kinds of problems we face, the kinds of relations of truth and power through which we are governed and through which we should govern ourselves" (1999, 188).

Thus, at the heart of the making of the new middle-class citizens as I observed them in Kunming is the formulation of a new kind of subject who is inspired by a different set of ethics than the socialist ones. Now citizens must learn to "rely on one's self" (*kao ziji*) rather than on the state to make the right choices, generate income, and regulate their own conduct. This peculiar form of self-governing in private communities that has gained popularity in Kunming and other Chinese cities is the implementation of the so-called civility pact (*wenming gongyue*), an agreement on a set of civic principles designed to guide the conduct of residents living in the same residential community (*xiaoqu*). Although it is not a formal legal contract, residents are generally compelled to sign it and conform to the regulations. What makes a civility pact work is not any external or administrative enforcement, but residents' self-awareness and willingness to scrutinize and modify their own conduct. Self-cultivation and self-control is touted as the emblem of the superior suzhi of modern middle-class Chinese citizens.[22]

Fieldwork in a Familiar/Strange Place

This book draws from ethnographic fieldwork I conducted in Kunming, the city where I grew up and have maintained close family ties and social networks. The intense part of the research was carried out during the summers between 2000 and 2006, but my understanding of the city and its changing social life extends far beyond this period. Even though I left for Beijing to study at Peking University in 1983 at the age of eighteen and then came to the United States to pursue my doctoral degree in 1990, I have returned to Kunming every summer over the past two decades.

Located on the Yun-Gui high plateau in southwestern China, Kunming is the capital of Yunnan Province and an ancient city established over one thousand years ago. The estimated population in 2008 was about six million including some three million registered urban residents. Unlike American cities, each major municipality consists of several levels of entities all subject to its control: the main city (*zhucheng*), secondary cities (*cicheng*), counties, and townships. Kunming Municipality, covering about fifteen thousand square kilometers, is composed of the main city, which includes four districts (Wuhua, Panlong, Guandu, and Xishan), and eight counties, some of which are being turned into secondary satellite cities. Of the four districts, Wuhau and Panlong used to be the inner core, marked roughly by the first ring road that replaced the old city walls. This core was where key administrative and commercial activities took place and it also was the most densely populated residential area before the housing reform. Although commercial housing developments have been built throughout the main city, the most aggressive expansion is in Guandu and Xishan— the two out-city districts that were once mostly farmland. Since the early 1990s, these two districts have become the primary sites of commodity housing construction. Due to its proximity to the scenic West Hills and Lake Dian, Xishan District in the west periphery has a high concentration of luxury town houses and villas along the newly widened Dianchi Road. In recent years, several major provincial and municipal government agencies originally housed in the inner core have been relocated to this area. Most strikingly, the northeast part of Guandu District has become now the largest bedroom community (*da woshi*) in the city, forming a second urban center in addition to the original city core that has now expanded to the second ring road.

During the Second Sino-Japanese War (1937–45), Kunming was quickly transformed into a modern industrial and cultural center as many industries, universities, and institutions in northern and eastern China fled the Japanese invasion and relocated to this relatively safe place. The sudden influx of capital, technologies, and talent brought about a short period of growth. But soon after the war ended, these entities and resources returned to their original locations, leaving Kunming's economy and cultural life stranded. For the following decades under socialism, Kunming and the entire Yunnan Province became rather isolated and underdeveloped—a place south of the clouds (what the word "Yunnan" literally means).[23]

Prior to the post-Mao reform, the tobacco and copper-mining industries were the pillars of the local economy. But the reform launched in 1978 quickly brought new opportunities to the region. Although tobacco and copper continue to be a vital part of the provincial economy, tourism, trade, and the service sector have become the new engines for economic growth. An expanded railway system, interregional highways, and improved air transportation now directly link Kunming to other cities in China and Southeast Asia. Further, due to its rich historical heritage and diversity of ethnic cultures, the province attracts millions of domestic and international tourists in search of the exotic "old China."[24] The rise of what has been broadly termed as the "consumer revolution" (Davis 2000) has led to an urban development craze and profound spatial transformations, involving massive demolition of the old and hasty construction of the new in the effort to become modern (*xiandai*) and catch up with more advanced, cosmopolitan places. As a result, the city is sprawling rapidly into the surrounding agricultural areas as numerous new residential neighborhoods with exotic names and bright colors are mushrooming. The old narrow alleyways and traditional residential houses are quickly disappearing, giving way to the frantic construction of multilane boulevards, gigantic shopping plazas, new housing compounds, luxury hotels, and neon-lit entertainment areas.

The booming economy has lured tens of thousands of migrant workers and petty traders from the surrounding counties and other provinces into the city. Meanwhile, social polarization has increased significantly between the urban poor (mainly consisting of lower-income families and laid-off workers) and well-to-do entrepreneurs and merchants, and between rural migrant laborers and officially registered permanent city residents. Multiple tensions between different interest groups—such as the conflicts between historical preservation and commercial development, between homeowners and developers—have emerged.

These rapid changes have turned Kunming into a strange place to me despite my frequent return visits. I grew up there between the mid-1960s and the early 1980s. In my memory, this is a quiet city full of distinct, traditional neighborhoods and narrow streets. But by the late 1990s the majority of the old neighborhoods and streets I used to walk through and visit had disappeared. The small nursery school on a quiet street that I had attended had been replaced by a high-rise apartment building. Numerous new roads have been built and are congested with private cars and cabs. These macro-level changes have also transformed the lives of my extended family and close friends. A classmate from high school became an instant multimillionaire at age forty-one by investing in the rocketing stock market. His family moved into a dream mansion in a well-protected elite community. He now drove a black Audi and would soon upgrade to a Bentley. But there are also those have been laid off, fallen behind, and struggle to make ends meet. One of my cousins, in his late thirties, was laid off due to the privatization of the factory he had worked for. He had a difficult time adjusting to the new reality of unemployment and tried to survive by moving in with his retired parents whose incomes were very limited.

My own family's living conditions have improved greatly in recent years. Since I was born, my family had lived in four different public housing units provided by my father's university. They were the typical kind of danwei housing—very small, bare concrete floor, and minimum community services. It was not uncommon to co-inhabit the space with countless hungry cockroaches. The first two units were flats without any running water or toilet inside. The entire housing block, in which they were located, was flattened in the 1990s and replaced by low-rise residential buildings. The last two units were slightly improved apartments equipped with a private bathroom and indoor running water. But recently I learned that these two buildings would soon be demolished to make way for the development of a private luxury residential high-rise. In 2005, my parents moved to a new residential compound built by a private developer although the purchase was collectively negotiated through the university. Their new home is much larger, brighter, and cleaner. Yet, as the cityscape and way of life they are familiar with are vanishing, there is an enduring sense of nostalgia for something lost as they live through the dazzling changes (see Zhang 2006). Like other families, we also went through the agonizing process of deciding which community to choose, how much we could afford, and how to assemble the money needed. After all, buying a home is the most important purchase for most families and usually exhausts all their savings. I spent hours discussing these issues with my parents and checking out several properties for them. My parents were considered too old to qualify for a bank mortgage loan. In the end, I contributed some money toward their purchase as expected from a filial Chinese daughter.

During my fieldwork in Kunming and even when I was physically far away in the United States, I often found myself entangled in exciting and at times stressful discussions of home purchase, forced relocation, employment problems, consumption, and coping strategies among my extended family and friends. Thanks to low-cost technologies such as the telephone, e-mail, and Skype, I was able to maintain close contact with them despite the physical distance. The boundaries between here and there, between fieldwork and private life have increasingly blurred. For me, this blurring is productive as it allows me to delve deeper into the lives of the people I study. To capture the pulse of this transforming city and reflect my deep entanglement with it, I wrote this book in a way that combined my anthropological research with personal experiences. As such, I am aware that my interpretation is derived from a particular subjective position and shaped by my mixed feelings toward the changes.

Studying the emerging middle classes is challenging not only because they are an amorphous social stratum but also because of their desire for privacy. In the beginning of the fieldwork, I was discouraged by the difficulty in gaining access to Kunming's middle-class families. A household survey or a random selection of households for interviews in any given community was nearly impossible. One could hardly enter the gated communities freely, let alone knock on the doors of the families inside without a prearranged introduction through a friend. Most families had an intercom connected with the metal gate of their building unit and refused to let in strangers. There was a strong sense of distrust and a desire to protect their privacy. What eventually enabled me to get into these fortified middle-class enclaves were personal contacts provided by my family and by high school classmates. In order to cover a wide spectrum, I tried to include informants from communities of different financial levels, geographic locations, and social components. The obstacles I encountered turned out to be an intriguing object of my inquiry that led me to explore the relationship between spatial exclusion and class formation.

My fieldwork relied on a combination of participant observation, semi-structured and informal interviews, and documentary research. I visited over thirty newly developed gated communities and ten older neighborhoods within Kunming and its suburbs. During my research, the two housing compounds where I stayed with my family provided a useful contrast in living situations: the first one was typical danwei housing, poorly constructed, crowded, and without many services; the second was a new private community equipped with what commodity housing typically offers today. I had ample opportunities to observe and interact with the people who lived there. Children's playgrounds became a convenient place to meet other parents and engage in informal conversations. Much of my time was also spent in interviewing about forty homeowners and management staff in several different communities. I also interviewed about ten developers and local officials involved in the construction of private new homes to understand their motivations, reasoning, and problems. In addition, I had many informal conversations with sales agents, security guards, and maintenance staff working in the private communities. I went on several special housing tours organized by the annual Kunming's home exhibition. As a potential buyer, I was sometimes pressed hard by the sales agents to sign an advance purchase contract because they desperately wanted to meet their sales target. When they found out my overseas background, they simply assumed that I had the cash needed to buy and pressed even harder. At other times I was largely ignored by the agents because I was not well dressed and did not appear to be someone who could afford the type of homes being shown to us. Class was very much at work on these housing tours as shown in agents' attempts to gauge potential buyers' class status and purchasing power and by their efforts to sell luxury homes through the notion of class membership.

Structure of the Book

To contextualize my ethnographic study in larger historical processes, chapter 1 traces the transformation of housing and land use by focusing on the rise and fall of welfare housing over three periods (the prerevolutionary era, the high socialist period, and the post-Mao reform era). I call attention to two simultaneous processes—the dispossession of state or public assets and the massive displacement of disfranchised urban and rural residents. Chapter 2 probes the gigantic machine of the real estate industry by looking at the daily operation of its critical components and the practices of its agents on the ground. It also discusses how the exploitation of migrant construction laborers and other workers in this industry takes place in the process of capital accumulation. Although my main focus is on Kunming, I also note the general trends in China at large.

The remaining five chapters explore the social, spatial, cultural, and political ramifications of the housing revolution in Kunming. Chapter 3 sketches an emerging, increasingly differentiated regime of living brought about by the booming real estate market. I ask why certain cultural concepts and spatial forms are constructed, promoted, and sold while analyzing the ways in which the equivalence of commodities works in the context of marketing private housing. I also address the contested relationship between privatized communal space, public life, and social entitlement. Chapter 4 takes up a core issue of this book—the relationship between class, space, and consumption. It analyzes the dual cultural process of space-making and class-making by examining how on the one hand self-conscious middle-class subjects and a distinct "class milieu" are being created under a new regime of property and living, and how on the other hand socioeconomic differences get spatialized and materialized through the remaking of urban communities. Chapter 5 offers a closer look at an unpleasant process that makes the middle-class lifestyle possible—the massive displacement and dispossession of ordinary city dwellers with a focus on the struggles of one Kunming family and an ethnic neighborhood. I unravel the power dynamics and the tensions between property rights and urban development, while highlighting several forms of civic activism that have emerged among the displaced residents. Through several ethnographic cases, chapter 6 tackles how a rising material culture reconfigures the intimate realm of self-worth, romantic love, and conjugal relationships. I show how owning a private house has become the decisive factor in constructing masculinity, considering whether to marry, and how it is a focal point of contention in divorce. Chapter 7 examines the logic and limits of "governing at a distance" in urban private housing regimes. I trace two parallel processes: the shift from direct state penetration into urban communities to the privatized local governing assumed by real estate authorities, and the subsequent widespread conflicts between property management agencies and homeowners.

The epilogue situates my study on housing, class, and urban governance in the context of a recent call for "building a socialist harmonious society" by the Chinese party-state. I suggest that the harmony discourse signifies an important shift in the technologies of governing as the reform regime faces soaring social inequality and mounting civic activism in the era of private property.

I

Farewell to Welfare Housing

Housing is no longer a welfare item; it is now a commodity!
A widespread government slogan

The rapid privatization and commercialization since the early 1990s has led to the disintegration of the socialist "urban public goods regime" (Solinger 1995) and the formation of a hybrid urban economic and distribution system. A new urban geography of class is emerging with a heightened popular consciousness toward private property ownership. The prerevolutionary time has often become a point of reference for people to talk about current changes. A popular rhyme in the reform era is, "Forty years of suffering no end; back where we started now we must bend."[1] What it suggests is not that China is simply returning to a prerevolutionary social structure and political system. But in the eyes of many ordinary Chinese, the emerging form of social and economic life no doubt resembles many elements of the old days. Private home ownership and commercialization of urban land are just two of the most palpable changes that indicate the end of the socialist mode of city life.

In this chapter I trace this historical transformation with a particular focus on housing and land use in order to contextualize my ethnographic study. By contrasting the high socialist period with the prerevolutionary time (prior to 1949) and the post-Mao reform years (1978–present), I seek to highlight both disruption and continuity in the system of housing and people's everyday experiences of it. Therefore, this chapter is mainly a macro-level historical recount of these changes. Toward the end of this

26

chapter, I will also bring our attention to how the master city plan for Kunming, which is premised on commercial developments and a modernizing ethos, gives rise to a new urban geography quite different from that of the prerevolutionary and socialist times.

Throughout this historical account, I seek to conceptualize the changes by suggesting that the commercialization of land use and the privatization of housing is a core strategy of post-Mao developmentalism that relies on the real estate industry as a vital growth engine. This mega-development, I argue, is built on what I call "late and postsocialist primitive accumulation," involving two simultaneous processes—the dispossession of state and public assets and the massive displacement of disenfranchised urban and rural residents.[2] As David Harvey has observed, "the turn towards state-orchestrated capitalism in China has entailed wave after wave of primitive accumulation," causing "a great deal of localized social distress and episodes of fierce, sometimes even violent, class struggle in areas desolated by this process" (2003, 153–54). The key to this primitive accumulation is the release into private hands of two sets of assets previously monopolized by the state—urban land and enterprises—at very low or virtually no cost. In other words, what makes the rapid accumulation possible is the chipping away of vast state resources by private entities, accompanied by the massive forced relocation of ordinary citizens to make space for real estate development. As a result of this grand reallocation of capital and resources, a glaring socioeconomic disparity is emerging. Moreover, the absence of property rights law before 2003 and a rather murky field of legal regulation have provided the necessary conditions for primitive accumulation in China. Although the state is making an increased effort to formalize and regulate the emerging land and real estate markets, local practices constantly ignore, evade, or derail government rulings to maximize capital accumulation.

The Rise of Welfare Housing

After the founding of the People's Republic of China (PRC) in 1949, the Maoist party-state strove to establish a new egalitarian society by eliminating all forms of private property ownership through nationalization (*guoyou hua*) of land, economic production, education, health care, housing, and other social services (see Meisner 1986; Whyte and Parish 1984). This approach was clearly influenced by Marx's declaration in *The Communist Manifesto* that "the theory of the Communists may be summed up in the single sentence: Abolition of private property" (cited in Tucker

1978, 484). Private ownership (*siyou*) was thus largely denounced as the evil cause of capitalism. In the cities, the socialist state became the sole legitimate owner of all land and assumed the primary responsibility for the welfare of its citizens through the newly established "urban public goods regime" that excluded rural residents outright (Solinger 1995; Zhang 2002). At the heart of this welfare regime was state ownership of land, public ownership of property, and state distribution of resources to official urban *hukou* (household registration) holders.[3] This regime became the pillar of a new urban socioeconomic order and the basis of the political legitimacy of the Chinese Communist Party (CCP). The Chinese term *fuli* (equivalent to "welfare") refers to a range of material benefits and free services that come with one's legal classification as an urban citizen and with employee status. *Fuli fang*, public housing distributed and managed by one's work unit, was perhaps the most important welfare benefit up to the late 1990s. Urban *hukou* holders were entitled not only to employment and public housing but also to low-cost services and goods heavily subsidized by the state. There was a strong sense of entitlement shared by urbanites who took state and danwei provision for granted. Welfare in socialist urban China, formed on the basis of collectivism and a state-planned economy, thus took on different meanings than it does in the West, where the concept is largely linked with social democracy and Keynesianism.

Kunming was no exception to these dramatic changes but took its own course. Unlike other major Chinese cities, Kunming was "liberated" peacefully and relatively late, in December 1949, when the provincial president, Lu Han, led an uprising and established a new Communist municipal government. When the new governing team led by the People's Liberation Army (PLA) entered Kunming, it took control over all major private finance, commerce, manufacturing, and retail companies in the province by nationalizing them into eight large state-owned enterprises. The danwei system was also established throughout the city. Prior to 1950, Kunming had been a hub linking China to Southeast Asia even though ground and air transportation to the inland was very limited. After 1950, it became rather isolated from the outside world as the central state decided to shut down many of these trade channels for national security reasons. A railway connecting Kunming to other parts of China was created in 1966 and slightly improved the situation.

For those who grew up under Mao's regime, public ownership was the norm and public housing was the predominant form. Concepts such as "private property," "privacy," and the "real estate market" appeared as not only alien but also as politically dangerous. Yet, for the older generation who had lived through the prerevolutionary period, during which private homeownership and the rental market were part of everyday life, the subsequent changes under socialism were dramatic. Some have compared the impact of the socialist housing reform on urban citizens to that of land reform on peasants in the countryside. Before 1950, most urban housing was privately owned and government involvement in this domain was limited.[4] Private housing was largely concentrated in the hands of a small group of landlords with large landholdings, however, leaving ordinary working-class families in poor, overcrowded conditions on the periphery of the cities (see Zhang 1998, 24–25).

In Kunming, there existed a clear spatialization of class. Merchants, entrepreneurs, local officials, military officers, and cultural elites owned sizable courtyard houses in the city core, where they were attended by their own private servants and protected by guards. Many of them also owned additional estates. Merchant families located in prime commercial districts often turned part of their house (the section facing the street) into a shop or shops (see Zhang 2006). Middle and lower-middle-income families generally had small courtyard houses; some were able to rent out a couple of rooms for extra income. My interviewees born in the 1920s and 1930s still had clear memories of the homes owned by their families. They could give me a detailed description of the houses and locate their family property on the city map even if many of these old houses had been demolished as a result of recent urban renewal. Working-class families, college students, and migrants usually rented rooms by using personal networks or real estate brokers. The private rental market was so lively and lucrative that the brokers had become a special class known as *fang yazi* ("housing ducks") who made a comfortable living on brokerage fees. The majority of the underclass lived in crowded, self-constructed shacks or mud houses just outside of the old city walls. A retired, eighty-year-old teacher described to me what these places were like:

> I was a college student and a member of the CCP's democratic youth league. So I was asked to visit the poorest in the city in order to spread the news from the party and mobilize the masses. My comrades and I went to the poorest areas or what we called "ghettos" near the Little West Gate, which separated the city from the outside. Along the old city walls, we saw huts, shacks, or simple mud houses put up by those struggling on the edge of society, including rickshaw pullers, newspaper sellers, street peddlers, fortune tellers, migrant workers, and so on. The conditions were miserable.

In the early 1950s, the CCP strove to nationalize the economy and eliminate private home ownership. Under the new policies, privately owned residential structures in Kunming were confiscated by the municipal housing bureau, which became the de facto landlord. Families that had owned their houses were allowed to retain only a small part of the unit as their own residence. The rest of the house was divided into several parts and assigned to other families in need of housing. These families were required to pay a very small fee to the city housing bureau. In some cases, the entire house was confiscated by the city government and the original owner's family was forced out completely. Although the great majority of private property was transformed into public housing, there remained a small percentage of private housing (*si fang*) in Kunming. Up to the late 1950s, people were still able to rent rooms informally by word of mouth, but the private "housing ducks" had largely vanished.

Kunming residents who had lost their family property during nationalization remembered their house and the takeover of their property clearly. For decades they had lived in fear generated by the often violent event. One of them, Song Ping, was a taxi driver in his fifties when I interviewed in 2006. His grandparents were considered capitalists because they owned factories and several houses in Kunming. During the nationalization in the early 1950s, most of their family properties were confiscated by the city government, but they were allowed to retain several rooms to live in. During the Cultural Revolution, some of these rooms were taken over by the workers and peasants who had seized political power. "I was still a child at that time, but I was already living in fear all the time," said Song Ping. "Because my family's class background was not good, my grandparents were subject to public humiliation while our house was divided and occupied by strangers. I have since then lived in the shadow of insecurity. My heart would tremble whenever I heard the beating of drums, dreading that another attack on my family was approaching." Even today he still does not like the sound of a gong and drum because it reminds him of that painful experience so deeply ingrained in his memory. I asked how he and his family felt when other people moved into their house. "Bitter, of course. But we dared not say anything; it was a state policy. Under the circumstances, we felt lucky just to stay alive," he replied.

It is not hard to imagine why tension grew between the original owner's family and incoming families sent by the city. The former tended to see the latter as invaders taking over their property but could not openly express their resentment. The original owners largely belonged to the relatively privileged, propertied class. But the new revolutionary order had denounced this class and displaced it to the bottom of the socialist class hierarchy. The incoming families were mostly poorer, working-class members who had no place of their own. They saw the original owners as societal parasites who had exploited others under the old system. Thus, they felt morally superior to the original owners and as deserving to use these houses. The tight living conditions also gave rise to conflicts between families. The now divided houses were originally built for single family use with one well in the center of the courtyard. When four to eight families came to live together, they had to share the limited common space and the well for water. Some families set up a small cooking area outside their room to maximize the use of space. If one family took up more space than others, made too much noise, occupied the well too often, or left garbage in the walkway, disputes and resentment would occur. Some families were placed in buildings originally designed as offices, schools, and for other functions. Sharing space and facilities in this situation also caused frequent conflicts (see Whyte and Parish 1986, 81).

Meanwhile, most Kunming residents were gradually brought into a new socialist mode of work and life, known as the danwei system, which combined workplace, residence, leisure, and basic community services. The state channeled large amounts of funds directly to the state-owned work units that were responsible for building housing compounds for their own employees. Before the post-Mao housing reform, 80–90 percent of urban residents nationwide lived in such danwei-based housing (Wang and Murie 1999a; Zhang 1998). In this system, access to housing was essentially tied to one's employment status, and family life became deeply intertwined with work as people living in the same housing compound belonged to the same work unit. The danwei resembles the basic building block of the Soviet city known as the *mikroraion* ("microregion or district"), initiated by the Nikita Khrushchev regime in the late 1950s. A typical *mikroraion* "comprised a neighborhood unit of living spaces in the form of blocks of flats, along with associated services, for perhaps 5,000 to 15,000 people. Pedestrian precincts linked restaurants, nurseries, kindergartens, club rooms, libraries and sports facilities, as well as educational, health, retail and cultural services" (D. Smith 1996, 75). The main difference between the two is that the danwei is typically walled and gated and all the services are provided by the work unit.

There was a high degree of uniformity in the spatial design of the danwei and its housing across Chinese cities. In his intriguing analysis of the genealogy of the danwei system, David Bray (2005) provides a detailed account of the distinct spatial form, architectural design, and rationale of the newly invented, socialist housing. He shows that danwei housing, which featured uniform, blocky, multistory buildings organized into gated residential compounds, was heavily influenced by Soviet urban planning (cf. Bater 1980 and Buchli 1999). According to Bray, two basic styles were borrowed from the Soviets: dormitory rooms with shared toilet, washing, and cooking facilities; and apartments with their own basic facilities that shared a hallway and main entrance. The two main reasons for adopting these particular housing forms were that they could be easily mass produced at a low cost and they served as a concrete spatial realization of the socialist principle of equality. The ultimate goal was to create a collective form of social life and egalitarian social relationships through spatial reorganization, while maximizing the use of space and minimizing construction costs. This type of housing was widely adopted by Kunming's work units, but because of the relatively lower population density in this city compared with Beijing and Shanghai, some one-story flats also were allowed.

The public housing system was firmly in place for about forty years, but it had many serious problems. First, due to insufficient state investment and rapidly increasing population pressure, there was a severe housing shortage and overcrowding throughout Chinese cities. The average living space per capita in urban China was 3.1 square meters in 1960, and then slowly increased to 3.6 meters in 1978 and 5.2 meters in 1985.[5] In Kunming, it was common for a family of five members to live in a small apartment of less than twenty square meters, sharing a single kitchen and bathroom with several other families. The situation in larger metropolitan areas such as Shanghai and Beijing was even worse and it was not uncommon for a family of three generations to live in one room. A piece of cloth was often used to separate sleeping areas among family members for privacy. In the mid-1980s, when I attended Peking University, a married junior professor with a child was normally assigned to one small room in a dormitory-style building and two single faculty members shared a room. Cooking was done with a small, movable gas stove in the dark, narrow hallway. Social friction and disputes between and within families frequently occurred as people tried to maximize their use of space by extending into what was considered public domain, such as the hallway and the shared water room.

Second, extremely low rent and heavy reliance on state subsidies resulted in poor housing maintenance and substandard living conditions. Once the buildings were constructed, little maintenance was provided by the danwei. As renters, occupants were unwilling to spend their limited income to keep the structure in a good shape. Further, one could not predict when his or her family would be asked to move as housing reassignments took place from time to time. But no matter how small, rundown, and transitory public housing might be, many people I interviewed had a sense of attachment to the place they called home. I grew up in a typical danwei housing system in Kunming and my family moved from one place to another within the same university several times from the time I was born until the 1990s. Despite crowding and material hardship, we became fond of some of the places. We especially missed the tiny houses on the campus where we grew vegetables and raised chickens in the outdoor space to supplement our family diet in a shortage economy.[6] My family also built a mud shack attached to the house, using it as a kitchen to extend our living space.

Third, there was inequality and disparity in the housing allocations between work units and among employees within the same work units. For example, larger work units with stronger government backing and greater resources tended to have better housing for their employees, while smaller ones with fewer resources could not afford to develop housing. Thus, for a long time the provision of housing was one of the most important criteria (sometimes more important than wages) that motivated people to seek work assignments with certain housing-rich danwei. This disparity was more pronounced in big cities such as Beijing and Shanghai where higher-level government agencies and leading national enterprises were located. Within the same work unit, not everyone was assigned the same type of apartment. Kunming residents frequently recalled that professional rank, administrative position, family size, length of time with the unit, and other factors affected the size and type of housing one might get. *Guanxi* (personal networks) was also critical in housing assignments. Thus, far from the ideal of fostering a sense of egalitarianism, the public housing system actually generated its own forms of hierarchy, unfairness, and resentment. These inequities continue to play out in an important way today and have given rise to uneven wealth accumulation during housing privatization.

The central state was aware of these housing problems and expressed its concern over the political implications in a document issued in 1978, fearing that the severe shortage and poor repair and maintenance of urban workers' housing and other facilities would cause social instability (see Wang and Murie 1999b, 102). Thus, beginning in the late 1970s and early 1980s, state investment in housing construction increased rapidly to ease the pressure. During this period, a large number of apartment buildings were constructed by major danwei that had the resources to do so. By 1986, the living space per capita in Chinese cities had increased to six square meters, yet for ordinary families in the metropolitan areas the situation did not improve much. To solve the urban housing crisis, the reform government eventually decided to abandon the welfare system and turn to privatization. In an official document detailing a 1987 government conference on urban housing reform experiments, the central state admitted to the public that "the current system of housing allocation and low rents is fraught with serious problems.... The burden of the state is getting heavier and heavier. Corruption in housing allocation is also becoming a serious social problem. Several decades of practice have proved that the current housing system cannot solve the problem in urban housing. We must seek reform." Kunming responded to this call but it did so slowly.

Commodifying Housing

In the late 1980s, the central state launched an initial housing reform that aimed to privatize existing public housing and eventually to commercialize the entire real estate market. The first important ruling, issued in 1988 by the State Council, called for a gradual selling off of danwei-controlled housing to their existing tenants over the following several years. Under the reform policy, families living in danwei housing were encouraged to buy back their apartments from their employers at deep discounts. The assumption was that turning tenants into owners would foster a sense of self-responsibility and allow danwei to assemble a large amount of cash for future investment in housing. Those who wished to rent or could not afford to purchase had to pay much higher rents.[7] Since the discounted purchase rate was so low, the majority of eligible employees chose to buy rather than rent in the end.[8]

But in the early stage of the reform, some work units and individuals were skeptical about privatization. This was particularly true to Kunming where the privatization of public housing occurred at a slower pace than other cities. Some danwei leaders there were not sure how their employees (especially those without adequate personal savings) would react to the drastic reform call after decades of public ownership. Retirees with limited incomes, single parents, and lower-income working families who had financial constraints simply did not have the money to pay for the purchase. The danwei leaders feared that a quick move would provoke resistance and even social unrest, and thus they preferred to take gradual, cautious steps. They emphasized that purchasing was optional, not compulsory. Liu Ping, a retired high school teacher and a divorced mother living with her disabled son, told me that she was extremely concerned when she first heard about the pending housing reform because she simply could not afford to buy the apartment: "I was afraid that eventually they would force everyone to buy. If I could not, I had to pay a high rent or might even be evicted. No one would lend me money since most families would be cash poor after their own purchase." A friend of hers, a young man working for a government agency, suggested that he could buy the unit under her name, while she and her son could live in his apartment located in an undesirable suburb. She refused because she was deeply rooted in the community where she had lived for over twenty years.

Some Kunming residents were also concerned about losing their lifetime savings if state policy changed later. There was a long history of erratic government policy changes during the prereform years that gave rise to such distrust. Several of my interviewees told me that they were highly skeptical about gaining full ownership of the unit they were about to purchase. They were unsure whether their work unit would insist on holding the final decision-making power over the right to transfer, sell, or rent it. They questioned whether the ownership they would purchase was true private ownership, or if the ownership would remain on paper only while their savings were taken away. Despite such doubts, most eligible families in Kunming eventually chose to buy their apartment. "I was watching my co-workers and neighbors," said a university professor. "Since they decided to buy, I did too. In China, you want to follow mainstream practices. If the policy changes later, we will all suffer. Plus, this could be my only chance to own some property as I certainly cannot afford to buy the high-priced commodity housing."

In addition to the sale of existing public housing, a new type of housing constructed by many city governments was also sold in the 1980s and 1990s. It was first offered at a full cost price, calculated on the basis of expenditures on construction, community infrastructure, and land lease. But it became clear that most ordinary families could not afford it, and thus a discounted price was introduced in 1982 (Zhang 1998, 135). Work units often absorbed part of the cost for their employees who purchased such housing. During the 1980s, thousands of elementary and high school teachers in Kunming purchased such newly constructed and subsidized housing and moved into what came to be known as the "gardeners' communities" (*yuanding xiaoqu*).[9] A typical one I visited was composed of twenty or more identical apartment buildings lined up row by row. The architectural form was very simple, not so different from the existing danwei buildings. Such communities were built exclusively for teachers, but the residents usually came from different schools. A conventional practice was to let those from the same school purchase units in the same building or in several adjacent ones so that neighbors were not totally strangers to each other. In the 1980s, many urbanites envied those living in this kind of community, which offered larger apartments and a better environment than older danwei housing had. But it did not take long for these residential buildings to turn shabby due to the poor construction quality. The paint of external walls became flaky and was washed away by the rains after several years.

Into the mid-1990s, housing privatization was finally in full swing in Kunming. During this period, the state issued a number of important rulings and regulations in order to push forward full-scale commodification. Two of them were most significant. In 1994 the State Council issued an important document regarding the decision to deepen urban housing reform. Its aim was to reinforce the principle of commodifying housing and to expand the sale of public housing. In 1998 another announcement urged all Chinese cities to speed up the reform toward monetarization (*huobi hua*).[10] The state called upon urban residents to discard their old socialist welfare mentality and to embrace private home ownership. A popular official slogan put it bluntly: "Housing is no longer a welfare item; it is now a commodity!" After late 1998, housing for most new hires in Kunming would not be assigned by their danwei; instead, they were required to purchase newly constructed affordable housing (*jingji shiyong fang*) coordinated by their danwei, or simply buy commodity housing on the market.[11] A new mechanism designed to help people on this path was a nationwide compulsory housing savings plan launched by the state in 1994, known as the Housing Provident Fund (Zhufang Gongjijin). Its aim was to combine mandatory individual contributions, employers' matching funds, and subsidized mortgage rates to enhance housing affordability (see Buttiner, Gu, and Yang 2004; Duda, Zhang, and Dong 2005; Mattias 2006).[12]

Three forms of homeownership were adopted by different work units according to their specific situations and different stages of the reform. (1) Employees who purchased public housing at a higher "market price" (*shichang jia*) obtained full ownership rights and could sell or rent their apartments on the market. (2) Employees who paid a lower "construction-cost price" (*chengben jia*) were granted full ownership rights, but within the first five years after purchasing they could not sell their housing on the market. (3) Employees who paid a much lower "standard price" (*biaozhun jia*) had only partial ownership rights, namely the right to occupy, use, or inherit among family members. Privatized housing under this condition could not be traded or rented on the market. Most work units in Kunming initially adopted the third model because they did not want to completely cede their control over housing. Some organizations such as universities and hospitals were more conservative than others, as they were reluctant to let "strangers" move into their residential compounds, which were well integrated into the danwei space. The attitude of the employees was highly ambivalent. On the one hand, they did not trust their leaders, who insisted on offering only partial ownership and thus demanded full ownership and control of their housing unit. On the other hand, they feared that their "pure" housing compounds would soon disintegrate if their neighbors started to sell or rent their units to "outsiders." As one professor said to me, "Can you imagine migrant workers and independent entrepreneurs you do not know someday living next door? They will not listen to the university. There will be no authority over them. It will be a total mess."

The property rights associated with the three types of ownership were extremely unclear. The majority of new homeowners I interviewed knew that they had the right to live in the purchased unit and could pass it on to their offspring, but they were not certain whether or when they could actually sell or rent it on the market later. As the reform deepened in the late 1990s, work units were under pressure from the authorities to fully privatize. Employees were required to pay additional money to gain unrestricted full ownership, guaranteed by the "housing ownership certificate" (*fangchan zheng*) issued by the city government. In some cases, however, the path to full ownership took much longer but no clear explanations for the delays were given by employers. For example, two of the universities in Kunming intentionally slowed down the process of acquiring the certificate from relevant city bureaus and did not provide their employees with the certificate until 2005. A senior university professor described to me his experience of the slow phased privatization:

My family was living in an apartment of roughly seventy square meters assigned by my university. Before the early 1980s we paid rent, but it was very little. Our salaries were also all very low. So it was equivalent to free housing, I would say. The first phase of housing reform started in the early 1980s by raising rents, but it was still not much, no more than fifty yuan per month. In the late 1980s, when the sale of welfare housing to state employees started, we were given preferential prices to buy our apartments. The discount was calculated after such factors as the length of time worked, professional title, and so on. The first payment I made was a little over ten thousand yuan in 1990, but I was given only 60 percent of the ownership while the university retained 40 percent. My university leaders did not want to give up control of the housing. I did not feel that I really owned it. Then, in the late 1990s we were asked to pay additional money. The total amount I paid was close to forty thousand yuan. We were promised the formal ownership certificate a long time ago, but it was only in the summer of 2005 that I finally got mine. It took a great deal of complaining, probing, and demands by the faculty and staff to reach this point.

As we spoke, he showed me the certificate he had carefully stored in an envelope locked in a drawer. Now, he said, he had begun to feel like a real owner because he could sell or rent it whenever he wished. For someone who had spent most of his life under socialism, he still could not believe that this was the reality.

Not all danwei followed the rules and price regulations set out by the state. Various forms of corruption invaded the privatization process. For instance, some enterprises simply sold their existing housing at extremely low prices, practically giving away such public assets to their employees. This was called *jianjia chushou*. Some danwei leaders acquired fairly large apartments with small symbolic payments, or illegally sold public housing to their unqualified relatives and friends. Such practices were prevalent in the 1990s and caused widespread popular discontent. The State Council was alarmed by the severity of this situation and subsequently issued an urgent notification to local governments in April 1998 in the effort to stop such practices that "have caused new social injustice and the loss of public assets." The memo made it clear that, if caught, the leaders who allowed such practices to take place would face civil and even criminal charges.

The sale of public housing not only increased local revenue but also significantly reduced government expenditure on housing construction and maintenance. It largely shifted the responsibility of housing provision from the government to individuals through marketization. Yet danwei continue to play an important role in this process even though they are no longer the primary or direct providers. Some of them in Kunming continued to build houses for their own employees by raising money from individual families to fund the construction (*jizi jianfang*). A large portion of commodity homes purchased by individuals on the market today are actually obtained in an organized fashion, with their danwei acting as their official representative to negotiate with real estate developers for better deals. If problems arise later, homeowners can band together through their danwei affiliation and assert stronger collective bargaining power. How do we explain the continued role of danwei in the realm of housing under privatization? First, danwei have long been reluctant to give up their role as distributors of public goods because this distributive power is a key source of authority for work unit leaders. Second, there is also pressure from employees demanding institutional protection and support in improving their living situation.

But the specific program used to privatize public housing also gave rise to inequalities in personal asset-building. Among the citizens eligible to buy back their units, those who occupied larger apartments—managers and unit leaders—were able to build more assets than those who had smaller ones. Some of the owners I interviewed have in recent years sold or rented out their units and used this income to finance the purchase of new, larger, and better commodity housing. But the newly hired employees did not benefit from the discount sale of welfare housing and have no assets to build on. In fact, younger professionals in Kunming today simply cannot assemble the amount of money required for a down payment to purchase an apartment within the first ten years of work. It is not uncommon for their parents to help finance the purchase, especially when marriage is pending.

Throughout the housing reform the term "privatization" (*siyouhua*) was carefully avoided in the official documents due to its problematic ideological insinuation of capitalism. The transfer of public housing into private hands was called the "sale" or "reform" of public housing. In reality, after a decade of what I call the "housing revolution," most publicly owned apartments in Chinese cities have now been privatized. The end of the housing allocation system also has paved the way for the rise of a commercial real estate industry that is producing private homes physically detached from any danwei and catering to middle-class families.

"New Land Enclosure"

The new real estate boom is made possible by a drastic shift in the way urban land is appropriated, a phenomenon that has been dubbed as the *xinquandi yundong* (new land enclosure movement) in China. The radical redistribution or the "grabbing" of land use rights by developers and the subsequent dislocation of millions of Chinese families in many cities has been compared by some Chinese scholars to the land enclosure movement that occurred in England during the Industrial Revolution. The historical image invoked here of *quandi* (land enclosure) powerfully highlights the rushed, hectic, unruly nature of land seizures in China today and underlines the greed that drives this new development craze. Thus, the purpose of the comparison is not to suggest that these two events, which took place in radically different historical times, represent a similar social formation or produce similar consequences. Rather, it is to emphasize the intensity, exploitation, and profound impact such land transformations have had on society (Hu 2001; Zhigang Wang 2001). The land enclosure movement in England, which involved the violent appropriation of public land by the lords and nobles for their private ends, produced a large number of landless working-class laborers for the developing industries (Thompson 1964). By contrast, the new land enclosure in urban China today does not generate a landless working class; rather, it leads to a form of capital accumulation that David Harvey (2003) has called "accumulation by dispossession"—a crucial process during neoliberal restructuring, by which large amounts of public assets and wealth are transferred from the masses to a small private social stratum (the upper classes).

One of the most effective means of capital accumulation during the post-Mao reform is the acquisition of land use rights and the forced eviction of urban residents on newly commercialized land. This process involves large-scale dispossession and displacement at an unprecedented speed. The use right of an enormous amount of land has been transferred from the state to private or quasi-private companies and circulated on the market. A large portion of the profits generated in this process have fallen into the hands of a small group of individuals. In this context, state ownership of land has lost its substantive meaning and becomes symbolic because what matters most now is the holding of use rights. It is in this sense that I regard this new land tenure system as a process of dispossession of state assets by private individuals and nonstate entities. Meanwhile, tens of thousands of urban residents and suburban farmers have been forced out of their homes and from their farmland to make way for commercial developments. Kunming largely conforms to this pattern of development with a particularly strong emphasis on inner-city redevelopment that has generated massive relocation.

The ruthless dispossession and displacement is backed up by an emerging pro-growth coalition between developers and local governments. These kinds of clientelist ties are becoming a more and more powerful force in urban Chinese politics (Wu 2004).[13] Through land development and redevelopment, city officials and developers are able to accumulate political capital and/or profits at the expense of the interests of ordinary city residents. The incentives for government officials to promote urban restructuring are enormous. With fiscal decentralization, local governments have gained more autonomy in decision making regarding land use and economic development, but at the same time they have to be responsible for generating their own revenue. A new strategy is to become a broker of urban and suburban land by selling use rights to developers. Use-right fees are levied in a lump sum at the time of the transaction, making it possible for local governments to assemble a huge amount of cash quickly to finance other projects. The income generated from leasing land accounts for a significant portion of municipal revenue. If party loyalty and ideological struggle used to be the basis for political capital under high socialism, today it is economic achievement and the ability to transform the city into a cosmopolitan center that count more in political advancement.

In Kunming, this emerging coalition is critical to all levels of political formation but is most clearly expressed at the level of district politics. A good example is that within the Guandu District, the largest real estate development firm (Guanfang) has become so powerful that it commands the district economy and is deeply embedded in the operation of the district government. On the individual level, government officials in certain key posts take large bribes from real estate developers in exchange for favors they provide in land use. For instance, the former governor of Yunnan Province, Li Jiating, and his son had close personal ties with several major housing-development companies in Kunming. One of the favors Li did for a developer was to give tacit permission for the construction of a high-rise luxury condominium complex near Green Lake—a designated primary culture and scenery protection site—even though the master plan clearly prohibits the construction of any high-rise buildings in this area. Li later was forced to step down in the wake of a number of corruption charges, many of which were tied to real estate.

This emerging coalition is powerful, giving rise to rampant corruption and the use of threats and violence to stifle popular resistance. It is not exaggerating to borrow Arundhati Roy's characterization of neoliberal privatization to describe China's new land enclosures: "To snatch these [public assets] away and sell them as stock to private companies is a process of barbaric dispossession on a scale that has no parallel in history" (2001). The massive displacement of ordinary citizens will be discussed in detail in chapter 5. In this chapter, I will focus on the dispossession of state land. How has such "land grabbing" (*qiangdi*) become possible in late socialist and postsocialist Kunming? What are the driving political and commercial forces behind this extremely lucrative yet risky business? How are these "unspeakable" profits created and channeled in this process? In order to answer these questions, we must first trace major policy shifts in land use on the national level and their local impact.

As the socialist housing system was put in place in the early 1950s, the real estate market was largely eliminated. The state declared itself the sole legal owner of urban land and did away with commercial land transactions. According to the PRC's Land Regulation Law, there are two forms of land ownership: state owned and collectively owned. The vast majority of urban lands are the first type, while most rural land and suburban farmland are the second type. The first chapter ("General Principles") of this law clearly states that "any *danwei* or individual is prohibited from occupying, buying, selling, or transferring land illegally." Although the state was the formal owner of urban land, in practice the land was owned by what Hsing (2006) calls "socialist land masters," including state-owned enterprises, governmental agencies, military units, universities, hospitals, and other entities, that had de facto control over the use rights of land allocated to them by the state. In Chinese cities, large-scale danwei, which functioned like miniature cities, controlled a large percentage of urban land to provide workplace, residence, service facilities, and leisure activities for their employees. However, these land masters could not transfer use rights or make commercial profits from leasing land before urban land reform. Their grip on the land allocated to them was firm and continued to be so in the territorial politics under commercialization.

In 1998, the Land Management Law (first issued in 1986) was revised to instate a critical change that separated the ownership of urban land from the use right. Although state ownership of land was firmly retained, the revised law allowed the commercialization of use rights for the first time. In the same year, a new government organ, the Ministry of Land and Resources, was created to oversee land use in the new system. Municipalities subsequently established their own land and resources bureaus to take charge of the emerging de facto land market. Another important ruling, the Temporary Rulings Regarding the Leasing and Transferring of Urban State-Owned Land Use Rights, was issued by the State Council in 1990. Later, the Urban Real Estate Regulation Law, which provides more specific operational rules regarding how to transfer land use rights for real estate development, was enacted in 1995. According to these new policies, the state can sell or transfer (*churang*) the use rights of state-owned land to land users with fixed terms; land users in turn must a pay fee to the state for the lease. Further, those entities that have legally obtained land use rights can also sell, exchange, or give away their use rights to other entities.[14] Three forms of transference of use rights through monetary compensation are formally recognized: auction (*paimai*), bidding (*zhaobiao*), and negotiation between two parties (*xieyi*). In the case of negotiations, the leasing fees cannot be lower than the minimum price set by the state; in the case of auction and bidding, the baseline must be kept secret. These policy changes represent the beginning of a radical departure from the old system of the administrative allocation of land for free and unlimited use. Now land use rights have become a special kind of commodity that can be circulated on the market and generate enormous profits.

Auction and bidding represent the two most drastic forms of land marketization. There are some important differences between them: public bidding is usually used for projects involving land whose use is restricted by the city planning bureau or for public projects for societal benefits (*shehui gongyi*). Its goal is to obtain higher but not necessarily the highest return for land use. Only certain qualified firms can participate. The rationale is that economic considerations should not be the chief factor in deciding which company is best for a vital public project. Auctions, however, can be used in cases involving land with no usage restriction. The purpose is to obtain the highest return. Any firm can participate in the auction and the highest bidder will become the new rightful user. Both types of transfer are handled through the municipal land transaction center, but the listings are also posted in the newspapers and on the Internet. Two of the most popular sites for land listings nationwide are ChinaLands.com (*zhongguo tudiwang*) and Land.SouFan.com (*soufang*), both of which provide a constantly updated list of parcels for sale nationwide.[15] The length of each lease is usually seventy years for residential construction and forty years for commercial or other types of construction. The use of public listings is intended to reduce the potential for corruption and the manipulation of land use by political authorities.

The first experiment in land auctions took place in the Shenzhen Special Economic Zone as early as 1987. The longest lease term granted at that time was fifty years. In the name of creating "special development zones," city and county governments in the Pearl River Delta region began to lease state-owned land to private investors, mostly to those from Hong Kong (see He 1998). In 1992, one-tenth of Hong Kong's market investments were channeled into the mainland's real estate development as a result of land commercialization.[16] Other parts of coastal China also began to engage in leasing land by creating special economic development zones. Xiamen and Fuzhou attracted large amounts of Taiwan's capital investments; Dalian, Tianjin, and Qingdao attracted Japanese and South Korean investments. Foreign capital invested in domestic real estate development became a major source of local government revenue in these areas. Inland cities moved relatively slowly and began their experiment with private negotiation rather than public auction. In Beijing, the first public auction of state-owned land took place as late as December 2003. Shunchi Zhidi, a Beijing-based real estate corporation, won the auction by offering the highest price of 905 million yuan for a lot of 308,700 square meters to be used for residential housing development.[17] This event, reported in the *People's Daily* (December 19, 2003), marked a new era of large-scale land commercialization. It is estimated that from 2001 to 2004, total land-lease deals exceeded 910 billion yuan nationwide and such earnings accounted for over 50 percent of the revenue of some local governments (Cheng and Zhang 2004).

In Kunming, the first land lease to overseas businesses took place in 1993 through negotiation. The city's real estate development bureau signed a contract with nine Taiwan- and Hong Kong–owned development firms. The municipal government in February 2002 issued detailed guidelines regarding how land auctions were to be carried out. Under these conditions, the exchange value of land skyrocketed. It was not uncommon that the use rights of a prime location in Kunming were transferred several times within a short period of time because of its rapidly increased value. Those entities in the early part of the chain, especially work units or private corporations that initially obtained the use rights through free administrative distribution or low-cost negotiation, were able to assemble sizable wealth through such transactions. As urban land became scarce, those with close personal connections with officials in charge of land use could quickly become multimillionaires by buying and selling land use rights. The frequent transfer of the same piece of land in a short period of time for higher and higher prices is called *chaodi* ("stir-frying land"). Land brokers can gain quick, enormous profits from such trading without actually going into construction. Another way to grab land is through covert transfers of farmland. Under the guise of developing "orchards" and "plantations," some local governments have illegally converted collectively owned suburban farmland into high-return commercial uses. To curb this problematic practice, the State Council issued a warning in 1999 to tighten the use of farmland. But such practices continued on the local level in many places including Kunming.

Behind the Unspeakable Profits

In the official discourse, auctions and bidding are touted as the first step toward a new market-based system of land use. This system is marked by three principles: openness (*gongkai*), fairness (*gongping*), and justice (*gongzheng*). The three *gongs* against potential favoritism aims to make land transactions more transparent and fair in the eyes of the public. Yet there exists a huge gap between the reality and the principles. Abuses of state resources were rampant during the commercialization of land.

The first and foremost problem was the "unknown loss or disappearance of state land-related resources" (*guoyou tudi ziyuan liushi*) that had occurred during the transference of use rights. The word *liushi* refers to a process of loss similar to constant, uncontrollable, and unaccountable soil erosion. A common cause was the "invisible transference" (*yinxing zhuanrang*), which ran counter to the principle of open, fair market competition. Under the name of fee-based negotiations, officials and developers formed alliances to appropriate state land by transferring the use rights to private firms run by their friends and relatives at an extremely low price (in some cases the fee was merely symbolic). The selling party and the officials in charge of approving such deals received handsome bribes or kickbacks while the buyers could turn around and sell the use rights at a much higher market rate or develop expensive commercial housing for huge profits. As a result, central and local governments received a significantly lower amount of land-related income than they could have. Meanwhile, massive amounts of land were falling under the control of nonstate entities. There was a public outcry to stop such colossal loss on the part of the state and to halt the uneven and unjust accumulation of private wealth. It was estimated that the loss of land-related income to the state due to corruption and illegal transfers easily exceeded billions of yuan each year. Some writers compared it to an unstoppable bleeding wound that would eventually drain state resources.

On May 31, 2001, the State Council issued an official warning in an effort to prevent further land loss by reinforcing land regulation. It stressed the importance of open, fair, and just market transactions and called for wider adoption of public auction and bidding. But this warning has not successfully stopped the "bleeding." In some cases, the frantic accumulation by dispossessing state land not only did not stop, it speeded up. As one reporter for the *China Labor Union* explained, "Since this is the last free lunch, officials and developers in Beijing have begun to rob land fanatically. Within only seven months in 2002, the amount of privately negotiated land transference exceeded 100 million square meters, equal to the total amount of land used for development in the past ten years. Now there is almost no unclaimed land left over within the fourth ring road."

There was also tension between the new market-oriented system and the old administrative distribution (*buohua*) system regarding land use that coexisted in the early 1990s. At the same time, the system began to shift toward a market-based form, but auction and bidding were still not common. Theoretically, the administrative allocation for free land use was allowed only for special, vital public projects, and it was illegal to transfer land obtained under these terms to a third party without the approval of the municipal or national-level government. But in reality, a large amount of land was still allocated for unqualified uses through the backdoor, or for a seemingly legitimate public project to provide a cover for private commercial development. Negotiated deals were largely reached through *guanxi* networks fraught with personal favors, kickbacks, and other illicit activities. Those who were able to obtain land through administrative allocation or negotiation were instantly in an advantageous position for market competition.[18]

The second problem with the new system was the frequent violations of the auction rules by local officials and developers. By manipulating the numbers and leaking inside information to certain bidders, the highest bidder might not be the winner. An insider could also offer the highest bid to fool the public but in the end pay a much lower price. Thus, auctions sometimes were turned into a way to cover up various illicit transactions. For example, the *People's Daily* (April 23, 2004) reported a notorious fraudulent land auction: in July 2003 the city of Xiamen hosted a heated public bidding for a parcel of land located in the city's most desirable financial district. It looked like the Jin Zhong Sheng Real Estate Company had won the bid with the highest offer of 27.8 million yuan. But this company had already been chosen by the district government prior to the bidding war and had made a secret agreement to pay only nineteen million yuan. After the bidding, the district government returned the amount of money above the originally agreed price to the company.

The third problem that impeded the new system was that developers frequently bypassed the city master plan or violated land management law. According to state statistics, there were over four hundred thousand reported instances concerning violations of land management law in China between 2000 and 2002, 15 percent of which involved local governments and danwei. As the next section will show, rather than guiding development, Kunming's city planning was dictated by lucrative development projects as government officials formed a coalition with developers.[19] The abuse of urban planning and breach of land regulation was not subject to accountability due to rampant corruption.

In sum, the new bifurcated land regime opened the door to multiple forms of transaction that went far beyond the state's ability to regulate and control this emerging market. The development and transaction of land-related resources over the past fifteen years has become a focal point of local politics, which has brought about new forms of alliance, competition, and contention among multiple players—namely entrepreneurs, governmental officials, danwei cadres, and foreign investors. Land has become once again a magical commodity and a source of enormous profits; controlling land becomes the fastest way to wealth, commercial development, and political power.

To what extent is China's privatization and commercialization of urban land and housing unique? Housing privatization was widely carried out during the economic transformations in the countries of the former Soviet bloc (Marcuse 1996; Struyk 1996). Russia pursued a strategy very similar to what China adopted—giving tenants in public housing the right to purchase the units they occupied at a deep discount. East Germany, however, took a rather different route of reprivatization through restitution—returning all property previously appropriated by the state to the original owners or providing original owners with compensation for the appropriated property.[20] Hungary pursued another form of restitution by transferring state-owned land and buildings to local governments, which were allowed to sell them off. Individuals who had lost their property were given compensation coupons to buy such state assets instead of being given their original dwelling units back. By contrast, restitution has rarely been implemented in China partly because property records were largely destroyed during the Cultural Revolution and partly because numerous families would have to be evicted with no alternative housing if such an approach were adopted. Restitution in the eyes of ordinary Chinese people can only create glaring disparities and symbolize a return to the prerevolutionary past dominated by class exploitation. The state thus put more effort into protecting the rights and interests of tenants in order to ensure social stability. China's housing reform is also marked by a strong government encouragement of purchasing housing rather than renting it.[21] By raising rents significantly while setting low purchase rates, the Chinese government prevented the situation that faced Czechoslovakia in the 1990s in which people preferred renting over buying due to low rent and free maintenance offered by state. Unlike many Eastern European countries that went further in privatizing land, China has sought to maintain a bifurcated system based on the distinction between state ownership of land and the commercializing of use rights in the urban areas.[22] This new system may appear conservative, but in practice it has enabled private firms to gain de facto control over a large amount of urban land.[23]

Recasting Kunming's Urban Geography

The rise and fall of welfare housing and the burgeoning market economy are closely intertwined with the changing urban geography of Kunming over the past several decades. The unique history and geographic location of this city have shaped its specific developmental strategies, which are centered on promoting tourism and border commerce. As a city in the southwest border region, Kunming's access to capital and the national/global market is different from that of Beijing, Shanghai, Guangzhou, or other southern coastal cities. It must reinvent itself by adopting developmental strategies that can capitalize on its unique history and location. Kunming experiences a double sense of lateness in that it needs to catch up not only with the Western world but also with the more developed coastal regions, special economic zones, and major metropolitan areas in China that opened up earlier and benefited first from reform. For decades Kunming has been regarded by people in the heartland and the coastal areas as a remote, underdeveloped, slowly changing borderland city. Anxiety about being late and the widespread desire to catch up have largely shaped local governments' decisions to wipe out old infrastructures deemed incapable of serving the new economy, which is centered on the service industry and mass consumerism. In this context, a new cityscape is seen as a crucial part of the making of a cosmopolitan, forward-looking Kunming. To speed up this transition, a radical approach involving the wholesale destruction of old structures and street patterns is preferred by the government to relatively gradual renewal strategies such as renovation or restoration.

A key objective of the 1993–2010 city master plan (*chengshi zongti guihua*) is to "redefine the nature of Kunming in order to set the proper goal of city development under new circumstances." Of its seventeen chapters, the first is devoted to highlighting three unique features of Kunming: (1) it is the provincial capital and therefore a political and administrative center in the southwestern region; (2) it is a heritage city with rich cultural and historical traditions; (3) it should be quickly developed into an international commercial hub by capitalizing on tourism, commerce, and trade. The third aspect is the focal point. An acute sense of being late in developing and a desire to catch up is clearly articulated in this opening chapter: "By 2020, Kunming should have moved into the ranks of highly advanced cities in the country in terms of its social, economic, and technological capacity.... This plan will lay the foundation to turn Kunming into an advanced international metropolis (*guojihua dushi*) by the mid-21st century." Although chapter 7 offers some basic ideas about the protection of historical-cultural heritage sites, it tends to focus on protecting parks, scenic spots, and reproductions of historical objects (such as towers, gates, temples, and arches) while largely ignoring the protection of the traditional residential/commercial neighborhoods—the living historical space. It only mentions several traditional neighborhoods in passing but completely overlooks the question of *how* to protect and restore these distinct neighborhoods. The plan is essentially a pro-growth blueprint premised on commercial development. The remaining chapters are devoted primarily to modernizing various aspects of the city's infrastructure and making more space for commerce, tourism, and mass consumption.[24]

Because of its richness in ethnic diversity and historical sites, Kunming was designated by the State Council in 1982 as one of the first twenty-four "renowned historical-cultural cities" (*lishi wenhua mingcheng*) in China. This special status brings a significant advantage in marketing the city as a desirable tourist destination, but historical preservation in some officials' eyes also hinders their ambitions for rapid commercial development and modernizing projects. Up to the early 1980s, a large portion of the century-old streets and residential neighborhoods still existed in Kunming.[25] In such neighborhoods, houses were located along the street and physically connected to one another. There was no clear spatial division between commercial and residential zones. A typical old house was a two- or three-story structure with wood panel siding and gray tile roofs. The ground-level rooms facing the street were usually used as shops. Other rooms were reserved for living quarters. The demolition of old neighborhoods and projects to widen streets began at a slow pace in the 1980s. As competition for urban land grew more and more intense, massive destruction of old neighborhoods and reorganization of city space began to take place in Kunming in the 1990s. Guided by the master plan, the majority of the century-old neighborhoods have been systematically demolished and replaced by multilane boulevards, massive shopping centers, office buildings, hotels, and new housing compounds. The demolition peaked between 1996 and 1998 as the city was getting ready to stage the 1999 International Horticultural Expo.

Justified in the name of modernizing the city and accommodating commercial growth, this time the scale of destruction was greater than ever. By mid-1999, Kunming appeared dramatically different. Old residential communities were replaced by large banks, hotels, department stores, and commercial plazas. Streets were widened, rerouted, renamed, or completely rebuilt. Many long-term residents told me that even they could not find their way around now. The state-controlled media and officials' speeches celebrated the restructuring as a giant step forward toward city modernization. Seeing the Expo as a rare opportunity to promote tourism, trade, and foreign investment, local governments invested heavily in real estate and construction. In less than three years, the total amount spent on such projects exceeded what had originally been planned to cover the next ten years. In a speech in 1999, Mayor Zhang Chenyin stressed the significance of "the city image project" designed to turn Kunming into a modern regional economic hub: "Recasting Kunming through a new face-lift and quality service sector is a critical way of displaying to the world our new economic achievement and forward-looking, open spirit." The obsession with being *xiandai* (modern) was clearly manifested in such phrases as "becoming a major modern metropolis," "to build a modernized city," or "developing Kunming into an internationally recognized modern metropolis." To be sure, the city and provincial governments were not the only ones that expressed such enthusiasm. Young people and the rising new middle class also embraced this vision of spatial modernization and were proud of the new cityscape. The media, the Internet, and the entertainment industry, which constantly provide images such as skyscrapers, freeways, shopping malls, and Western-style villas, are the main source of their imagination of *xiandai*.

In the summer of 2000, the grand restructuring suddenly slowed down as the State Council announced that all the officially designated "renowned historical-cultural cities" would be inspected and reevaluated.[26] If a city failed to protect its historical sites and structures, the special title would be revoked. Because many of the urban redevelopment projects had destroyed heritage sites in these cities, local governments began to panic. Kunming was no exception. Since tourism is now a vital part of the Kunming-centered regional economy, losing the special status would have had a direct negative impact on the entire provincial economy. In order to show that something was being done for historical protection, the city government hastily created a special agency in charge of heritage preservation and took three symbolic steps, developing plans to (1) rebuild several key historical symbols that had been destroyed; (2) preserve three remaining century-old streets: Luofeng Street, Huashan South Street, and Huashan East Street; (3) and restore the only traditional neighborhood left in the city, Jingxin Street. A special fund of six million yuan was allocated for these projects. The city master plan also was revised to reflect an increased awareness of the need for historical preservation. The chief director of the Kunming City Planning Bureau claimed that the guiding principle for urban development is "to strengthen the protection of our renowned historical-cultural city" while "balancing the relationship between protecting historical-cultural sites and modernizing the city" (Li 1999, 26). Ironically, and unfortunately, the concern for preservation appeared at a time when most of the old neighborhoods had already been destroyed—when there was not much left to protect.

THE master plan is more than simply a blueprint or ideal of modernity; it has concrete social, political, and economic consequences. It guides urban development, channels the flow of capital, and defines who can live where. While bringing enormous profits to some real estate developers, entrepreneurs, and government officials, it displaces and marginalizes others. Since the 1980s, millions of urban Chinese families have been forced out of their homes and relocated to poorly constructed communities on the outskirts of cities without adequate services such as public transportation, schools, hospitals, and food markets. In Kunming, the makeover for the 1999 Expo forced tens of thousands of ordinary residents (mostly factory workers, service sector employees, and small-business operators) out of prime commercial districts and into poorly planned relocation communities in the western suburbs. It was very difficult for relocated families to commute to work or to schools that were located far away from their residence. Small-business owners mostly lost their businesses as their shops were eliminated along with their old homes.

A result of the privatization of housing and large-scale relocation is the spatialization of class in the city. The newly rich, which includes business elites, the higher-level managerial class, and well-positioned officials, are taking over prime locations in the urban core, while lower-income families are being pushed out into the peripheral areas. This new geography of class is manifested in a highly differentiated pattern of residential communities that offer quite different living space and lifestyles.

2

Unlocking the Real Estate Machine

"What is the national symbol of China today? Cranes!" This popular joke vividly shows that contemporary Chinese cities are under permanent construction. Indeed, cranes and scaffolds have become an integral part of city life since the 1980s while skyscrapers, shopping malls, hotels, and residential compounds mushroom in the cities. The scale and speed of such construction has been unprecedented in modern Chinese history. The rapidly expanding real estate industry is hailed as the most powerful growth engine of the Chinese economy in the reform period. In Yunnan Province, the gross output value of construction increased from about 212 million yuan in 1985 to 3.1 billion yuan in 1999 and then to 4.48 billion yuan in 2004 (*Yunnan Statistical Yearbook* 2005). One of the remarkable changes is a shift from the domination of state-owned enterprises in construction to the coexistence of state-owned, semiprivate, private, and foreign-owned firms. This growing industry has not only stimulated mass consumption in multiple domains (such as housing, interior design, remodeling materials, and so forth) but has also provided millions of jobs through its labor-intensive construction, sales, and property management sectors. It is through this gigantic machine that capital is accumulated, cities are reconfigured, and middle-class dreams are realized.

How does the real estate machine actually work on the ground? Who are the key actors in this sector? In this chapter I offer an ethnographic account of the daily operation of several critical components of this machine in Kunming by focusing on the practices of their agents: developers, planners, mortgage lenders, sales and advertising staff, construction laborers, and interior remodeling workers. I seek to understand the nature and social location of these actors and show concretely how they got where they are and how they make things happen. Property management staff—another important component—will be discussed in detail in chapter 7. Although no city is "typical," Kunming in many ways represents the national trend of real estate development. Its pace, however, is slower and the incorporation of foreign capital is less intense than it is in Beijing or in Shanghai and other coastal metropolises. Although my account primarily draws from my observations and interviews of firms and agents based in Kunming, it also incorporates relevant anecdotes from other cities that received national attention. In order to situate my ethnographic case, I move back and forth between a locally specific account and national-level policy changes that set the conditions for Kunming's development. Three analytical issues are central to my account: (1) the hybrid nature of the real estate firms and the implications of this for understanding the relationship between the state and capitalism; (2) the role of political capital in the working of the real estate industry and the formation of a powerful pro-growth coalition between developers and local government officials; (3) the question of labor exploitation that is often masked in the tale of China's extraordinary economic growth.

Hybrid Practices of Developers

As a whole, housing developers constitute one of the wealthiest and powerful social groups in the cities today. The firms they operate through are complicated and vary in nature. During my fieldwork in Kunming, I encountered an intriguing phenomenon: although most people perceived that the new commercial housing belonged to the private sector, and that related transactions and management matters were done through nonstate, market mechanisms, in reality only a portion of these development companies were wholly privately owned. Most of the major players before the late 1990s were by legal definition state-owned enterprises (*guoyou qiye*) created by local district governments, yet they operated along the lines of the private enterprise model. Meanwhile, it was common for some private firms to mimic certain disciplinary practices and the organizational culture of the socialist danwei in their management.

Unclear Ownership, Flexible Operation

The four largest real estate companies in Kunming were supported by and named after the governments of the city's four core districts (Guandu, Panlong, Wuhua, and Xishan). They maintained close ties with the district governments, which granted them better access to land and other key resources. In turn, the district governments benefited from the sizable revenue brought in by such lucrative businesses. These real estate enterprises consisted of many subsidiary firms of a mixed form of ownership (*duozhong jingji chengfen*) and acted as independent, profit-seeking commercial entities.[1] These firms had very little to do with their parent companies, as long as they provided a required percentage of annual profit. They also could subcontract their work to smaller, private construction and remodeling teams. In general, they had their own budgets, hiring policies, and rules of profit-sharing—just like private enterprises.

Let us take a closer look at the most powerful developer in Kunming, the Guandu District Real Estate Development Corporation (hereafter referred to as the Guandu Co.). This firm was initially established in 1986 as a typical, small, state-owned enterprise, overseen by the Guandu district government. It was a time when commercial housing had just begun to emerge and market competition was low. But this firm was unprofitable for the first five years and had changed its management four times. With such a bad reputation and huge debt, the company was on the brink of bankruptcy in 1991. That year, the district government appointed a new general manager, Liu Chenwei, in an effort to save the company. Liu was a daring middle-aged entrepreneur who had years of experience as a manager in the private sector. According to his chief assistant, Mr. Zhao, Liu was determined to change the way the firm was run through aggressive personnel and salary reforms. First, he did away with the "iron rice bowl" (*tiefanwan*) employment system and adopted a new hiring system based on merit and ability. Second, he implemented a highly differentiated salary system as an incentive for employees to work their way up in the company. Third, by offering generous bonuses and other attractive benefits to employees, and by tying these rewards directly to the firm's performance, he fostered a new kind of work ethic that greatly enhanced employees' creativity and efficiency. In only two years, this company successfully completed the construction of several large residential communities in the northern suburbs of the city. This type of commodity housing was geared toward lower-income families, and it was sold very quickly. The firm made profits for the first time and gradually became the "big brother" (major player) in Kunming's emerging real estate industry. Zhao's account clearly idealized Liu and largely attributed the firm's success to his leadership. But he did not mention the clientelist networks Liu had built with local officials and the corruption involved. For example, Liu was able to seize and convert sizable farmland for housing development at very low costs because of his ties with the local government.

In 1994, the Guandu district government approved a proposal by the Guandu Co. to reorganize itself into a much larger, higher-level corporation with multiple ownership forms and multiple businesses. With a steady 15–20 percent increase in annual profit, the company had a profit of eighty million yuan in 1995. The newly organized corporation had a large administrative headquarters and owned three sets of entities: ten subsidiary enterprises organized into "limited corporations" specializing in construction, property management, and entertainment; four "joint shareholding enterprises" (*cangu qiye*) in the hotel and cement manufacturing businesses; and six residential community management committees. The ownership of these subsidiary entities was ambiguous, as they contained many private subcontracting businesses. But this did not seem to be a problem for the managers of these small companies because for them the legal definition of their companies was far less meaningful than how they were actually run.

In 2000 I interviewed Mr. Lu, the head of a remodeling company affiliated with the Guandu Co. I was a bit confused about the ownership of his company because he had once said that it was his own business, but then at another point he mentioned that it was a state-owned enterprise belonging to the Guandu Co. I asked him to clarify the nature of his company:

> Does it really matter? I do not care whether it is state or private and I honestly do not know how to classify it. If you really want to go by the legal definition on paper, we are called a "shareholding company." Every employee is allowed to own certain shares and is given a salary, but at the end of the year we divide the bonus according to rank. Every year my parent firm [the Guandu Co.] gives my company a starting fund of over one hundred thousand yuan and the priority for getting several major project contracts. But that is it. We are on our own from that point. If we do a great job and make more money, we get to keep more. My parent company does not care how I run my company as long as it gets a handsome share of my profits.

I also asked Mr. Lu whether he wanted to set up his own private company someday since he had accumulated a lot of money and certainly had the financial capability to do so. "No, because the company I am managing now is almost like my own company," he said. "Moreover, I have all the advantages of being attached to a large, government-supported corporation—accessing start-up funds, getting otherwise competitive projects, and enjoying local government protection in any bureaucratically related matters." As a general manager he received the largest portion of the total annual profit of approximately ten million yuan. His only concern was that he could be fired if his relationship with the parent company deteriorated, or if he failed to deliver the expected profits. But he assured me that this would not happen because he had strong personal ties with major decision-makers and his business had been lucrative over the past eight years. I later found out that his father was a close friend of one of the founders of the Guandu Co., who got him into his current position. To be fair, Mr. Lu was also a qualified candidate, as he had obtained his bachelor's degree in architecture and design from a renowned Chinese university. He quit his teaching post at a local college to lead the remodeling company. When I met him, he was only in his mid-thirties and was already considered highly successful. He owed a black luxury Buick and two up-scale condominiums (one for himself and one for his parents). In order to take advantage of both the existing state sector and the expanding private sector, many entrepreneurs, as he did, used flexible, hybrid ownership forms to maximize their competitiveness and profit-making in a mixed economy.

The 1980s and 1990s were also a period in which government agencies and nonenterprise entities, such as schools, hospitals, and the military, plunged into the market to seek new ways of making profits (*chuang-shou*). This created a rare environment for the proliferation of innovative alignments between private businesses and state elements.[2] In more recent years, the ownership form of Chinese enterprises has undergone profound transformations. The 15th Chinese Communist Party Congress in 1997 announced that shareholding itself should not be labeled as "socialist" or "capitalist"; rather, it can serve as an important operational element of the new economy. Thus, shareholding, a system of capital assemblage initially introduced to the mainland from Hong Kong and adopted first by *minying* ("nonstate-owned and run") companies, was for the first time recognized as a legitimate form of public ownership in China. It was further promoted by the 16th Party Congress in 2002 as a way of reforming and organizing state firms. This was the larger context in which shareholding became a highly popular system adopted by both state and private sectors in Kunming's real estate industry. The operational models of the two sectors increasingly resemble each other. It has become more and more difficult to speak of a purely state enterprise due to the existence of a diversified form of capital.[3]

Mimicking the State-Owned Enterprise Culture

Over the past fifteen years, the number of private developers that are not formally affiliated with any government entity or state enterprise has been increasing steadily in Kunming. This type of development firm can be divided into two kinds: relatively permanent, full-scale private companies and smaller "project-based companies" (*xiangmu gongsi*). For the former type, shareholding is the most widely adopted form of ownership. Although they are privately owned and managed, their roots can be traced back to the state-owned enterprise (SOE) reform. Although heavily influenced by business organizations and practices from Hong Kong firms, they also adopt certain organizational features (such as CCP membership and ethics) of state enterprises. Before the establishment of public auction of land, private firms were not in a position to compete with the major players, backed by the district governments, because the latter could obtain prime land at extremely low prices.[4] But in recent years some private developers have been growing rapidly and have become highly competitive.

Linyuan, a prominent real estate development corporation in Kunming, was founded in 1993 through a "closed shareholding system," which meant that no additional shareholders were allowed, while any transfer of shares had to be approved by the board. The primary shareholder, Mr. Dong, who later became the sole owner and chief executive officer, had worked as a lower-level cadre in one of the city's district governments. When the SOE reform began in the early 1990s and many state enterprises were transferred to private hands, he seized the opportunity to take over the real estate company originally run by the district government. Because he had inside information about the pending reform, he was able to assemble ten million yuan from thirty-three private shareholders—mostly his friends and relatives. He started by building and selling affordable housing (*jingji shiyong fang*), which was encouraged and subsidized by the government.[5] Even though the profits were smaller than those from developing luxury housing, this type of housing was more affordable and sold quickly. Linyuan gradually established its reputation and trust among the public.

When I first interviewed Mr. Dong in 2002, his firm already had an asset base of three hundred million yuan and employed 180 salaried staff and workers. His office was modest but comfortable, located in a small building used for sales in a newly constructed housing compound. He wanted to be on-site to oversee things directly. With the growth of the firm's capital, he had also begun to diversify its operations by creating several smaller companies that specialized in coal mining and selling Ford cars, medicine, and media products. In 2003 he combined all the companies into a large entity called the YingDi Group. A year after this restructuring, the assets of the group had increased to one billion yuan and the firm had about one thousand employees. I interviewed him for the second time in the summer of 2006. The headquarters of his enterprise had moved to the eighteenth floor of one of the tallest downtown buildings. His office was spacious, with a sweeping view of the city, and was tastefully decorated with a tea ceremony area.

Like state enterprises, Dong's corporation has maintained a personnel file system (*dangan*) to keep track of employees' backgrounds and behavior. To my surprise, it also has a Communist Party organization branch of one hundred members, with Dong acting as its top leader. Party members gather periodically to study relevant government policies, engage in collective activities, and conduct moral education. They are expected to take a leading role in reinforcing disciplinary rules in the company.[6] As part of the party activities, Dong led a team on a special tour of Yanan (considered the birthplace of the revolution) and the Red Army's Long March Path in order to learn about the CCP's history and revolutionary spirit. Some participants probably treated this event as a tourist opportunity, but Dong himself seemed to take it seriously. He believed that young people today needed faith and discipline regardless of whether they work for a private or a state unit. I was a bit surprised by his attitude and he noticed my reaction. He smiled and leaned back in his luxury black leather chair, saying, "The party organization helps the company to oversee and regulate workers better. It also teaches self-discipline, and offers an organizational structure that people are familiar with. But of course we do not hold political and ideological struggle meetings as in Mao's time." After a pause, he continued, "Party leadership is the mainstream politics in Chinese society. I do not want my company to exist outside the mainstream or far away from society. My enterprise is a cell of society and should stay within the mainstream." Mr. Dong insisted that the attempt to make a clear distinction between state and nonstate firms today is not meaningful:

> We are not radically different from state enterprises. For instance, we are also conducting the propaganda of "building a harmonious society" within our enterprise as promoted by President Hu. State firms also use the shareholding system and are driven by profits like us. The fundamental difference I see is where the profits go. For us, the profits and risk all belong to shareholders; for the latter, they all go to the state.

Linyuan's practice indicates that socialist organizational and operational traits have not entirely faded away in the private sector. Indeed, many private firms model their organizational culture and activities after the socialist danwei. New entrepreneurs in the reform era may adopt capitalist corporate business practices, mainly from Hong Kong, Taiwan, Germany, Japan, and North America, on the one hand, and utilize socialist organizational culture and certain familiar socialist ethics to shape their firms, on the other hand.[7] Such bricolage of old and new, Chinese and foreign in business practices and social values is a distinctive feature of the market economy with Chinese characteristics that blurs the boundaries between capitalism and socialism.

Although private firms are more flexible in their operations, they can be in a disadvantaged position when competing with government-sponsored developers in securing the use of land and bank loans. This is how Mr. Dong explained it in a 2002 interview:

> In the case of private firms, the local government can only benefit from our taxes, but not our profits. But the government can get both the profits and taxes from state-owned real estate enterprises. Therefore, firms with local government backup frequently get preferential treatment in access to land and money. By contrast, it is very hard for us to get land at good locations in the city. I have to use less desirable suburban land to build housing.... When we first started, we could not get any loans from banks; all the shareholders borrowed money from friends and relatives. It was highly risky, but all investments have risk.

What he described here regarding land competition was particularly true for the 1990s, during which most land transfer cases took place through closed-door negotiations between interested parties. Developers with local government support clearly fared well. Since 2002 the state has pushed hard for public auctions, giving private developers a better chance to compete in the emerging land market. But land prices have also skyrocketed under the new auction system. For example, Dong has obtained two pieces of land for his recent housing developments through auctions, but the cost was high. The first lot of 141 *mu* was near the second ring road within the city and he paid 1.45 million yuan per *mu* in 2002.[8] He built a massive compound of high-rise condominiums on it. The second lot was in the western suburbs, on which he built an upscale community of town houses. Even though it was outside the urban core, it cost him one million yuan per *mu* in 2005.

Like other private entrepreneurs, Dong borrowed his initial capital from kin and friends because bank loans were largely inaccessible to private individuals.[9] As his enterprise became stronger and rich in assets, he was able to secure bank loans for new projects. However, personal connections were still very important in getting larger and better loans. As a self-made, successful entrepreneur in Kunming, Mr. Dong's biggest dream was to "create a firm like the Ford Company that can last for over one hundred years."

A One-Person Show

Project-based companies emerged and played an active role in the early phases of real estate development in Kunming. They were usually created by one or two individuals for a specific housing construction project and the operation was small and temporary. Such "companies" had no permanent office or staff and subcontracted the construction work to migrant teams. Entrepreneurs who operated this way tended to have special personal ties with government officials in charge of city planning and land allocation. They were less constrained by official rules, and more aggressive in giving bribes in order to speed up paperwork or obtain land at a better location. Once construction was complete and the housing was sold, these companies could disappear. The head of a project company could make a large sum of money on one single project and move on to other types of businesses.

Ms. Wang, in her early forties, was one of the few female developers I met. She owned a project-based company in the city. After a hectic day packed with business activities, she finally agreed to meet with me at 10 p.m. in a small teahouse on the first floor of the building in which she lived. Sipping a delicate cup of hot Yunnan black tea, she told me how she got into the risky real estate business. She was once a sent-down youth during the Cultural Revolution and then became a factory worker upon her return.[10] After the college entrance examination was restored by Deng Xiaoping, she had an opportunity to go to college and later became a reporter at a major Chinese newspaper agency. But she was not happy with the meager income her state job offered and decided to "jump into the sea" (*xiahai*) in 1998 to start her own business. In three years, she registered a small real estate company and developed a residential community of some four hundred households in the western suburbs—a sprawling area of new construction. Like other smaller private developers, she faced two major challenges. The first was to acquire land in a good location, which inevitably involved the use of *guanxi* networks and bribery. She had some powerful friends in the city's land planning bureau. She did not want to go into the details, but she assured me that without these connections nothing could have been done. The second was to acquire capital for the construction and the first project required 160 million yuan. Since most small start-up firms usually did not have any collateral, major banks were reluctant to provide any loans. Ms. Wang borrowed from friends and two smaller banks at very high interest rates, somewhere between 20 and 30 percent. Sometimes the money did not arrive on time and the whole project had to be put on hold. She recalled one such challenging moment:

> One year the construction had already started, but the loan we needed did not go through as expected. The bank had promised me the loan earlier, but later withdrew the offer. It was a cold winter and it was snowing. Several hundred contract workers were waiting on-site. I was so upset but could not do anything with that bank. I had to use all my backdoor connections to get the money from other channels in order to buy materials and pay workers. I just could not see my project die like that. This kind of situation is a true test of one's ability. If you do not have strong connections, you simply cannot survive the real estate business.

In our conversations, she frequently referred to the absolute necessity for bribery in order to get things done although she was unwilling to specify the occasions and amounts. In her view, bribing your way through was the norm, not the exception. Just recently her brother, who also owned a project-based company, was trying to build a high-rise for condominiums and offices in the downtown area and ran into serious financial trouble. During construction, they found that the ground was not stable due to unexpected mud-rock flows. As a result, the bank withdrew the second loan. She had to help out by taking loans against her property for her brother's company. By the time I met her, she had made a fortune and owned two large private housing units and a car with a personal driver. When I asked her whether she would stay in the real estate industry, her answer surprised me: "No, I am going to turn to other types of business. I think real estate in Kunming is overheated. In fact, the entire Chinese real estate industry is a bubble economy, which will burst sooner or later. I'd better stop now and take the money and run."

Facing fierce market competition, real estate developers, regardless of their ownership form, have largely embraced the principles of commodity production and maximizing profits by adopting a flexible hiring and contracting system. To reduce labor costs, most of them rely heavily on subcontracting with smaller construction teams of rural migrant workers. Government-sponsored developers have reinvented themselves to become more flexible and competitive by mimicking the organizational structure and operational mode of private firms. Private firms at the same time do not completely discard socialist ethics and the party's discipline techniques.

Given this complex situation, binary categories such as "the private" versus "the state" or "the capitalist" versus "the socialist" cannot adequately illuminate the ways emerging real estate firms operate in China today.

Further, political capital generated from formal government sponsorship or informal personal ties with local officials is crucial for real estate development for three reasons. First, the land regime is still largely state controlled even though a market mechanism has been introduced. Second, the municipal and provincial governments have considerable power over all development projects. Finally, real estate development has become one of the most important sources of revenue for local governments and provides sideline incomes for officials.[11] These factors have created the conditions for the interdependency and mutual protection of political and corporate interests. In recent years, there have been some new changes in the way political capital operates. Several developers with direct and strong support from certain central government agencies have come to invest and develop in Kunming. Using power and pressure from the top, they are able to manipulate local government agencies and obtain large pieces of land for moderate prices. These new "outside" private developers have now become powerful players competing with the local-based ones in Kunming's real estate world.

The Use of Mortgages

An important component that makes the real estate machine work is emergent bank loans to developers and individual home buyers. Corporate loans emphasize the good credit of the company and its ability to pay the loan back. Banks often have to undertake an extensive evaluation to determine the probability of the success of a proposed development project, using a developer's total assets as collateral. But credit (*xinyong*) in China is also established through personal connections (such as friendship and past business interactions between the CEOs of the two entities). Individual consumer loans became available in the late 1990s and are largely confined to the purchase of houses and automobiles. In September 1998 the People's Bank of China issued a milestone document titled "Individual Home Mortgage Regulation Rules," which formally endorsed home mortgages to qualified individuals. The basic qualifications for a borrower include a permanent urban *hukou;* a steady occupation and income, good credit, and the ability to pay back the loan; a home purchase contract or agreement; and a 30 percent down payment. It is up to the bank to decide what kinds of jobs and income are considered steady and to evaluate the applicant's ability to pay. Generally speaking, the interest rate for home mortgages is set by the central bank and has been relatively stable over the past ten years, at about 5 percent. Only two minor increases were made in 2004 and 2005. In more recent years, commercial banks are allowed to make some adjustments within a 10 percent range but cannot go below the bottom line set by the central bank.

So how do banks that operate in Kunming compete to get customers under such tight control of mortgage rates? Mr. Lin Jun, the division head of a fast-growing commercial bank in Kunming, explained to me that "most major banks in the city use the lowest rate allowed by the central bank. So we have to compete through better advertising and special services. For example, we make the application procedure easier, charge fewer fees, and/or set up convenient desks in the new communities during the selling period." But providing quality service is not easy. One of the obstacles facing many banks is an old mentality shared by the staff, who think that they are doing a favor to the potential customers, rather than trying to win their business. To change this attitude, banks conduct periodic staff training sessions to cultivate a new culture of customer service. "Treating customers like God" is a basic principle adopted by many banks. The staff members are taught how to be friendly and responsive by greeting customers and smiling a lot.

Another common strategy is to team up with the developers to recruit borrowers. "If my bank provides a loan to a developer to build a new community, he or she often promises to introduce the buyers of that community to apply for my loans," said Mr. Lin. "We might get invited to set up service desks in their sales office and meet their customers directly." Since the rates offered by different banks are more or less the same, home buyers are likely to use the most convenient agencies to apply for mortgages. This way they can accomplish two time-consuming tasks (purchasing a home and obtaining a mortgage) at one stop.

During the early stages of implementing the mortgage program, rules were relatively stringent and it was not very easy for individuals to qualify for a loan. But in more recent years, there have been many more application sites people can go to and the procedure is simpler. For example, Kunming's home buyers like to go to the Housing and Real Estate Transaction Center, a centralized place where real estate–related business is conducted. This center is located in a six-story building at the heart of the old downtown district. One morning when I arrived at about 10 a.m. there were already several hundred people there filling out forms or waiting in lines. The first floor was occupied by the convenient service offices of several major banks (such as the Construction Bank and the Industrial and Commercial Bank) that process mortgage applications and withdrawals from their Housing Provident Fund. The second through the fourth floors were used for processing property transfers and public notaries. This setup, known as the "one-dragon style service" (*yitiaolong fuwu*), was meant to provide convenience for consumers who engaged in independent transactions.

Another popular form of mortgage service takes place in a collective fashion. When employees from a danwei purchase commodity housing from a developer as a collective group, banks may get permission from the work unit to send a team in to take applications and answer questions. This is not only convenient but also carries a greater degree of trust in the eyes of applicants because these agencies are screened by their danwei and used by their co-workers. One day in 2004 I accompanied a divorced, middle-aged college professor, Chen Hong, to apply for a mortgage loan on her campus. There were two desks set up separately by the China Merchant Bank and the China Construction Bank, which offered virtually the same interest rate. After chatting with her friends there, she decided to choose the Merchant Bank because she already had an account with this bank and it owned the only two ATM stations on the campus.[12] The application form was ten pages long, with numerous conditions and clauses, and the notary document was seven pages long. Chen did not take much time to read them but only checked a few key factors such as the amount of the loan, the interest rate, and the term. She then asked the two friendly representatives to point out where she should provide required information and completed both forms in ten minutes. I was surprised by her action and noticed that other people there were doing the same thing. I asked her why she did not bother going over the form carefully to make sure that everything was all right: "That is not necessary. I trust what my danwei brings to us. Since we are all using the same form and get the same terms, if anything goes wrong, I am not alone and my danwei will take care of it for us. These banks know that and dare not take advantage of us."

Although bank mortgages have made it possible for many middle-income families to reach their homeownership dream, Chinese borrowers often feel anxious about being in debt and paying long-term interest. Most Kunming residents I spoke to chose the term between eight and fifteen years even though the thirty-year term was available. As soon as they had saved enough or could borrow additional money from close relatives, people would want to pay off the entire loan. There was a strong desire to get out from under the debt even if it meant leaving little money in savings. "I just do not feel like I really own the house if there is a mortgage on it," said Chen Hong. She initially took a 140,000 yuan mortgage for twelve years at the low rate of 4.2 percent. But two years later, she took out almost all her savings and borrowed twenty-thousand yuan from her parents to pay off the loan. When I saw her again, she was very happy and more relaxed. "Finally I feel that this is my house now! You cannot imagine how great this makes me feel," exclaimed Hong. "I consulted several friends and they all said that I should use my savings to pay off because the mortgage interest is too much." Like Hong, the majority of urban Chinese today see owning a house as the biggest and most secure investment in a changing economic environment. In their eyes, money can come and go, but a fully paid house can stay there for a long time and bring stability and respect to one's life.

Advertising Dreams, Selling Homes

Being able to sell housing units quickly at a profitable rate largely determines whether a real estate project is successful or not. Home buyers usually took into account of the following factors in their decision making: (1) location and price; (2) apartment and community design; (3) the reputation of the developer and the services promised. Among these factors, only price is relatively fixed while everything else can be manipulated through representation. In Kunming, housing units in the new communities were often sold before the completion of construction. Thus, buyers can only see architectural and community design through drawings and miniature models. If a developer can produce desirable images and disseminate them as widely as possible, more potential buyers will be attracted. Typically, before the construction begins, the real estate firm holds a press conference followed by aggressive newspaper and TV advertising. Some also hang large eye-catching banners and billboards throughout the city. The press conference is not only an important opportunity to introduce the project to the public but also a way of demonstrating the support of local government agencies and of strengthening the reputation of the developer. A common practice is to give each reporter attending the event a "red envelope" (*hong bao*) of 100–300 yuan as a token of appreciation for their presence and a hint that favorable coverage is expected.

In August 2006, I attended one such press conference hosted by the Silver Sea Real Estate Corporation to announce its plans to build a massive residential community around a small lake. More than two hundred people attended the event at one of Kunming's five-star hotels. The host of the housing show of the Yunnan provincial television station was invited to be the guest host. The theme of the press conference was "The Return of the Dayan Lake—The Rebirth of a Natural Lake in the City." The tiny lake referred to here was used as the selling point and presented as a means of returning to nature and serenity for the future residents. The development's master plan, rather than considering the potential damage to the natural beauty of the lake, presented the development as a noble preservation effort. In the beautifully printed booklets handed out at the conference, all the pictures used to illustrate the future community life were lifted from other places; some were created by using special digital technology to combine scenes of other places with a drawing of the anticipated buildings. There were also thirteen diagrams of the condominium models on the last two pages of the pamphlet.

The press conference featured five keynote speakers. The CEO of the development firm first introduced the project and called for public support. An expert from the provincial bureau of urban design followed, praising how much the new development would contribute to the beautification of Kunming's urban space. Then an official from the city environment protection bureau talked about the importance of wetlands and confirmed that the new development would create a better environment for the city. The chief planner from Hong Kong gave a detailed account of the four basic concepts she had used in the design process: nature, culture, taste, and responsibility. Finally, a well-known retired university professor briefly traced the origin of Dayan Lake and the history of Kunming as a water city. He was asked to reflect on the cultural and historical sensitivity of the developer, but surprisingly he also offered some of his own critiques of recent redevelopment projects in the city and called for better preservation of nature and cultural heritage sites. The next day the major local TV stations and newspapers reported this event and applauded the development project as sensible and environmentally friendly. A full-page, prominent advertisement ran for about two weeks in several newspapers, including the most widely read paper, the *Spring City Evening Daily*.

With the increased demand for real estate advertising, agencies specialized in making ads are also flourishing. This is an extremely lucrative business that does not require a lot of start-up capital. Fengchi, known for making creative posters and billboards, is one of the major agencies in Kunming and it controls a significant portion of real estate advertising in the city. One of the cofounders is a university professor who started this line of work as a moonlighting job in the late 1990s. He accumulated a sizable amount of money in just a few years and is now a wealthy man with political clout in the city.

Even with aggressive advertising, the hard work of selling ultimately falls on individual sales agents. Typically, when a new residential compound is put on the market, the developer sets up a sales office on-site and hires its own sales staff. Although there were some male agents working, most of those I met were women in their twenties or thirties. These young women float between new construction sites and are referred to as *shoulou xiaojie* ("young ladies specialized in selling homes"). The term *xiaojie* carries a sexual connotation and occupies an ambivalent position between legitimate and illegitimate services.[13] *Shoulou xiaojie* usually do not have much prior work experience, but they must be pretty and charming. Their work pays well but is also unstable, stressful, and short-lived. As one such woman put it: "We are eating out of our youth (*chi qingchun fan*).[14] Look, the youngest in our company is only nineteen. The qualifications to do this kind of work are so low that one can begin to work after only a month's training and make a relatively good living. But once you reach thirty, the company tells you to leave because you are not good anymore." *Shoulou xiaojie* must work very hard to meet the minimum sales target set by their firms. Their incomes depend on commissions as the base pay is extremely low (often less than three hundred yuan per month). Companies usually require that each agent sell at least 3–5 units per month. If this target is not met for three months in a row, the agent will be fired without pay. Sometimes it takes a while to get a contract finalized and the money deposited, and this delay can become a big challenge. "During this period, I was always extremely anxious because I had not had any deal finalized for two months. I was about to lose my job and thought I could not last anymore and would go crazy. At that crucial moment, one customer signed the contract and gave me new hope," recalled Miss Liu.[15]

During my fieldwork I accompanied several potential buyers on their trips to hunt for suitable housing. Some of them were serious about buying a place soon; others just wanted to get familiar with the market for a future purchase. Occasionally I went alone to look at new properties because my aging parents were interested in buying a place at that time. One day in August 2000 I went to Jade Garden, an upscale housing compound widely advertised in the city. Although it was still under construction, the sales had already reached their peak. As I walked into the office, I saw eight agents—all young women in blue uniforms—talking to customers. They were extremely attentive, willing to answer all questions, and providing information that customers requested. Each customer was given a bag of carefully designed and tastefully printed literature and as well as a ten-minute video compact disc introduction to the compound. The advertising materials made great use of the fact that Jade Garden was adjacent to the city's beloved Green Lake and created an illusion that the lake was part of the community life offered. In the center of the room, there was a model of the entire community and several models of the different kinds of units offered. The agents frequently used them to explain the spatial layout, including a children's playground, underground parking, and green space. Even though the apartments cost between five hundred thousand and one million yuan, some wealthy customers could make a decision right there and signed the contract with a deposit. Most customers collected all the information they needed and went back to discuss it with their family members.

Kunming's housing market has been largely a sellers' market due to the high demand. Most newly built units in popular locations are completely sold within a year of completion. But competition remains and it is harder to sell the luxury models than to sell the low- and medium-priced ones. For the young saleswomen I met, the actual day-to-day work of selling was exhausting, tedious, and stressful. Not only did the sales staff not have any job security but also they were under enormous pressure from the firm to sell more units and to do so quickly. If one could not meet the monthly quota, she risked being fired. Even though the profit from each sale was huge, the agents only received a small fraction of it. On average each agent would meet eight to ten potential buyers every day and had to remain enthusiastic even though they had repeated the same information over and over. As the sale approached its end and fewer customers came, most agents would be laid off and then must look for other projects.

Once I checked out a luxury condominium high-rise in the heart of downtown with a female informant interested in buying a place. This stand-alone eighteen-story building was surrounded by noisy department stores and shops. There was no garden, swimming pool, or other kinds of communal space. But some buyers liked its convenient location in the central financial district and were willing to pay a high price. When we got there, most units had already been sold—there were only three left. The sales office was quiet and we were greeted by two young women. One of them took us to see a model home designed to accentuate what locals considered Western-style lavishness (*haohua*). The living room floor consisted of large, light yellow granite slabs. All the bedrooms had hardwood floors. Ornate lighting fixtures were installed throughout the house. The two bathrooms featured a Jacuzzi, granite vanity top, glass shower enclosure, and Italian tiles, things that were rare and an extravagance in the eyes of most Kunming residents. The model house was to demonstrate to potential buyers what a dream home could be. But what buyers would actually get was a "bare/naked apartment" (*maofang*) without any basic finishing details. Upon request, we were allowed to see one of the unmodeled units. It was like entering a different world, with concrete floors, unpainted walls, and nothing else! The glamour of modern luxury living had suddenly vanished. It is estimated that it normally takes an additional one third of the cost of the home purchase price and two to three months to get a decent remodeling job done before a family can move in.

The saleswoman was polite and patient, but at the same time she was also trying to figure out whether we had the financial capacity to buy. She asked what price range we were looking for and how soon we could make the decision. She did not ask about our occupations directly because one could make substantial sideline incomes that are not reflected in their formal occupation. Instead she was observing our reaction carefully to see whether we were taken aback or felt at ease when she told us the cost of each unit (five hundred thousand yuan or more). My friend gasped gently. The agent sensed that we were not in this price range and quickly wrapped up the tour.

Some sales agents I met on the shopping tours were snobbish, especially if they were selling upscale housing. They were warm and responsive in the beginning, but once they sensed that you were not in the right market they would not waste any more time. So how did they make this judgment? Some simply looked at the car a customer drove. If it was a Lincoln, Mercedes Benz, Audi, or BMW, they would rush out with a very warm greeting. If it was a Santana, Toyota, or Mazda, a lukewarm greeting was given. If it was a taxi or bike, they would put that customer on a low priority. Customers were also judged by their clothing and the way they acted. A few minutes of conversation could also reveal much about one's background and economic status. But these indicators were not always reliable and misrecognitions did happen:

> One day several salespersons were sitting and chatting in the office. A man who looked like a peasant migrant worker showed up on his bicycle and wanted to see some model houses. Most agents ignored him and continued chatting. One of them, a young female agent, took him for a quick tour out of politeness. It turned out that this "migrant worker" was really the boss of a well-known Taiwanese enterprise. He was happy with the new housing community and decided to buy all the units on one floor. The woman was thrilled, while the others were shocked and regretted their misjudgment. (*Yangzi Evening Daily,* June 30, 2004)

In this highly feminized sector, the ability to sell relies heavily on one's beauty, youth, and personality performance, involving a kind of short-lived affective labor. The good earnings often come with an acute sense of insecurity, stress, and alienation. Young saleswomen must know how to sell not only houses but also their attitudes on the sales floor by putting on pleasant smiles and acting deferentially in front of potential buyers.[16] As soon as they get married or want to start a family, many of them quit to look for other kinds of work that might offer more stability. The gendered nature of this realm is further reflected in a sharper contrast between buyers and sellers. While most agents are young women, their customers are mostly middle-aged men with purchasing power. Although women (wives, lovers, or mistresses) may come along, they are usually not the final decision makers. Thus, the underlying assumption of employing mostly young women is that male buyers not only come to buy housing but that they also expect to enjoy a special, pleasurable service that boosts their ego and legitimates their status.[17]

Labor's Lot: Sweat, Blood, Liminality

The construction of new housing depends on the hard and dangerous work of millions of migrant workers. Although the buildings they create are highly visible in the urban landscape, they remain an invisible social group living under substandard conditions. To earn a modest income they must endure harsh working conditions and rely on their "blood and sweat" (*xuehan*). In Kunming, as in other Chinese cities, most construction workers are male rural migrants in their twenties and thirties. Part of the unspeakable profits of the real estate industry comes from the exploitation of migrant laborers through low wages, unsafe work conditions, long working hours, denial of benefits, and lack of job security. My account focuses on the conditions of the construction workers and their struggle to make a living in a world that depends on their work but treats them as mere laborers. I start with a few stories that took place in other Chinese cities because they made the national news. I then move to my own observations in Kunming.

January 2004. Pu Yongqin, a Sichuan construction contractor, fled with over one hundred thousand yuan of "blood and sweat money" he owed to several dozen peasant workers who worked for him on a housing development project in Ningbo, Zhejiang Province. He subcontracted a portion of the work and received a lump sum payment from a large construction firm, but he did not pay his workers for several months and suddenly vanished with his wife.

September 2004. Five hundred peasant workers finally won a lawsuit and received a one million yuan payment for their unpaid wages owed by the developer. More than one hundred workers showed up at the middle court in the city of Maanshan to celebrate the victory. The workers' representative was so excited that he kissed the one million yuan check.

August 2006. A group of angry peasant construction workers in Shijingshan District, Beijing, climbed to the top of an unfinished high-rise and threw metal pipes, bricks, and wood blocks down to the street. They were protesting because the contractor they worked for had fled without paying them after several months of hard work. The police came but could not quell their outrage. These migrant workers were demanding that the top district official step in to solve the problem. They claimed that their families back home desperately depended on their wages.

Long delays in, or denial of, wage payments by their contractors or developers is a common problem faced by migrant construction workers.[18] In China, the actual construction work is mostly outsourced by large firms to smaller construction teams that employ young rural migrant men. The heads of these teams, known as *baogongtou,* act as labor brokers. Typically such contractors are also from the countryside and tend to have more migration and urban experience. They recruit poor young men from their own village or county who have no special skills to work in the city because their families are struggling financially. Their average monthly wage in Kunming is between four hundred and eight hundred yuan, but getting this much or any money at all is not guaranteed. A contractor usually gets paid in a lump sum by the construction company for the work he agrees to perform. The decent ones pay the workers and still make money. But some choose to run away with the money and not pay the workers after the construction is done. The ultimate beneficiaries of this subcontracting system, however, are the larger construction companies that get the bids for the projects and then farm out the actual work to the smaller teams of peasant workers.

In addition to keeping wages very low and denying payments at times, minimizing the cost for labor maintenance is another way to increase profits. In Kunming and Beijing (where I conducted my previous fieldwork on migrants), I visited several construction sites where workers lived in makeshift huts (*gongpeng*) that had been poorly assembled with wood sticks and asbestos shingles. Because there were no windows, it was very dark inside the hut. Wind could easily blow through the walls; rain often leaked through the roof. On rainy days, *gongpeng* were flooded or surrounded by water and mud. Due to Kunming's mild weather, workers there are luckier than those in Beijing where the temperature can drop below 10 degrees Celsius in the winter. Without adequate heating devices, workers must stay close together to warm one another up with their bodies. Summer is also challenging as the temperature in some cities reach 40 degrees Celsius. It is extremely difficult to fall asleep in a crowded, poorly ventilated hut.[19]

Overcrowded housing is a common problem facing construction workers. It was not uncommon to see fifty people crammed into a room of thirty square meters without any privacy. Their beds were made of bamboo sticks and a piece of hard cardboard. Their safety was at risk and tragedies took place under certain weather conditions. For example, Shenzhen was hit by a typhoon on September 2, 2003, during which twenty-one people died, twenty of whom were construction workers who died when their poorly fabricated *gongpeng* collapsed. Due to the poor hygienic conditions (lack of bathrooms and running water), contagious diseases can easily break out. Food poisoning occurs frequently. In August 2003 forty workers got food poisoning on a Shanghai construction site and forty-nine on a Beijing construction site; in October 2003 sixty workers fell sick on a Jiangxi construction site. When I visited the construction sites in Kunming, I saw meals being prepared outside without basic hygiene standards and no refrigeration. As raw food was left at room temperature for a long time, bacteria could thrive. To save money, contractors were likely to buy cheap and poor quality food for workers. The daily meals for construction workers were very simple, consisting of rice or steamed buns and boiled or pickled vegetables. Meat was considered a rare luxury. Not getting enough to eat was a common complaint among migrant workers.

Accidents at construction sites take place all the time since safety procedures are virtually nonexistent or not followed. A young migrant worker told me that "there is no such thing as safety training. My boss just handed a helmet to me on the first day and told me to start. This helmet is supposed to protect my life and I am supposed to watch out for myself." A thirty-seven-year-old Henan migrant worker, Zhen, fell from a scaffold twenty-four meters above the ground after it collapsed in August 2006. He was buried under a pile of iron pipes and four of his co-workers fell and died instantly. He was taken to the hospital and survived. "For those of us doing this kind of work, it is entirely up to fate," Zhen told. "If God lets me survive, I can make some money to support my family. You just do not know when death will come. Few people care about our lives in this society." During his twenty years of construction work, his head was once hit by a falling metal pipe and he fell three times from broken scaffolds. Sometimes he wondered why he was so lucky and had thus developed a strong faith in fate (*ming*).[20]

Construction workers constitute an underclass in contemporary Chinese cities because they have virtually no chance for upward social mobility and live under extremely poor conditions. Although their labor is indispensable in the making of urban China, they remain forever the invisible, floating "outsiders" and mere laborers in the cities. This sense of liminality and placelessness is well articulated by a poem, "The Song of *Mingong*," that was collectively created by and circulated among some peasant workers:

> We are roaming about
> From the eighties to the next century.
> We see this city changing with each passing day
> In a myriad twinkling lights
> But not a single light belongs to me, brothers,
> Not a single light belongs to us.

Modeling the Middle-Class Dream

Every weekday morning around 8:30 a.m., several dozen migrant workers would arrive on bicycles at the gate of a newly constructed housing compound, waiting to be checked in by the security guards. Some were chatting with each other and others were busy finishing their breakfast— a steamed bun or egg pancake sold by peddlers at the corner. They were going to work in the new homes purchased by urban middle-class families to transform the bare housing (*maofang*) into "private heavens."

Buying a new house is the beginning of another costly process of modeling and remodeling (*zhuangxiu*) to turn the place into a livable and comfortable home. Its importance to individual families and the entire housing industry is reflected in the fact that the labor and material cost is roughly one third of the housing purchase expense. Depending on the size of the house, a *zhuangxiu* project takes one to three months. The high demand for remodeling and the amount of money homeowners invest in it have given rise to a sizeable, profitable sector specialized in providing tiles, natural stones, wood flooring, paint, lighting fixtures, bathroom and kitchen equipment, and so forth. Interior modeling workers are mostly semiskilled rural migrants. Like construction workers they constitute an indispensable part of what makes middle-class lifestyles possible, yet they are socially invisible in the cities and are seen as a potential source of danger to the safety of urban families.

There were over two thousand *zhuangxiu* companies in Kunming as of 2006. The largest and most well-known ones employed thirty to one hundred workers and staff and work primarily for hotels, office buildings, and upscale villa communities. These large companies can afford to

Figure 1. Migrant workers entering a middle-class housing compound to start remodeling work.

Figure 2. Home interior design that reflects the taste of Kunming's new middle class.

Figure 3. Migrant workers transform a "naked" house that was recently purchased by a wealthy family into a private domestic paradise.

spend a huge amount of money on advertising their work, but actually farm out some of the projects to informal migrant teams. The majority of the *zhuangxiu* workforce operated on a much smaller scale and on a temporary basis. Even though some of them were called "companies," they were not registered nor did they have offices. Typically, when a contractor found a remodeling job, he would use his own relatives and, if necessary, hire two to four additional workers chosen from a well-established network of semiskilled migrants from the contractor's native place.[21] Most of them had acquired skills in carpentry, plumbing, and tile and electric work through informal apprenticeships; some learned as they worked. Kunming's *zhuangxiu* market was dominated by migrants from Sichuan and Zhejiang provinces. Zhejiang migrants had a reputation for providing better quality work due to their long tradition of carpentry in certain regions. But in more recent years, the share of Sichuan migrants in this business grew significantly because their labor was cheaper.

During my fieldwork, I came to know several remodeling workers. Some of them worked for my informants who had recently bought new homes;

two worked on the new homes my parents and my sister purchased. Chu Shifu (Master Chu) was an independent contractor whom I came to know very well because he worked on my parents' and sister's homes for four months. His story was similar to the experiences of many migrants who ended up in this business:

> I was born in 1976 and began to learn carpentry from my father when I was thirteen. But I was not interested at that time and did not really learn the skill. My hometown was in rural Guangan, Sichuan. We were very poor and many of us had to leave home, looking for work outside. Most young people in my village dropped out of school and left for work outside. In 1991 I went to work as a carpenter in a local township chemical factory. It was a backbreaking job and I sometimes simply could not lift the stuff there. Two years later I went to Guangzhou and worked in a plastics factory run by a Taiwanese boss. I worked in construction there with several folks from my hometown. We usually got up at 3 a.m. and worked until 5 p.m., making only ten yuan a month. We never had enough to eat. When hungry we drank tap water. We dared not dream of tea or other things. At that time I learned that without special skills I would never be able to make a living. So I returned home and began to focus on learning carpentry from my father.
>
> A year later, a fellow villager who had been in Kunming for several years asked me to come to work for his remodeling team. That was the time the *zhuangxiu* craze just began to take off nationwide. So he was doing very well and was expanding his business. After working for him in woodwork [installing wood floors and making furniture] for several years, my skills improved a lot. I made fifteen hundred to eighteen hundred yuan a month. But I could make a lot more if I set up my own business. So I tried in 2003, but things were not easy. The most difficult part was to find customers who would trust you enough to give you a project. People like us are highly mobile and do not have a license. We are called the "guerrillas" team. I understand why many urban residents do not trust us because they think we will take their money and run away.
>
> I had to do a good job and prove myself. I started with some families I had worked for before and asked them to introduce me to their friends and relatives if they liked my work. I gave warranty to all the work I did. If any problems occurred later, I would return to fix them for free. Still, it was not easy. Sometimes I had no work for two months. But gradually I was able to build up a network of customers and establish my reputation.

Networking with customers was crucial for the success of small remodeling businesses. Chu Shifu was introduced to my parents by a neighbor who had hired him, and then my sister hired him. Later, they introduced him to three more families. The quality of Chu's work was not the best, but his price was very competitive compared with what a larger company would charge. Since middle-income families like my parents did not have a lot of disposable income, keeping the cost down was their foremost concern. Equally important was that they felt that they could trust him because he was introduced by a friend. As promised, Chu promptly came back four times to fix plumbing problems that occurred later. This satisfied my parents greatly.

According to the estimates of several contractors, there were roughly fifty thousand Sichuan migrants in Kunming doing *zhuangxiu* work. They were concentrated in the following low-income communities: Baima, Honglian, Chuanfang, Guandu, and the North Train Station areas. Many were waiting for jobs and were grateful if they were picked up by a contractor. The spontaneous labor market formed on the basis of native place and profession provided a flexible, cost-effective way for small contractors to recruit labor. But it also meant that the workers lived on highly unstable incomes, with little protection against illness and other potential misfortunes.

Mobile, smaller modeling teams must operate in a flexible way to reduce cost. The workforce Chu Shifu assembled consisted of about nine people—an electrician, three or four carpenters, two tile workers, two painters, and his father. Chu oversaw the projects and was responsible for designs; his father did carpentry and also took care of miscellaneous jobs. Other workers were called on a temporary basis and were paid for the specific work they performed. "My pool of laborers is relatively stable. I normally choose them from the same group of fellow natives whom I know well. This way I know the quality of work I will get and they are confident that I will pay them. But if one does not have the right skills, even if he is my relative I will not hire him. At most I will use him for simple jobs that require little skill, for example knocking out walls or cleaning up," said Chu. I asked him why he had not created a formal company or whether he would consider doing so in the near future since his business seemed to be growing. He said no and cited several reasons. If he had a formal, larger company, costs associated with office rent, staff management, and advertising would increase significantly. The operation would become much less flexible, particularly regarding hiring. The earnings would be subject to taxation. Without personal connections with the local political and business worlds and without a large amount of capital, migrant contractors such as Chu would not be able to compete with the more established local firms.

THE emerging real estate industry as I observed it in Kunming displays a pattern of two opposite movements involving capital and labor. On the one hand, capital keeps moving up and becomes concentrated in the sectors controlled by developers, architects, and community planners; on the other hand, labor moves downward to small, flexible teams that tap into a rural migrant workforce to reduce costs and shed welfare responsibilities. This pattern of development, with a capital-intensive top and a labor-intensive bottom, marks China's postsocialist capital accumulation and economic restructuring. Yet the centrality of this massive labor force tends to be erased in the grand narrative of urban development and the real estate boom.

3

Emerging Landscapes
of Living

"Home buyers in the 1980s focused on the physical house (*fangzi*) itself; home buyers in the 1990s looked for community greenery (*lühua*); home buyers in the twenty-first century underscore cultural taste (*wenhua pinwei*) and new concepts of living (*linian*)." This is a popular saying that I frequently heard from Kunming residents. It nicely encapsulates the shifting desires of Chinese home buyers over the past three decades. With the rise of private home ownership and class distinctions, a differentiated regime of urban living is emerging.[1] It involves a new set of spatial forms of dwelling and emerging concepts of living. A private home is not only an important investment but also a salient site for articulating cultural distinction, social entitlement, and life orientation. How are such notions as *wenhua* (culture), *ziran* (nature), and *linian* invoked and deployed in the making of the new regime of living? How do the contradictions between the attempts to transplant the Western modern housing styles and the desires to preserve Chinese cultural elements play out in architectural design and planning? What is the relationship between differentiation and the equivalence of commodities in shaping property value? How is the boundary between private and public space shifting due to the demand for privacy and fear of crime? I explore these questions through a concrete study of Kunming's diverse new properties with a focus on design, architecture, and lifestyle. It is in this arena of producing and marketing distinctive estates for different clients that we get a glimpse of how culture and economy articulate with each other to shape the new landscapes of living.

A major tension in the production of new forms of living derives from the friction between real estate developers' efforts to use Western architectural designs and foreign place names to appeal to middle-class consumers, and a nationalistic sentiment expressed by some local governments and intellectuals who see the trend of "going foreign" as nonpatriotic and disturbing. For example, the Kunming Municipal Government actually took action to curtail foreign naming, revealing a broader strife that exists between nationalist pride and the pursuit of Western modern styles. Despite such concerns, foreign naming continued to flourish in Chinese cities, especially in Beijing and Shanghai, as the two cities aspire to become leading global metropolises with a vibrant cosmopolitan life.

Another tension I seek to grasp is how the dialectics between universal exchange value and the particularity of commodity form works out in China's real estate market. I examine two simultaneous processes. The first is a process of *differentiation* expressed in housing styles and cultural tastes. Developers seek to produce an array of residential forms and concepts of living in order to harness and kindle the never-ending, divergent needs and desires of consumers. Such differentiation marks the formation of a mass consumer society, in which competing commodities are advertised and sold through the notion of distinction and choice. To make housing products more marketable and valuable under intense market competition, culture and nature are appropriated as the raw ingredients to produce distinction. Yet, there is another process of at work: *equivalence*. As Karl Marx explains in *Capital,* "The equivalent form of a commodity, accordingly, is the form in which it is directly exchangeable with other commodities." Despite the differentiation expressed in cultural and spatial forms of living, the ultimate goal of the developers is to maximize the exchange value of commodity housing. Although the principle of equivalence is central to commodity production, the selling of commodities relies on the appropriation of distinctive cultural images and concepts of living. It is through this dual process of differentiation and equivalence that different cultural forms and elements of nature are brought into the market sphere of transactions and profits.

This dual process is an integral part of contemporary consumer capitalism. In his insightful analysis of advertising in contemporary India, William Mazzarella has argued against a totalizing discourse on late capitalism by highlighting the persistent tension between the concrete and the abstract, the particular and the universal crystallized in the commodity image under globalization. "Nowhere is this clearer than in the production of advertising, where the value is generated precisely out of provisionally harnessing the unpredictable concretion of images within linear narratives" (Mazzarella 2003, 45). His insight is useful in understanding the cultural logic of Chinese real estate development and marketing. Developers and marketers know too well that the exchange value of commodity housing can only be realized and maximized when the commodity itself is able to harness consumer desires through concrete and tangible cultural forms that reroute consumers' attention away from mere abstraction. Thus, it took less than a decade for the Chinese real estate market to shift its focus from selling the house to selling the images and *linian*.

"New Housing Movement"

As more new homes become available and the housing market becomes more competitive, what strategies do developers use to make their products appealing and thus sell well? How do buyers make their decisions on which home to buy when facing myriad choices? On one level, housing is a form of commodity whose exchange value is determined by the abstract human labor invested in it. On another level, developers must manufacture and promote the distinctive features of their products through branding and advertising in order to maximize their profit margin. The word "manufacture" here carries two meanings: the physical construction of residential communities, and the social construction of uniqueness and desirability using exaggeration, fabrication, and idealization. The double sense of manufacturing has generated a new social movement that aims to promote new ways of thinking about residence and living across urban China. It is in this context that the "new housing movement" emerged.

The "new housing movement" was initially launched in 2000 by the China Urban Real Estate Developers' Network (CUREDN), which was organized by a dozen powerful nonstate real estate enterprises. The founding president, Wang Shi, was the head of a well-known, Hong Kong–based, transregional real estate firm.[2] The goal was to cultivate a sense of culture, order, and idealism in a field dominated by profit-seeking, market calculation, and corruption. In that summer, CUREDN held a high-profile forum in Shanghai, during which some five hundred participants discussed what the concept of "new housing" meant to contemporary China and how it could reshape urban living and real estate practices. The forum unveiled the "Shanghai Manifesto," which outlined the three basic principles of the "new housing movement" (see Shan Xiaohai 2001). First, the new housing should be created for ordinary people, rather than for a few privileged elites. Second, the new housing is not merely a place to live but should promote a new culture of living based on a mindful awareness of human existence and nature. Third, a new order of doing business must be established to ensure fair market competition as well as to protect architects' creativity.[3] The emphasis on ordinary people, a culture of living, and business order reflected a spirit of idealism, in sharp contrast with the stark reality of a real estate world characterized by the blind pursuit of profit at the expense of ordinary people's interests and a lack of cultural considerations.

This initiative attracted the attention of architects, planners, sociologists, economists, and information technology workers in many major cities. Was this new housing movement led by a few powerful developers a genuine effort to explore new forms of living for ordinary people, or was it simply an attempt to create business alliances and develop a new consumer market? The critics regarded this initiative as an effort by a few developers to entice a group of lower-income consumers who had been ignored in the early phase of the commodity housing development. "By now most rich people in China have already bought their own homes and solved their housing problem. Thus, it is no longer easy to get money out of their pockets. Now it is time for developers to turn their eyes toward the ordinary people and find new ways to convince them to spend their hard-earned 'blood and sweat money' (*xuehan qian*) on new housing," explained the author of an article titled "Whose Housing, What Is New?" (Shan Zhenping 2001, 250). In this writer's eyes, the so-called new housing movement was a covert move to "steal" money from lower-middle-class families by turning them into consumers willing to spend their life savings to attain a new way of living vaguely depicted as "humanistic and cultured" (*renwen*).

The vision of new housing promoted by this movement is just one of the many emerging concepts of living (*juzhu linian*) that middle-class Chinese are pursuing today.[4] In what follows, I will show how several popular forms of living are created in Kunming and how culture and nature are deployed in the making and selling of commodity housing. When these ideas and concepts are adopted by different developers and put into practice, they sometimes become rival forces in the battle to win consumers' hearts and money. My analysis draws from my ethnographic material as well as a special weekly column, *Loushi* ("Real Estate Market"), that is featured in several major local newspapers in Kunming. It provides an important entrée into how various concepts of living are created and disseminated as this section contains not only housing advertisements but also lengthy review articles about new properties written by professional journalists. Consumers read these writings regularly and treat them as an authoritative way of elucidating the new concepts of living exemplified by the new communities.

Selling *Linian* and Lifestyles

As the popular saying presented at the beginning of this chapter suggests, in the beginning of the housing reform what mattered most to urbanites in buying a place to live were physical, pragmatic elements such as the size, floor plan, and location of the property. Although these basic factors continued to be important, buyers in the 1990s began to pay greater attention to the landscape and environment of the community, not just their own dwelling units. *Lühua,* which refers to both the ratio of green space and the quality and design of lawns, shrubs, trees, and flowers in a given community, became a most important criterion for assessing the desirability of an estate. Davis Fraser translates *lühua* as "oasification" and suggests that "oasification commodifies green, pleasant aspects of a constructed nature to create a buffer zone between the individual apartment and its larger social and spatial contexts" (2000, 27). This feature is particularly attractive to urban Chinese because green communal space was largely absent in their everyday life under socialism.

Into the twenty-first century there has been a new shift from practical matters to relatively intangible concerns. Two notions are particularly central in the marketing of commodity housing in this era: "culture," which refers to a myriad of relatively elusive factors such as taste, lifestyle, class, and status; *linian* (combining two words, "ideal" and "concept"), which signifies "a stark departure from the outdated idealism of communist utopianism" (Wu 2004, 227). Today, selling homes largely depends on one's ability to package distinctive cultural concepts into the products, and link property value to lifestyle aspiration. Despite the very different emphasis in each period (from the materiality of housing to environment to culture), there has been a constant underlying assumption of free consumer choice throughout the reform years.

Transplanting Western Modern

A prominent image frequently packaged in new commodity housing and sold to Kunming home buyers is *xiandai* (modern). It is often used interchangeably with the term *yangqi,* meaning "foreign flavor" or "overseas taste." The conflation of these two terms indicates that being modern is intrinsically tied to foreign influences, or more precisely to Western influences. As I have argued elsewhere (2006), *xiandai* is increasingly expressed and realized through urban planning and home architectural styles that negate traditional and Soviet-style spatial forms. The vision of modern living today is sold through the construction of properties that claim to adopt authentic foreign architectural motifs and promise to offer an aura with an exotic, modern flavor.[5] This phenomenon is not unique to Kunming, but represents a nationwide trend that has been observed by other scholars (see

Fraser 2000; Wu 2004). The architectural motifs that signify modern are usually drawn from North America and Western Europe. In Beijing and Shanghai, due to the high concentration of financial capital and a transnational business class, new urban mega-projects for upper-middle-class Chinese and expatriates have sought well-known, high-priced international architects to "brand" their design and assert their authenticity (Ren 2008). Although these signature projects are extremely expensive, they have become a high-status symbol and emblem of Western modern styles.

In Kunming, however, the projects that claim to transplant Western modern styles are less concerned with authenticity and do not much resemble the original design. At best, they are an approximate reproduction of what is broadly perceived by locals as Western-style housing. Few developers have commissioned international architects (except for a few Hong Kong–based planners) for their design due to the extremely high cost. In some cases, the foreign atmosphere is simply created by giving the property and streets foreign names. To generate more foreign flavor, property advertisements tend to feature images of Caucasians and foreign residential landscapes. I visited about eight gated communities in Kunming that were named after a foreign place or claimed to have used a Euro-American motif in design (British, French, Norwegian, Mediterranean, Californian, and so on). But to me these were just ordinary, contemporary single-detached homes, town houses, or luxury apartments commonly found in the West without any distinctive characteristics. They were mostly designed by domestic architects who borrowed certain design features from the West or Hong Kong that gave a very different feel from that of traditional Kunming houses or socialist housing. I was not sure why a property was named after a particular country since it had very little to do with the architectural style of that place.

The naming of properties is a contentious issue worth further investigation. Typically there are two types of foreign-flavored names used by developers in Kunming. The first is related to foreign places, such as "Think UK," "Norwegian Forests," "Californian Maple Garden," "Bohemian Garden," "Marco Polo Peninsular," "Greenwich," and so on. The second is a hybrid form, mixing English words with Chinese words, for example, "BOBO *Ziyou* (Freedom)," "GOGO *Xinshidai* (New Age)," and so on. Even if some of them do not make any sense in the Chinese translation, the very use of English words signifies a development's modern, unconventional, and cosmopolitan orientation. New developments (especially upscale ones) with a foreign-flavored name are widespread and it is estimated that more than one third of the new developments in Kunming fall into this category. One of them, Think UK, a large compound of high-rise

Figure 4. Villa dream: Western-style townhouses in a wealthy, protected suburban development near Lake Dian.

condominiums, invoked a strong negative official reaction in 2005. This compound, constructed by a real estate firm owned by Mr. Dong, is located near the second ring road, an area that was once considered an undesirable place to live because it was far from downtown. But with the rapid urban sprawl of recent years, this area has been completely transformed. Farmland and factories have been replaced by new hospitals, schools, and commercial facilities. This area is now considered part of the new urban core and a convenient place to live. Think UK consists of some three thousand condominiums and about one hundred commercial stores located on the ground floor of these high-rises. As the largest high-rise residential community in the city, it targets white-collar professionals and middle-class families. Its advertising motto is "Think UK—a Fashionable Living Community, a Globalized Dwelling Place." The community is thus marketed as a modern, cosmopolitan place that integrates residence with commerce. The image of the British national flag is used in newspaper advertisements and street banners. When I was conducting fieldwork in the summer of 2006, many people in Kunming told me that it was bizarre to see United

Figure 5. Streets in Think UK named after British places and names, such as Palm Spring Park, Windsor Rose Garden, Victoria Garden, England Apple Park, and Cambridge Library (top down).

Kingdom symbols flying in a Chinese residential community and to hear someone saying, "I live in Think UK." This unusual use of foreign names and symbols generated a great deal of curiosity and conversation among Kunming residents.

It is interesting to note that Mr. Dong named two of his recent upscale developments (Think UK and Greenwich) after English places and one (Lennon Villas) after the English celebrity, John Lennon, the Beatles singer. In an interview, he explained his motive to me:

I follow what the consumer market demands. It is called *shishang* ("trendy"). I do not like to be trendy myself, but if the market wants it, I will provide it. When I started to build this large complex of condominiums, nothing like this on this scale existed in Kunming. I was the first one to try and it was risky, so I needed a trendy name to attract buyers and make people think it is something cool. Why British names? It was fortuitous because the words and images just came to my mind and I knew it was one of the trendy things today. Now just imagine the effect: there are three thousand units there. Assuming each family has about three members, there are a total of ten thousand people involved. If they all talk about this place to their friends and acquaintances, that is like free advertisement for my firm.

Think UK embraced foreign naming fully. Not only is the community named after the United Kingdom but all the streets and communal spaces inside also are named after an English place: Victorian Garden, Cambridge Library, England·Apple Orchard, Windsor Rose Garden, Hyde Park Health Center, and so on. These are by no means grand streets, gardens, or parks; they are merely short, narrow roads ranging from one hundred to three hundred yards and small communal spaces. The English names, however, are intended to give people an illusion of being in a foreign milieu. The security guards dressed in a peculiar type of red uniform also remind some of colonial Hong Kong. Experiencing the exotic this way largely depends on one's imagination of a place one has never been to. What matters here is not authenticity (e.g., whether the landscape really resembles that of England); rather, the imagined experience or feeling (*ganjue*) of being there can be comforting to some. As one resident put it, "I have never been to England and probably will never go there, but I feel like I am there just by looking at all the street signs of English places. It is not the same but I still enjoy it."

In 2005, a debate took place on the Internet. Under a column called *Qiangguo Luntan* ("Forum on Strengthening China"), which is a public debate/commentary space sponsored by China's official newspaper, *People's Daily,* a netizen criticized the practice of foreign naming and specifically referred to Kunming. Even though this commentary did not represent the paper's editorial position, it was widely circulated and had far-reaching effects. The Kunming municipal government quickly responded by banning the use of foreign names for ongoing and future developments. The municipal party secretary, Yang Chongyong, warned: "This practice signifies the degeneration and loss of decent Chinese urban culture. Kunming must immediately correct such blind worshiping of Western things and fawning over foreign powers." He then called for respect for traditional Chinese culture and indigenous local practices.

The Kunming government's order provoked different reactions and ignited a nationwide debate on this matter. Many older Kunming residents and intellectuals applauded the government's ban and claimed that it was time to stop the virtual colonization of the city. One retired college professor in her early seventies told me: "This is a good step. Otherwise, I will get more and more confused. My daughter recently moved into a new xiaoqu called Bohemian Garden, I think. She told me that her friend just bought a house in another xiaoqu called Marco Polo Villas. I sometimes get these names mixed up and do not know which 'country' they live in." This woman had taught foreign literature in a local college and thought it was hilarious to see foreign names popping up in her own hometown.

But there were also those who did not believe that government intervention could ultimately change a practice driven by market forces or alter a
popular mentality. Foreign names would reappear as long as they could
facilitate sales and make some people feel good. A legal scholar pointed
out that even though it was a display of bad taste and poor cultural judgment, developers had the right to use whatever names they wished as long
as their actions did not cause direct damage to the sovereignty and dignity
of the nation. The government could only provide guidance; it had no
right to impose a ruling. Representatives of some real estate companies
also defended their choices. Li Yan, the manager of the sales department
of Think UK, said: "Kunming is trying to merge with the global world
(*yu guoji jiegui*), so we should be able to pick and choose the good things
from the outside world and blend them with local culture. The design and
naming of our shopping streets and community is merely meant to incorporate some English cultural flavor. If some citizens find our ideas hard to
accept, that is just too bad." There was indeed a contradiction inherent
in the Kunming government's policy. On the one hand, the government
denounced foreign naming; on the other hand, it had earlier endorsed a
slogan, "Turning Kunming into the Geneva of the East," as its long-term
development objective. The use of Geneva, a European city, as its source
of inspiration, albeit adding the word "East," was a reflection of the very
mind-set that has been called into question.

Some intellectuals attributed the trend of foreign naming to China's nou-
veau riche culture and a neocolonial mentality. Professor Yu Kongjian of
Peking University remarked: "This [using foreign names] is derived from
a national mind-set of a country that lags behind or hopes to develop.
We can also call it a neocolonial cultural mentality.... We hope that this
stage will soon pass. Once a nation becomes truly strong and has gained
greater self-confidence, it will not worship foreign names."[6] Further, he
explained that this practice was a product of the *baofu* (suddenly rich) age:
when some people suddenly became rich but have no culture or education,
they worship money and take the West as the icon of affluence and status. Professor Guan Yuda of Yunnan University called the excessive use of
foreign names "a superficial form of utopian culture" that simply equates
Western or overseas lifestyles with success, respect, and high status. He
also noted that since most Chinese people could not easily go abroad,
living in a community with an overseas atmosphere partially might help
fulfill that dream. This dream of the West has found its way into the recent construction of nine new towns in the Shanghai suburbs. According
to NPR reporter Louisa Lim (2006), each of these towns is built in the
distinctive style of a European city in order to attract wealthy buyers who

are willing to move out of overcrowded Shanghai. Thames Town, for example, is meticulously modeled after a British town, Lyme Regis, and was
designed by the British company Atkins. This is a wholesale copy that "features cobbled streets, half-timbered Tudor houses, Edwardian town houses,
and a covered market with a clock tower and weather vane on top" (Lim
2006). What one resident said to Lim represented a common viewpoint of
homeowners there: "I like it here because it's *like* a foreign country." Some
critics, however, bemoan these copies of European towns as a form of self-
colonization.

Fulong Wu, who studied Western architectural motifs in Beijing's new
housing regime, argues that "transplanting cityscape is a conscious action
by developers to exploit globalization and thereby overcome the constraints
of local markets" (2004, 227). By steering consumer desires, developers
hope to exploit a specific market niche—the urban newly rich—by selling
them a new vision of the good life and cosmopolitan urbanity.[7] Although I
agree with this assessment, I also want to bring our attention to the social
conditions and ethos that make the cultivation of certain consumer desires
possible. There are at least two primary forces behind the transplanting
of Western modern styles to Chinese residential space. The first is a commercial one centered on real estate developers who wish to increase profits.
The second is a popular mind-set that conflates the modern and the good
life with the West. This mind-set has long historical roots in Chinese history, which have been explored by other scholars (see Huters 2005; Zhang
2005). When these two forces converge, it creates an ideal condition under
which the appropriation of Western spatial forms and lifestyles thrives.

Creating "Vernacular Modern"

Although transplanting the Western modern dominates Kunming's new
housing scene, there have also emerged other kinds of architectural and
landscape designs inspired by ethnic cultures based in Yunnan Province
and by traditional Chinese garden motifs. The ethnically influenced new
housing developments seek to create a comfortable living space that is seen
as both modern and distinctively local. "Vernacular modern" is achieved
through fusion, which combines different local cultural elements and physical materials to create something new rather than claiming authenticity
(cf. Brumann n.d.).[8] The meaning of "vernacular" (*bentuhua*) is not fixed.
In some cases, it refers to local ethnic architecture or native flora that can
be used in the landscape; in other cases, it refers to traditional Chinese
garden designs as exemplified in some south coastal areas such as Suzhou.
This kind of commodity housing caters to consumers looking not only for

modern comfort and class status but also for the beauty, peace, and balance offered by traditional or ethnic architectural designs.

Appropriating ethnic residential forms is more popular in Kunming than in other cities due to its geographic location in a province known for ethnic diversity. There are over twenty ethnic groups in Yunnan, among which some distinctive, elaborate housings architectures (*minju*) have long existed and been recognized by the Han majority (see Li, Chen, and Wang 2000).[9] Among them, the Bai, Naxi, Dai, and Yi ethnic dwellings are particularly distinctive and elaborate. In addition, the traditional Chinese cultural notions of the yin-yang balance and the natural flow of *qi* (energy) are also incorporated into the design. I would like to discuss two kinds of fusion below: one is elitist, featuring luxury single-detached homes that draw architectural inspiration from a particular ethnic housing style; the other is more common, featuring apartment complexes that combine multiple ethnic cultural elements with rudiments broadly recognized as traditional Chinese designs.

The most prestigious, ethnically inspired new housing in Kunming is Naxi Xiaoyuan ("Little Naxi Style Garden Houses"), consisting of sixteen sizable courtyard houses that cost two to three million yuan each. Located in the new northern residential development zone of the city, Naxi Xiaoyuan was constructed by the powerful Guandu Co. When I visited it on a warm summer afternoon in 2000, the construction had just finished but 80 percent of the units were already sold. A staff member from the developer's office, Mr. Wang, accompanied me on a tour of the property, which he was quite proud of. As we stepped out of the car, I was immediately taken by the distinctive architecture of the courtyard house in front of my eyes. It was nothing like what I had seen elsewhere. The basic color tones of the entire structure were white and blue. The external walls were painted artistically, featuring delicate geometric patterns; some showcased traditional Chinese ink paintings of plants and flowers. The raised roof was made of neatly placed half-round light blue tiles, finished with overhanging curved lines at the corners. As we walked up to the main gate of a courtyard house, Mr. Wang carefully unlocked the door, which was made in a traditional Chinese style of two large pieces of solid wood painted in black with two metal rings at the center. In the old days, the rings were used for knocking, but today they were merely decorative. I noticed that a high-tech intercom doorbell system was installed on the right side of the wall for homeowners to screen visitors.

The courtyard inside was nicely landscaped with dark blue bricks on the ground and trees and bamboo plants. The door of each room consisted of four beautifully carved, Naxi-style wood panels, something that one would typically see in an antique furniture store today. But what really surprised me was the interior of this model house. The living room floor was made of large blocks of light yellow granite with small black stone insets. The ceiling featured a style called *diaoding* that is typically found in luxury hotels. At the center was a grand, flashy lighting fixture meant to provide a splendid aura. Mr. Wang turned the light on and said: "Look! It is completely modern and comfortable inside. We are trying to blend the beauty of traditional ethnic architecture with a modern practical way of living. This is what some rich people want today because the fusion style is unique and reflects our provincial cultural characteristics." The communal space was equally impressive, displaying meticulously maintained lawns, trees, ponds, and fountains. "Our goal is to make people who live here feel that they have returned to nature even though they live in the heart of the city," said Mr. Wang.

Such tastefully designed, elaborate courtyard houses were no doubt built for a very small group of consumers—the newly rich. As claimed in the advertising brochure, this exclusive community was meant to serve as a "status symbol" for its owners as it displayed not only wealth but also cultural taste (*wenhua pinwei*). Houses built in the vernacular-modern style are usually more expensive compared with Western-style villas because they require more craftmanship, artistic details, and labor. Further, the cost of land for building Naxi Xiaoyuan is high since it is low density and located within the city core.

The other kind of ethnically influenced housing involves the technique of bricolage. Rather than following a particular ethnic residential form, it combines diverse features that are viewed by consumers as "vernacular." Sunshine Garden, developed by the Qingfeng Real Estate Firm, provides a good example. I visited it three times and interviewed two residents who were introduced to me by a friend. The average price of an apartment in Sunshine Garden was around three hundred thousand yuan, which was within the middle range of commodity housing prices in Kunming. It is difficult to characterize its architectural and landscape designs, but it definitely has a vernacular flavor.

First, the design of the buildings' roofs resembles that of *zhulou*, the Dai ethnic minority's bamboo houses. It is done in an abstract form, and the material used (tile) is radically different from the traditional bamboo. However, this design differs from the typical concrete roof commonly found in other new developments. The developer was highly protective of the "innovative design" and tried to prevent visitors from taking any pictures. I was not aware of this policy and nearly got myself in trouble. As I was walking with my two informants in the garden, I took my camera out and began to take pictures of the buildings. Since they were both very proud of their new community, they encouraged me to take a lot of pictures. A uniformed security guard on patrol suddenly ran toward me and yelled, "Stop! No photographing is allowed here." I was baffled: "Why?" One of my informants, a private businessman in his early thirties, stepped forward and said, "I live here and she is my guest. We can take whatever pictures we want because this is my home. What rights do you have to interfere?" As most new middle-class homeowners who have paid a lot of money to purchase a home do, this man had a strong sense of entitlement and felt that this place belonged to him. The security guard backed down a little and explained: "Sir, I am sorry that I did not know you live here, but this is not my idea. I am just doing my job. This rule is set by the bosses of our company because they do not want other developers to copy our popular design." He turned to me and said: "Please just don't take any more pictures. Otherwise I might lose my job. If my bosses see it, they will think that I do not perform my duty." I felt sorry for this guard caught between his bosses and homeowners. I assured him that I would stop and not give any pictures to other firms. I later learned that in a highly competitive housing market, some developers had actually sent undercover agents out to gather popular designs. But I wondered whether, if the camera belonged to my informants, they would have had the right to take pictures of their own homes and community. *Interesting!*

Second, instead of replicating the so-called Continental European style of grand lawns, the design of the common space was modeled after southern Chinese gardens that featured small creeks, lily ponds, miniature bamboo bridges, and pavilions hidden among thriving plants and trees.[10] I later learned that the developers and designers had considered a range of choices and finally decided on an architectural style that was at once modern, natural, and "Oriental" (*dongfang qingdiao*).[11] Against the popular trend of copying the West, Qingfeng wanted to distinguish itself from other developers by going vernacular, or *bentuhua*. To create a *bentu* environment, they tapped Yunnan's rich natural resources—plants and rocks from the ethnic regions. Known for its great botanic diversity, Yunnan Province is praised as "the kingdom of plants." During the construction period, the developer sent teams of workers to various remote mountainous areas to obtain and transplant a variety of rare species of plants native to the region. For example, a couple of *Banna rong*, a type of beloved fig tree native to the Xishuang Banna region, were carefully shipped over hundreds of miles and transplanted in Sunshine Garden. In the end, more than twenty species classified as "precious or rare" (*zhenxi*) found a home in Sunshine Garden's miniature kingdom of native plants.

In addition, the company made an unusual effort to bring in Yunnan native rocks to enhance the *bentu* atmosphere, including famous Jinsha rocks from Hutiao Xia (Tiger Jumping Gorge), Jianchuan ink-colored stones from Dali, multicolored rocks from Dongchuan, and limestones from Dianzhong (Zhang et al. 2000). Each piece of the Jinsha rock weighed eighteen tons and took more than twenty workers to pull it out of the torrential river. This attribute of *bentuhua* went hand in hand with the notion of *shengtai* living, as both envisaged a living environment close to nature. I asked some residents what attracted them most about this style of vernacular modern. Some said that they felt at home and comfortable with the fusion of modern construction and local aesthetics. Some indicated that their elderly parents who lived with them really preferred the *bentu* style and would not feel like they were living in a foreign place. As a retired teacher once told me: "If I had money and choices, I would definitely go for a community with a vernacular atmosphere. I can envision myself strolling along the streams and over the wooden bridges, watching water lilies blooming, and taking a rest in a Chinese pavilion. To me, that is a beautiful way to live. I just cannot picture myself telling my friends that I live in a place called Marco Polo or Bohemian Garden." Clearly, there is a special niche in the housing market for those who prefer vernacular modern.

Shengtai *Living: Commodifying Nature*

One of the most popular *linian* of living today in Kunming is the idea of a *shengtai* residence. It is closely tied to the notion of *lühua* but suggests more than that. The word *shengtai* can be roughly translated as "ecology" or "ecosystem," which accentuates a balanced natural environment. Originally, it was used in the context of protecting rain forests, animal life, and natural landscapes from being destroyed. Then, *shengtai* quickly became a fashionable term referring to a new type of residential space, which allows human beings to return to nature by providing a close, harmonious relationship with the environment. A new term, "special zones of eco-living" (*shengtai tequ*), was coined to describe this way of living. The "natural world" envisioned is by no means natural; it is a human-made environment that features plants, trees, ponds, and fresh air, or proximity to forests, mountains, lakes, and rivers.

Kunming is located in a large basin on a high plateau surrounded by mountains and hills. Historically, the city was also known as a water town (*shuicheng*) with many small rivers, ponds, and lakes. Even though many of them had dried out over time, the largest one, Dianchi Lake, has remained and has nourished a distinct regional culture and social life. These mountains and water bodies (real or imaginary, present or past), well documented in literary writings, are now deployed as elements of nature by the commodity housing regime. The western suburb around Dianchi, for example, has been turned into a site for experimenting with shengtai housing. A number of new residential developments, such as Oriental Rose Garden, the World Expo Garden, Jindian Forest Park, Lakeside Dream, Country Golf Villas, and Splendid Manors, all claim to be exemplars of this new concept of living. Their key selling point is "being close to nature" or "living amid a natural world." Built on a suburban hill or near a small lake, these properties tend to have quiet surroundings and more green space.

Country Golf Villas is deemed one of the largest shengtai communities in Kunming. It covers an area of six thousand *mu,* consisting of over four hundred of what Chinese call "villas" (Western-style single-detached homes). The green coverage of this property is as high as 82.5 percent, and the entire community is surrounded by hills and woods. There are human-made miniature mountains, small waterfalls, creeks, and walking paths inside. The fresh oxygen produced by plants and trees is accentuated in the advertisements. A newspaper review of Splendid Manors paints a poetic picture of this property: "By living here, one is in intimate contact with greenery, bright flowers, sunshine, and fresh oxygen. At night one can watch city lights flickering and stars blinking in the sky, while being soaked in the gentle breeze of nature." World Expo Garden is another new residential development built on the concept of shengtai living. A full-page advertisement in the *Spring Evening Daily* illustrates how the notion of nature is appropriated by the real estate industry as an invaluable commodity. On top of the page are several large Chinese words printed in a bold, orange font—"We Only Have One," followed by an image of the blue Earth. Three capitalized English words in green lettering, "MAN AND NATURE," serve as the background while the Chinese translation, *ren yu ziran,* is printed over the image of the Earth. Below is a paragraph explaining the uniqueness of this property and the ideal vision of living it offers:

> The essence of an ideal life is the harmonious coexistence between man and nature. Where is the natural way of living accompanied by mountains and waters? Will we be able to find any natural fresh waters in our future homesteads? The unique place that can accommodate human beings in nature is here—the World Expo shengtai zone. It is adjacent to several thousand *mu* of Jindian forests and provides 9,965 square meters of fresh water originating from the nearby White Dragon Pond.

Interestingly, this notion of harmony between man and nature has also found an important place in the state's official discourse on governing through harmony.

In the above portrayals, nature (*ziran*) is appropriated as a precious commodity to be sold. This cultural appropriation of nature (sometimes involving the reproduction of nature through landscape artifacts such as human-made ponds) is a key element in producing and increasing property values. Such discourses on nature or living close to nature are partially derived from the traditional Daoist philosophy of life. The highest state of being pursued through Daoism is the seamless merging of nature and human, and the ultimate return to nature and truth (*fanpu guizhen*). This ideal is reflected in the popular concept of shengtai living, embraced by certain social strata in search of distinction, cultural taste, and a higher state of being. Shengtai living also draws on recent global environmental discourses about the importance of green projects, but it uses them in a peculiar way. Ironically, the very encroachment of new developments into natural surroundings destroys nature itself. The outsized villas and cookie-cutter town houses represent anything but the harmony between nature and the human world as envisioned by Daoists or environmentalists. In a way, the celebrated "eco-living" and the desire to embrace nature too often turn into a destructive force because in the process of creating private green utopias, nature must be violated, transformed, and commodified. In order to become a marketable product, the advertised "natural environment" must also be privatized so that it can be possessed and consumed by those who can afford it. Thus, the construction of the private oases ends up promoting a politics of exclusion in the name of green living. This process is not unique to China, but widely found in other parts of the world.

The notion of shengtai living is by far the most successful *linian* that appeals to a large number of home buyers in Kunming. Why do so many consumers look for closeness to nature in choosing a residence? Is this preference merely produced and manipulated by developers to serve their interests? My fieldwork suggests that while housing advertisements and real estate columns are a powerful tool of manufacturing consumer desires, we must also situate the popular yearning for "green" nature in a historical context against Chinese people's experiences of an impoverished, "gray" urban life under Mao.[12] During my interviews, I asked the homeowners to describe the housing and community they lived in before the economic reform. Besides crowding and poor construction, the lack of color and the absence of green space in their communities was what stood out in their memories. They frequently referred to "gray concrete buildings" and "bare roads" in describing their living environments under

Figure 6. Bohemia Garden: an example of *shengtai* living that provides a natural, green environment.

the danwei system. The current longing for green space thus represents the denunciation of the impoverished gray past and the desire to launch a new, enriched way of living. It is against this historical background that the notion of shengtai living has gained such great momentum.

The Lure of Privacy and Freedom

The commodity housing market also targets a small yet fast-growing section of the Chinese population—young, single urban professionals who wish to have a place of their own. These people, mostly under the age of thirty, have accumulated some money, but not enough to purchase a larger place over two hundred thousand yuan. They either rent or live with their parents, having little privacy or control of the space they live in. Given this situation, some real estate developers have begun to build what is called *danshen gongyu* ("apartments for singles") for this market niche. Typically, the size of an apartment like this ranges from forty to sixty square meters, suitable for one person to live in comfortably. The cost is around one hundred thousand yuan, which is within the reach of young professionals with mortgage assistance and parental help. Since such apartments are too small for a family, most buyers will upgrade to a larger and better place eventually. How do developers market this type of housing? What concepts do they employ to lure younger buyers? The most frequently invoked notion in advertising *danshen gongyu* is the personal freedom bestowed by a space of one's own.

Free Harbor is one such development that caters to unmarried professionals in Kunming. Its dramatic, sixteen-page advertising brochure starts with a "Freedom Manifesto" in the form of poetry. It claims that "the dream of youth is eternal freedom, the foundation for courage and faith in one's life." By declaring that Free Harbor is a space that can provide such personal freedom, the advertisement depicts it as "the oasis in the urban desert." There is also a list of quotations about the importance of freedom by three renowned people familiar to Chinese middle-class readers: Zhuangzi (one of the founders of Daoism in China), Jean-Jacques Rousseau (the French philosopher), and Spartacus (the leader of the famous slave uprising in ancient Rome). It is striking to see such a dramatized call for freedom in a real estate advertisement. Yet its intention is not to engage in any political debate on freedom, but to convince the consumers that personal freedom can be realized in "a private space of my own." Another peculiar image, *buluo* (tribe), is also used to describe the people who would come to live in this community—"the tribe of freedom"—to highlight the point of having a free spirit. The use of such "evocative words and suggestive images" has its own seductive power, as suggested by Pierre Bourdieu in his study of real estate advertisements in postwar France (2005, 24). This is because "the readers, armed with their previous experiences, both of the ordinary, and also the literary, would project onto the text/pretext the aura of correspondences, resonances and analogies which make it possible for them to recognize themselves in it" (2005, 24). In the case of Free Harbor, the production of the aura of personal freedom was vital in marketing relatively small, private dwelling spaces to young, single urban professionals.

The hodgepodge of writings, citations, and images put together in this advertisement sometimes may not seem to make much sense, but the message is clear that true independent life begins with a space of one's own and buying a *danshen gongyu* is the entry into personal freedom and modern life. This is potentially an enticing message to many young people in Kunming who have long lived under their parents' roof in crowded danwei apartments. For those who do not want to be entangled in the web of familial and danwei relationships, *danshen* apartments provide a space "without the city's noise and without a father's disciplinary gaze and a mother's nagging." They believe that a private space beyond social constraints will give rise to a true self and a free spirit. This longing for privacy can be read as a reaction to the deprivation of private space characteristic of high socialism.

Shifting Private/Public Boundaries

Although the emerging landscapes of living offer a variety of new visions of urban life for consumers of different socioeconomic locations and cultural tastes, the nature of communal space in these new communities has become blurred and contested. Is this space public or private? Who has the right to access such space and decide what the best use of it is? During the course of my fieldwork these questions ignited heated debates among property owners, developers, and urban planners. The new Property Law enacted in 2007 requires that all common building structures and spaces (such as green fields, roads, and other open space) in a community belong to the homeowners collectively. Before this law was enacted, the ownership of the communal space (*gonggong kongjian*) within a commodity-housing compound was not clearly delineated. In addition, one must also consider the social practice of communal space as it has been shaped historically. Even though commodity housing was sold on the principle of exclusiveness, existing social relationships and other factors often created conditions that allowed "outsiders" to come in and share the new space and facilities. In what follows, I will discuss three cases that represent different circumstances under which the use of privatized communal space was conceived and contested by those living inside and outside it and how the language of rights was invoked. I will also briefly note the implications of this new spatial order for thinking about citizenship and entitlement in the postsocialist era.

"Not a Free Park"

Longfeng is a large new middle-level residential compound consisting of about one thousand commodity housing units. It is located near the second ring road and adjacent to several older danwei housing compounds inhabited by factory workers and college professors and staff. I lived there during the summer of 2006 and thus had ample opportunities to observe the social dynamics within this compound. Even though Longfeng is by no means a luxury development, it stands out among other older housing compounds because it provides a nicely landscaped communal garden, outdoor exercise equipment, and a Western-style children's playground. Ever since the construction was completed in 2005, it has become a de facto "free park" for nearby residents who frequently come to take a stroll after dinner or bring their children to play. The central garden features a man-made pond with bamboo bridges, pavilions, and fountains. The hundreds of goldfish living in the pond have become a local attraction as people nearby come daily to feed them with bread, crackers, and steamed buns. In the early evening, the bridge over the water gets crowded with people watching the fish.

Near the pond, there is a large, high, stone-paved platform that can be used for multiple purposes. One morning I was awakened by loud music. When I looked out from my window on the sixth floor, I saw two dozen women in their fifties or sixties doing a popular Yunnan fan dance for exercise. After that, they came almost every morning. Another group of women showed up around 7 p.m. for their evening exercise. Some residents living near the central garden became increasingly annoyed as the loud music disturbed the serenity they cherished. They talked to the property management staff and demanded their intervention to have the exercisers change their location or lower the volume of the music. They alleged that some of the women were "outsiders" who did not live in the compound and thus had no right to be there. But the management staff said that it was not so easy for them to single out the "outsiders" because some of them were invited by their friends who lived in the compound. In the end, the staff agreed to ask the exercisers to make less noise and be more sensitive to the residents living nearby but they allowed the gathering to continue. One unhappy resident blamed the security guards for not fulfilling their duty to protect the private residential space: "Look! Our xiaoqu is becoming a free park. It just does not make sense that outsiders who did not pay a cent can also come to play, stroll, and exercise in our space. This place should be for the residents only because we, the homeowners, paid for everything." This sense of exclusive entitlement to the privatized communal space is shared by many middle-class homeowners I spoke to. The more upscale a gated community is, the stronger such sentiment manifests itself.

Another source of discontent resulted from the use of communal facilities, especially the playground. Longfeng is a large compound containing more than one thousand families, and there are at least several hundred children living there. But there is only one playground plus a sandbox. Located on the east side of the central garden, the playground is a popular site for children who come to enjoy the slide/climb structure, two swings, and a seesaw. This type of playground, which has a well padded ground and bright colors, is relatively new to China and does not exist in the older danwei communities. Kids living in the surrounding areas who have no access to such play facilities are intrigued by it and want to come and play. During our stay in Longfeng, my four-year-old daughter would go to this playground after dinner every evening. It was also a great opportunity for me to talk to other parents and grandparents there. From our conversations I found out that almost half of the people there did not live in this compound. One girl who frequently played with my daughter lived in a nearby older teachers' housing. Her mother told me: "We first came to visit a friend who lived here. Then my daughter discovered this playground. Now she wants to come every evening. The guards at the gate now probably think we live here because we come almost every day." The playground typically became very crowded from 6:30 p.m. to 9 p.m. every day. On average there were twenty to thirty kids, most of whom wanted to get on the two swings. Sometimes friction took place as children became frustrated with the long wait. A couple of parents complained in private that the reason it became so overcrowded was that too many "outsiders" took advantage of the place. But since many of these "outsiders" were also friends and acquaintances of some homeowners within Longfeng, they felt that they had the right to visit and enjoy the facilities. Keeping them out altogether might hurt the social relationship between some residents and their friends. Further, there was a persistent socialist sentiment of sharing communal space and facilities despite the privatized nature of the new property regime. Thus, what a public or private space means legally and socially is a contested matter in everyday life.

"Simultaneously Open and Closed"

Recall Think UK, the luxury condominium complex I discussed earlier. The struggle over the use of communal space was especially pronounced due to the unique combination of residential space and retail shops within this community. Unlike other commodity housing, Think UK is designed as a "simultaneously open and closed community" consisting of two different parts: residential buildings and commercial retail space. To provide a measure of security, the residential buildings are grouped into several enclosed units (*zutuan*) with code-protected gates. But the communal space in the xiaoqu is open to the public because of the presence of some three hundred retailers. These hair salons, DVD stores, boutique shops, restaurants, bakeries, and bookstores all depend on customers inside and outside of the development. This mixed-use design has created a conflict of interest, unforeseen by the homeowners at the time they purchased the apartments. When I interviewed Mr. Fang, the head of property management at Think UK in the summer of 2006, he confirmed that this conflict was the most difficult problem facing his team, a dilemma he had been unable to solve:

> Every evening, hundreds of people from the nearby working-class communities would pour into our xiaoqu because they have no other places to go for their pastime. We are the only xiaoqu in this area that offers a pleasant environment with trees, lawns, flowers, nicely paved paths, and entertainment facilities. People come for a stroll, visit the shops, sit on the benches, and use the exercise facilities. It is quite a scene! Business owners love it because they want more potential buyers. But our homeowners are unhappy. They frequently confronted me with this question: "Are the communal space and facilities our private property?" I said: "Yes!" "Then that means other people should not use them, right?" they pressed. "Correct!" I said. "Now so many outsiders are using them. How do you explain this situation?" they pushed further. "What you just said makes sense logically. But when you purchased your housing and signed the agreement, you were notified that this was designed as an open xiaoqu. So you should know what that means," I replied. That was the best I could do because I understood why they were upset. They are the ones who pay for all the space, facilities and maintenance cost. But the majority of people using them are the outsiders. But I cannot keep the outsiders out because, first of all, the shops would have no business, and second, their faces are not marked "outsiders."

According to Mr. Fang, the developer and his management team had not figured out a solution yet. Some suggested enclosing the facilities with fences and gates so that only residents could have access; nonresidents could only come in for shopping. Meanwhile, there was constant pressure from the business owners who wanted to keep an open and inviting atmosphere for consumers. They argued that blocking off the facilities would send a hostile message and thus turn away a lot of potential customers. During the World Cup, an extremely popular event for Chinese, some retailers had set up a couple of large-screen TVs in the central square for public viewing. As most games took place late at night, between 2 a.m. and 6 a.m., the loud cheering noises of the soccer fans disturbed the residents in adjacent buildings. Disgruntled residents took their complaints directly to the headquarters of the developer, threatening a lawsuit to protect their property, which in their eyes had been turned into a "free park" (*mianfei gongyuan*). The developer eventually offered private compensation to the affected homeowners to assuage their anger. But the tension over the use of communal space and facilities continued to surge from time to time.

Parking space was another sensitive issue. Since not every family had bought a permanent underground parking space due to its high cost, some simply parked in unreserved spaces. But oftentimes there was no space left for the residents during the day when shoppers were also allowed to park in those spaces. Mr. Fang explained: "This xiaoqu can only accommodate about four hundred cars. When the number is reached, our guards have to turn away incoming cars even if the drivers live here. Some residents just do not understand and do not want to cooperate. They become angry and shout at our guards: 'This is my home! Let me in!' If we do let everyone in, can you imagine what it will be like? Total chaos!" Throughout the interview, I could sense Mr. Fang's deep frustration as he was facing an impossible situation created by the developer—namely, the need to satisfy the demands of both the shop owners and the homeowners who co-inhabited this space yet had radically different interests. When retailers' demands for openness and a larger consumer crowd clashed with homeowners' demand for security, quiet, and exclusiveness, the developer and property management agents could only temporarily mitigate the tension. Yet the root cause persisted and the problem would come back to haunt this community.

"Visually Open"

The ambiguous boundary between public and private space/property was one of the focal points of discussion during a press conference held by the Silver Sea Co., which aimed to establish good public relations for the firm (see chapter 2). The Hong Kong–based chief designer of the master plan proudly described what the new community would look like. One of the features she highlighted was a beautiful lake scene of clear water, dancing willow branches, and swans. Trying to sell this place as if it were a public space for all citizens to enjoy, she exclaimed that "this scene would no doubt become a public attraction, adding an enormous amount of beauty to the city of Kunming."

During the open question session, however, one reporter asked several pointed questions: "It is not clear to me whether the man-made lake in this new development belongs to the developer, the homeowners, or the city. Who will be in charge of maintaining this space? Is it going to be open to the general public or only to the residents who live there? Who is entitled to this new resource?" The CEO of the development corporation appeared uncomfortable. He stood up slowly and reluctantly confirmed that the community would not be open to the public due to the lack of re-sources to keep the place safe and clean. But he added that "even if people cannot come in physically, they can still share and enjoy the pleasant lake view from the outside." He then quickly turned to other questions. In this peculiar vision of the relationship between the privatized space and the public, the "outsiders" must be physically kept out of the private property; only their gazes are allowed to travel through the fences and gates. This spatial design is called "visually open to the outside" (*shijueshang duiwai kaifang*), which, the chief designer claimed, would provide necessary secu-rity for the residents and at the same time allow the public to appreciate the beautiful scenery, albeit from afar. "Visually open" turns out to be a way to justify the privatization of public land in order to create a private paradise for a few privileged individuals. In the end, only private property owners would have true access to their paradise, while others can merely admire it at a distance.

The Economy of Fear

Despite the diverse forms of new living, a common concern among the residents is the fear of crime, and a common solution to it is to fortify their newfound paradise with walls, gates, and new technologies. Security is heavily marketed as a desired feature and privilege of the new residential space. It is in this sense that I argue that fear, or what Caldeira (2000) terms "the talk of crime," has its material consequences. Fear has not only reshaped Kunming's urban landscape but also propelled the growth of a new economic niche that specializes in supplying private security materi-als, technologies, and laborers.

Theft and violent crimes (such as robbery, kidnapping, and murder), which were relatively rare under Mao's regime, are reemerging in reform-era Kunming as well as in other Chinese cities.[13] Meanwhile, mass media and new communication technologies help accelerate and expand the ex-posure of crime-related information to the public. Due to such heightened fear and anxiety, the police and community watch organized by retired elderly people are no long sufficient to meet the increased demand for security, especially in the new residential enclaves. As a response, private security and new technologies of surveillance have assumed a pivotal role in maintaining order and ensuring the safety of gated residential communi-ties. It is estimated that throughout China there were over fifteen hundred registered security service companies with a total of about one million employees in 2006. *Baoan,* which means "protecting safety," is a relatively new concept that emerged in the late 1980s. It is associated with the notion of commercialized service as opposed to *gongan* (public security) provided by the government. Under socialism, every large and midsized danwei had its own security office in charge of everyday social order and the staff were permanent employees whose training, salary, medical benefits, and pension were all taken care of by their danwei. But this system became more and more cumbersome and costly in a market economy. Beginning in the 1990s, many work units started to seek a more cost-effective model for providing security by turning to the market.

The supply of private guards became available in the 1990s as Chinese cities were flooded by rural migrants willing to work as cheap laborers. The young, unmarried male migrants became candidates for jobs with commercialized security services. The first formal baoan company in Kunming was the Kunming Security Guards General Corporation established in the late 1990s as a subsidiary of the Municipal Public Security Bureau. Soon the district-level public security branches also formed their own auxiliary baoan firms, many of which were simply contracted out to private owners. Thus, on paper these entities were state owned and affiliated with the public security agencies, but in reality they were run as profit-making organizations after the private enterprise model. The employees were predominantly low-wage rural migrants hired on a temporary basis and could be "rented out" by banks, hotels, factories, universities, and other entities.[14] It was estimated that there were more than ten thousand trained security guards working in Kunming's baoan companies by 2007, not including those hired by developers or organizations on their own.

The private security industry is a lucrative business based on the exploitation of cheap migrant labor. A firm can usually train young migrant men in the military style within three months and lease them out as "professional" security guards. Typically a baoan in Kunming gets about six hundred yuan per month from the firm but the actual user pays about nine hundred yuan to the firm. A small part of the three hundred yuan will be used to pay for the workers' accidental death insurance and overhead, and the rest will be pure profit. More and more developers and enterprises today like to use such security services because they are not held responsible for anything other than paying wages.

The privatization of security services has important moral and cultural implications. Although baoan interact with the police from time to time, these two are distinctly different entities in terms of their authority as defined by law. Private security guards are not law enforcement agents. Even though they can arrest security violators in their territory of duty, they have no right to detain anyone overnight and must immediately turn them

Figure 7. Iron window bars provide a form of self-protection in a lower-income neighborhood.

over to the local police. But in practice this is not always the case, and the power of baoan varies greatly depending on the context. In some upscale communities and powerful corporations, security guards retain a great deal of authority in dealing with those who are deemed to be disturbing the private order and the safety of their clients. Even though baoan are not allowed to carry guns, they can engage in other forms of violent acts to deter the unwanted others. Further, in the new regime of living, as Pow (2007) notes, baoan occupy an ambivalent position: they are the agents who secure the good life of civilized enclaves, but they are also regarded as the inferior "moral other" due to their rural *hukou* status and their perceived lack of suzhi.[15] Their job is to prevent and reduce criminal activities for middle-class residents, yet they are seen by the same group of people as a potential source of criminality due to their liminal status in the city. Their very presence is a source of anxiety as well as comfort. As one elderly woman resident put it: "The security guards do help improve the safety of our compound because outsiders and criminals are less likely to come in due to their presence. But deep inside I always have a shadow of doubt. You just cannot trust them completely. They are poor and might be tempted by the wealth around them. I have heard of several cases of theft and robbery and many people suspect that they are all inside jobs." This woman's narrative reveals a contradictory feeling toward baoan: a sense of dependency and deep-seated distrust. No matter how helpful they might be, migrant security guards are not seen as "true" members of the community and they are perceived as unable to resist the temptation of illicit acts to gain quick money.

The fear of crime and the desire for self-protection have also boosted the growth of an industry specialized in manufacturing and selling safety materials, which range from heavy-duty iron doors and window bars to video intercoms and surveillance cameras. As an important criterion to evaluate the quality of a property, home buyers typically want to know what kinds of safety devices are available and what security services are used. It is interesting to note that in the 1980s and 1990s, the use of fancy safety bars was seen as a status symbol for a family; today, it is the absence of bars that has become the symbol of status and good taste. Only in lower-income communities that lack private security measures do residents still use a metal door in addition to their existing wood door and iron bars to protect themselves. By contrast, the mid-level and upscale communities today have video intercoms for all households and surveillance cameras in communal spaces. Such high-tech features are visibly marketed in the brochures distributed to potential buyers. These emerging fortified middle-class enclaves have also become a fertile ground for producing a new middle-class culture, which will be explored in the next chapter.

4

Spatializing Class

One afternoon in the midst of a light summer rain, three of my former high school classmates came to pick me up in a silver Passat to see a new upscale housing compound called Spring Fountain in the western suburb of Kunming. One of them, Ling, who was recently promoted to the head of a local branch of a major bank, had recently bought a home there. When our car was approaching a large iron gate, a billboard caught my attention. In Chinese, English, French, and Korean, it read "Private House, No Entry" (see figure 9).[1] Two uniformed security guards stopped us and asked some questions. From the back seat, I heard Ling telling them his house number and then they waved us through.

With the emergence of a differentiated geography of living, a new social stratum, the "new middle class" (*xinzhongchan jieceng*) is in the making.[2] Today urban Chinese no longer shy away from status recognition and are eager to seek differentiated lifestyles and cultural orientations through a variety of consumer choices. The reconfigured residential space, among others, is vital to the formation of a new urban middle-class culture. In this chapter I seek to demonstrate how private home ownership and increasingly stratified residential space serve as a tangible ground on which class-specific subjects and cultural milieus are fostered. In his study of new residential communities in Beijing, Luigi Tomba (2004) argues that one of the reform regime's goals has been to create a consumer-oriented professional middle class. Thus, he sees the rise of the middle class partly as a result of intentional social engineering involving various public policies to reallocate resources and adopt new zoning practices. Although Tomba's structural-oriented analysis of social engineering is valuable, my account focuses on the process of self-making among social actors. I highlight the dual cultural process of space-making and class-making by examining how on the one hand self-conscious middle-class subjects and a distinct "class milieu" (*jieceng wenhua*) are being created under a new regime of property and living, and how on the other hand socioeconomic differences get spatialized and materialized through the remaking of urban communities.[3] I also consider how rapidly expanding housing advertising becomes a vital engine in manufacturing and disseminating the dreams, tastes, and images of a new middle class.[4]

The question of middle-class making and its intrinsic relationship to spatial production has been explored by many scholars in diverse social contexts. For instance, the growing body of literature on gentrification and gated communities in North America suggests that the desire of the middle classes to cultivate a secure and distinctive lifestyle is the driving force behind the practice of gating and the recent return from suburbia in an effort to revamp inner-city neighborhoods (Davis 1992; Ley 1996; Low 2004; N. Smith 1996). In particular, Setha Low's ethnography (2004) shows how gated communities offer a contained physical and social space, in which a distinctive middle class way of thinking about what constitutes values, decent tastes, happiness, and the good life is produced and reproduced through everyday life. In his account of the remaking of the central city in Canada, David Ley (1996) argues that this new wave of gentrification is propelled not only by economic calculations (cheaper housing and less travel time and expense), but more important by a post-Fordist cultural orientation of living among the "cultural new class" that is more urbane and cosmopolitan.[5] It is this attention to everyday cultural processes of space-making and class-making that I turn to in developing my analysis.

In what follows, I will first sketch out the newly stratified residential space in Kunming by focusing on three levels of communities that local people frequently refer to, and then turn to an ethnographic account of how middle-class subjects and a middle-class cultural milieu are cultivated within these places. I also analyze the role of real estate advertising in shaping the cultural meanings and images of the new middle class. Toward the end, I offer a brief account of the emerging class distinction between the "masters" and the "servants" within upper- and middle-level communities, and some reflections on the implications for rethinking the cultural politics of class, space, and consumption.

Stratified Living Space

If the sociospatial form of Chinese cities under socialism can be characterized as relatively "homogeneous" based on occupation and danwei, it has been greatly transformed into a heterogeneous one since the 1990s (see Wu 2008b). The mass development of commodity housing in particular has generated a highly stratified and segregated residential regime demarcated by gates and private wealth (Davis 2002; Fraser 2000; Siu 2005).[6] The significance of residential location (rather than occupation) in identifying one's socioeconomic location is reflected in the question people commonly ask while meeting another unfamiliar person. Under Maoist socialism people would ask "what danwei do you belong to?" But now people are more likely to ask, "What xiaoqu [residential community] do you live in?"

In contemporary Kunming, the striking differences between wealthy and lower-income neighborhoods can hardly go unnoticed.[7] Lower-income housing consists of mostly matchboxlike apartment buildings that are poorly constructed and maintained. There is little public space between buildings and virtually no green space. The low-quality exterior paint is easily washed away by the rain, making the surface of buildings look like "crying faces with running tears" as one informant put it. By contrast, the upper- and middle-class neighborhoods are spacious, clean, and well protected, featuring different architectural styles and made of better construction materials. There are also well-kept lawns, flowers, and trees, which present a particularly attractive environment for home buyers. The bright and cheerful colors of the new commodity housing make them stand out as dreamscapes in the city landscape. What further differentiates the new residential regime from the old one are the following factors that may not be so visually obvious: property values, community services, and the social composition of the residents. Let us take a closer look at both the physical and social attributes of the three levels of communities commonly differentiated by Kunming residents.[8]

"Gardens" and "Villas"

The newly constructed luxury neighborhoods are commonly referred to as "gardens" (*yuan* or *huayuan*). One kind consists of condominiums in high-rises or multistory structures in gated communities located within prime downtown areas or the core urban districts; the other consists of town houses or detached single-family homes located in the developing inner suburbs. Chinese people call the latter *bieshu* ("villa"). In some large metropolitan areas, such as Beijing and Shanghai, luxury single homes have also been constructed in the outer suburbs. These are all commodity housing that can be bought and sold freely by private individuals. The price varies greatly from city to city and has increased rapidly over the past ten years.[9] In Kunming as of 2007 each unit of such luxury housing cost

Figure 8. Jade Garden: an upscale housing complex located near the central financial district and Green Lake.

seven hundred thousand to 1.5 million yuan depending on the size and location. Some of the larger single-family houses in more exclusive communities could cost as much as two to three million yuan. These numbers were far beyond the reach of the majority of local people although similar homes cost twice or three times as much in larger metropolises such as Beijing, Shanghai, and Guangzhou.

Jade Garden, located near Green Lake in the very popular Wuhua District, is one of the upscale gated communities that I frequently visited. Because it is near the central financial zone, adjacent to a picturesque lake park, and within the best school district, Jade Garden is one of the most expensive and sought-after properties in the city. It consists of a high-rise tower and several large six-story buildings, forming a completely enclosed residential compound of some two hundred units. Each unit is 150 to 180 square meters, which is considered spacious by Chinese standards. The initial sale price per unit ranged from four hundred thousand yuan to eight hundred thousand yuan depending on the view. By 2007, however, the resale value had nearly doubled. This housing complex is run by a private property management agency that is known for its high-quality customer service, which is modeled on its Hong Kong–based parent company. It has an indoor swimming pool, a gym, a clubhouse, and meticulously maintained landscaping.[10] Like most other upscale compounds, this private enclave is protected by surveillance cameras and private security guards. Residents have their own keys to open three sets of gates: the large metal front gate (closed at night), the building unit gate, and the house door. During the daytime, the main gate is open but the guards stop and question anybody who does not appear to be a resident there. I was stopped twice and had to wait until they called my friends and confirmed that I was indeed their guest.

Although the residents in the upscale neighborhoods are all considered well-to-do, their occupational and educational backgrounds are diverse and can hardly be considered members of the "elite." As merchants, entrepreneurs, or what David Goodman (1999) calls "owner-operators," they tend to be lumped into two categories: *zuo shengyi de* (those doing business) as opposed to those working in the state sector, or *da laoban* (big bosses) as opposed to the wage laborers in the private sector. Their success is often attributed to the fact that they started their business relatively early and thus were able to take advantage of the emerging private economy for fast capital accumulation before the market competition intensified.

Mr. Zhou, a homeowner in Jade Garden, ran a specialty clothing business, which was well known among middle-class families and expatriates interested in high-quality, Western-style leisure and outdoor clothing. Zhou, in his late thirties, graduated from college in 1987 but decided to give up his intellectual career for private business in 1991. He started as a *getihu* (individual businessman) and was able to pull several thousand yuan together for a start-up business. His operation was small in the beginning and he rented a stall of less than ten square meters on a street near a local university. Four years later, the city government decided to widen several roads and thus demolished all the stalls and shops on them, including his. By then he had already made some good money and was able to rent a larger store on a main commercial street. Between 1995 and 1997, his business took off and he made about one million yuan annually. He attributed his success to three factors: knowing how to select high-quality products in classical leisure styles, offering superior customer service, and starting the business early. When I met him, his business had grown into a three-store operation with ten employees. His story reflects the common experience of many successful private entrepreneurs whose commercial

Figure 9. A sign that reads "private house, no entry" in French, Chinese, English, and Korean at the entrance to a luxury gated community.

Figure 10. JinKang Garden: gating and security services are a symbol of status.

endeavors have evolved from a one-person show to a small private business. Although they are by no means super wealthy, they can live a very comfortable and stable life.

When he met me at the compound gate, Mr. Zhou indicated that he preferred to conduct the interview in the communal garden, not at his home. After we sat on a bench and talked for an hour, he became more comfortable with me and decided to invite me into his home. He had a spacious condo on the tenth floor with a sweeping view of Green Lake. A young live-in nanny greeted us at the door. She was responsible for cooking, cleaning, and taking care of his infant son. The furniture inside was nice but not lavish. He showed me all the rooms and said, "I enjoy a comfortable life and the privacy here, but I am not after an extravagant lifestyle." His entire family could easily have lived on the income generated from his retail clothing business, but his wife wanted to have a career and decided to continue working as a cashier at a major bank. As we sat down on the black leather couch, I noticed a Bible on the coffee table and a statue of the Virgin Mary on the bookshelf. Because these items were not common to find in Chinese families, I asked him whether he was a Christian. "Yes, my wife and I are both sincere believers in God, but we do not go to the church. We have a small group of friends meeting at our houses regularly. If you are interested, you can join us," Zhou said. I later found out that informal Bible study groups were spreading among the urban middle class and that new private communities provided a safe haven for such activities due to less governmental surveillance.

"Middle-Stratum Neighborhoods"

The "middle-stratum neighborhoods" (*zhongdang xiaoqu*) consist of commercially developed housing, but the ways in which the families obtain them vary greatly and the social composition of the residents is complex. It is estimated that more than half of the units within this category are sold as straight commodity housing to private buyers in Kunming. The rest are bought in bulk by large danwei, which then sell them to their own employees with a subsidy (see also Wang and Murie 1999a, 1999b; Zhang 1998). Prices ranged between two hundred thousand yuan and five hundred thousand yuan in 2007 depending on the size, quality, and location. Normally danwei are able to negotiate a better price than what is offered to individual buyers. Communities at this level are also gated and protected by security guards, but the control is not as stringent as that of the upscale ones. A well-dressed person with an urban professional appearance is likely to

Figure 11. Sunshine Garden: a middle-level private housing development in the western suburb.

be able to pass the gate without being questioned by security guards. Catering to emerging middle-class families, these neighborhoods tend to see a concentration of smaller firm managers, independent business owners, highly specialized professionals (such as doctors and lawyers), and intellectuals who make substantial sideline incomes.[11]

Ms. Tang lived with her husband and daughter in a 110-square-meter condo in Riverside Garden, a large newly constructed residential community in the developing northern part of the city. This area used to be farmland, but it is now covered by new gated communities. Before purchasing this home, the Tangs had lived for over ten years in a small, rundown apartment assigned by her work unit. After graduating from college in late 1980s, Tang became a high school teacher, bringing in a monthly salary of about fifteen hundred yuan. Her husband, also a college graduate, first worked for a state enterprise and then "jumped into the sea of private business" to work for a small firm that sold personal therapeutic equipment. He soon became the marketing manager of this national distributor's regional office, earning five thousand to ten thousand yuan a month depending on his sales. When they made this new purchase in 2001, the Tangs had saved enough cash for a large down payment (50% of the total two hundred thousand yuan) with a ten-year mortgage.

Tang was delighted at the much larger living space and better residential environment. When she gave me a tour of her new home, she was particularly proud that her daughter could now have her own room—a private space decorated the way she liked. This was a dream Tang always had for herself when she was growing up, but it could not be realized in the old days under the socialist regime. She told me that she was the one in charge of decorating their house and had spent a lot of time on selecting furniture, curtains, bedding, and so on in order to give their home a personal character (*gexinghua*). Although she greatly enjoyed the newfound privacy and autonomy, Ms. Tang sometimes felt isolated because she did not know her neighbors well and no one seemed to be interested in making friends. She expressed a sense of disappointment because she felt that her neighbors "are not well-educated and their suzhi is low." One of the examples she gave me was that some residents within the compound let their dogs run loose and shit everywhere while no one would clean up after them. Her perception echoed a popular view among Kunming residents that those in upscale and middle-level new housing compounds were rich in money but relatively poor in suzhi. And this view reflected a general mentality shaped historically that tends to associate businesspeople with low suzhi.

The social atomization experienced by some in their new communities may not be shared by those who have developed other forms of connectivity and interaction outside the residential space, however. Some of my informants reminded me that although they might not interact with their neighbors, they had shifted the focus of their social life to other relationships and associations. For example, one male resident who worked at a bank said that his social world was centered around his old friends from high school because they did not have any direct conflict of interest and the friendships were pure and long lasting. They regularly got together for dinner, evening tea, and golf. On the weekend, he took family trips with his friends' families. He said that he hardly had time left over for cultivating meaningful relationships with his neighbors after all these activities. Only occasionally did he have a nostalgic moment for the old neighborhood where he grew up and played freely with other kids.

"Gongxin Xiaoqu"

Lower-income neighborhoods are generally referred to as *gongxin xiaoqu*, which literarily means salary/wage-based communities because most residents there live on relatively fixed incomes (ranging from meager to moderate salaries or wages). These are housing compounds funded and constructed under different circumstances. The first type consists of lower-cost yet reasonably nice housing developed by commercial real estate companies under direct contract with specific danwei. It is priced at a little less than two hundred thousand yuan per unit. The second type is created by the municipal government to house relocated families that were pushed out of the city core as a result of several large-scale urban redevelopments in the 1990s (Zhang 2006). The third type of housing is built under the "Stable Living Project" (*anju gongcheng*) promoted by the state. It gives developers special loans, tax breaks, and other benefits in order to keep the costs down, but requires that these housing units are sold only to qualified lower-income families at an affordable price. The socioeconomic composition of the people living in these salary/wage-based neighborhoods is diverse and includes factory workers, clerks, service sector workers, school teachers, and migrants. In recent years, as a result of the state-owned enterprises reform, many factory workers have been laid off and no longer receive any stable income.

Jiangan Xiaoqu was a large lower-income community located in the northern part of Kunming. Ten years ago, this entire area was farmland and considered a suburb. The first several residential buildings were constructed by the Panlong District Real Estate Development Company in the early 1990s for some three thousand relocated families that had been pushed out of the inner city. Later on, this company constructed eight more apartment buildings for nearby universities and factories. Local farmers whose land was appropriated for housing development were compensated with an apartment for each family. Initially the work units assigned these housing units to their employees as part of the socialist welfare package, and later on employees were asked to buy back the ownership from their danwei at an extremely low rate. The average size of each apartment (typically two to three bedrooms) was between forty and sixty square meters. In recent years, social polarization within the community had deepened. Many worker residents were laid off by their failing state enterprises and were struggling to make ends meet. Others had gained more money and had been able to move into better and larger commodity housing elsewhere by renting their Jiangan units to relatively poor migrant workers. The task of maintaining social order and managing the community became more challenging due to the large number of absentee landlords and a high turn-out rate of renters.

Theft was considered a major problem for two reasons. People of different kinds frequently moved in and out of this rural-urban transitional

Figure 12. Poorly constructed, lower-income housing without walls and gates.

zone, making it difficult to keep track of the residents living there. More important, the police were virtually absent for many years because this area was considered rural and thus was not fully incorporated into the existing urban jurisdiction. A small police station was finally established a few years ago, but its presence was relatively weak. The property management agency was supposed to take charge of public security and community services, but its manager claimed that it was impossible to fulfill such responsibilities due to the lack of funding, particularly as it frequently encountered strong resistance from local residents while collecting the regulation fees. Further, I was told that the security team was substantially understaffed and could not afford any high-tech surveillance devices. Individual families were thus left to protect themselves by installing metal bars around their windows and balconies. Residents in the eight buildings initially owned by a university organized mutual watch groups and installed metal fences and gates around their buildings. These gates were locked between 11 p.m. and 6 a.m., but were open during the day. The

Figure 13. Men playing Chinese chess in an open community space in a lower-income neighborhood (Jiangan Xiaoqu).

new measures helped reduce theft, but they did not enhance the residents' sense of safety; the presence of fences and gates only reminded them of the poor security conditions.

Unlike the fortresslike upscale neighborhoods, however, Jiangan was a more open and lively community. There were no walls and surveillance cameras. Every day elderly men would gather around small stone tables in open public areas to play Chinese chess and smoke pipes; retired women and men would congregate to sing Chinese opera. There was a well-used community center consisting of a reading room where residents read newspapers and magazines and several rooms were designated for senior and youth activities such as dance, painting, calligraphy, and other enrichment classes.

As a partial response to the visible stratification of urban neighborhoods, the state and local governments have tried to adopt a new policy of mixed housing by requiring developers to construct a certain percentage of affordable housing units (fewer than ninety square meters each) in every new xiaoqu. The aim is to ensure that lower-income families are not completely excluded from the new commercial housing market, and that the residential community will not become entirely class based. But this policy is not effectively implemented due to commercial resistance and corruption. Another mechanism designed to help middle to lower-income people to buy commodity housing is the compulsory housing savings plan, the Housing Provident Fund, which combines individual contributions and employers' matching subsidies. But this project in practice ends up helping the employees of larger and stronger public enterprises and institutions much more than those in smaller, private firms or the self-employed (see Ya Ping Wang 2001).

No longer "comrades" (*tongzhi*) who shared their danwei-based housing as in the socialist time, residents in the new communities are "strangers" to each other, surrounded by walls and gates. Are they capable of developing any sense of common social and cultural identification beyond material wealth and consumption? Can we speak of any identity of interests, habitus, dispositions, or even an emerging class consciousness among these "strangers"? Can shared spatial experience lead to a particular kind of class-specific subjects? The next two sections seek to grapple with these questions.

Exclusivity, Privacy, Atomization

The Spring Fountain complex I visited with my friends had about 150 households and was not considered large in comparison with some recent mega-developments. But it was nicely designed and full of trees, grass, and flowering plants. The center of the compound featured a goldfish pond, a Chinese-style pavilion, a miniature stone mountain, water lilies, and fountains accompanied by light Western music. These things were not merely an aesthetical veneer, but important in locating one's jieceng. The condo my friend, Ling, had purchased was spacious, about two hundred square meters, with three bedrooms, a large living room, a dining area, and two bathrooms. Although impressed by the landscaping and large living space, my other two friends began to feel a bit uneasy. One of them, a woman, worked for the provincial government's health education institute. The other, a man, had changed his job many times. He first worked as a civil servant in the local government and then quit his job to work for a small computer firm. After the firm went bankrupt, he drifted for a while and finally found an office position in a private company. With their fixed salaries, they would not be able to afford such a place. The woman said with a sigh, "My place has none of these, but is surrounded by street noise, dust, and cooking smells from the street hawkers outside the window." She continued in a slightly teasing tone that even though they still considered Ling a close friend, he really belonged to another jieceng now:

> Even though before I knew that he [Ling] made good money, I still felt he was part of us because he lived in a community not so different from mine. We could go knock on his door whenever we wanted. But now things are different. Every time I come here, the security guards would stop and question me, especially because I do not drive a private car. I would not want to come to visit him here as often as I did before. It just makes me feel inferior and out of place.

Their sense of exclusion and uneasiness mainly derived from their inability to acquire a place that demands consuming power beyond their reach, a place that so tangibly demarcated socioeconomic differences through concrete spatial forms. Further, through much enhanced new surveillance devices (heavy metal gates, cameras, laser sensors, professional security guards, and so on), upscale communities heightened social isolation and segregation as they excluded unwanted intruders outright. Such exclusion was often justified by the fear of urban crime and by a neoliberal rationality that valorizes private property, personal wealth, and the pursuit of a privileged lifestyle at the expense of public space and social intermingling. Through highly visible spatial demarcation, it externalizes and foregrounds previously invisible or less pronounced socioeconomic differences. Community was thus deployed as an active element in structuring class differences.

Places like Spring Fountain were largely perceived by urbanites as *furen qu* (wealthy district) where wealthy people congregate, yet within these places there was a strong sense that social and cultural cohesion was lacking among the residents. One question I asked my interviewees was "do you feel that you have something in common with others living here?" Nearly all the answers were "no" or "not much." Many, including Ling, used the word *za* (diverse, mixed) to describe the social components of their community:

> People here have quite different social backgrounds and experiences. They are indeed a hodgepodge (*da zahui*). The only thing they have in common is money and consuming power. But I guess a jieceng is much more than that. Perhaps, after one or two decades of living together these people will gradually form some sort of common lifestyle, tastes, and dispositions. But for now I do not feel that I share much with my neighbors.

Residents in the private communities I spoke to had a strong desire for privacy and rarely interacted with one another. Among some thirty people I interviewed, only two said that they had visited their next-door neighbors once or twice to see their interior remodeling before the families actually moved in. The rest of them said they never did. One elderly woman who lived with her well-to-do son's family told me that her son specifically warned her not to invite neighbors in or to say much about his business because strangers were not trustworthy. I asked where they would seek help in case of an emergency. None of my interviewees mentioned neighbors. Some said they had their own car and did not need others to help with transportation. In case of a medical emergency, they said they would rather call a fee-based ambulance service. Others said that they would rather hire a *baomu* (domestic worker) to take care of a sick family member than ask for help from neighbors. As one woman explained, "I do not even know my neighbors. On what basis do I ask for help?" Then she continued:

> We used to live on a danwei compound and knew almost everyone. We paid visits to neighbors and friends in our spare time. But since I moved into this new community, things have changed. I have not been to any neighbor's home so far. They would not invite you. At best they say hello to you when running into you outside or playing with kids at the playground. I would not feel comfortable going to their home or chatting as we really have little in common. After all we are strangers to one another.

What we see is a double process at work: the spatial differentiation of people by community based on private wealth, and the atomization of individual families within each housing compound. Anthropologist Liu Xin calls those without organic connections "serialized individuals" because "there is no commonality among them except for their physical adjacency and proximity" (2009, 193). In a different context, in postwar France, Pierre Bourdieu describes a similar process of atomization in the suburban single-family housing communities, which in his view offered only a mirage of the good life. For him, those who were drawn into this type of living arrangement were "deprived of the relationships that formed within their neighborhoods, particularly in and through trade union campaigns, without being able to create—in a place of residence where socially very homogeneous individuals are gathered together, but without the community of interests and affinities that ensue from belonging to the same world of work—the elective relationships of a leisure community" (Bourdieu 2005, 189).

The intense desire for private space and the atomization of families that I describe here must be understood in light of the historical memory of the socialist form of living. In his detailed account of the cultural politics of gated communities in Shanghai, Choon-Piew Pow (2006) provides an insightful analysis of why privacy is highly valued today and what privacy means to the residents who seek seclusion behind the gates. He contrasts new gated communities with Shanghai's traditional neighborhoods, in which communal/domestic boundaries are frequently transgressed due to the lack of personal space (see also Pellow 1996). Middle-class home buyers are obsessed with privacy because they see the possession of private space as a form of liberation from the old, socialist way of life. Pow identifies four layers of meaning in the privacy pursued by urban residents: the privacy of individuals within the household, the privacy of households within the community, the privacy of the housing compound from the outside world, and the privacy of households from state control. The new commodity housing is particularly appealing because it offers not only private property ownership but also private space and privacy beyond the public gaze. It is in this context that developers explicitly market private homes as a "perfect, independent space" or a "private oasis" where one can experience the pleasure of living a new middle-class life. Owning one's own home, spatially and socially detached from the danwei, is taken by many as an ultimate liberation because it enables one to break away from various social constraints and surveillance. As one woman who owns a suburban town house with her husband phrased it, "Every day I come home, I feel so relaxed and liberated. I do not have to see or deal with my co-workers or bosses. As I close the door behind me, I feel like I'm entering a different world, an oasis so serene, and it belongs only to my family." For her, detachment does not mean being cut off or abandoned; rather, it is liberating and reviving because a space of one's own allows the private self to flourish.

Cultivating Jieceng through Consumption

Residents in upscale communities often feel compelled to engage in conspicuous consumption. The ability to consume properly is taken not only as the measure of one's prestige (*zunrong*) and face (*mianzi*) but also as an indication of whether one deserves membership in a particular community. If one's consumption practice is not compatible with the kind of housing/community one purchases, one would be seen as "out of place." Such pressure does not emanate from any identifiable organization or written rules, yet it is all-pervasive and imbued in the everyday cultural milieu. Home ownership and community choice constitute the core of this new consumer culture, while private car ownership, a home's interior design, children's schooling, leisure activities, clothing style, and food choices are also important spheres through which jieceng is performed and conceived.

Ms. Liang and her husband had just bought a home in the luxury Jade Garden development. Although only a high school graduate, her husband was able to make substantial money from his small-scale gasoline and industrial oil trading business. She explained to me how they ended up here and her perception of the suitability of their lifestyle for the new place:

A few years ago, we already had saved enough money to buy a unit in another upscale community, but we eventually decided on a lower-level community. Why? Because even though we could afford the housing itself, we could not afford living there at that time. For example, while most families drive their private cars, I would be embarrassed if I have to ride my bike to work every day. Even taking a taxi is looked down upon there. If our neighbors see my parents coming to visit me by bus, they will be laughed at too. Since my rich neighbors go to shop for shark fins and other expensive seafood every day, I cannot let them see me buying cabbage and turnips. Every family there seems to be competing with one another. If you do not have that kind of consuming power, you'd better not live there because you will not fit in well.

By the time I interviewed her, her family was in a stronger financial situation and thus she felt that they were ready to live in an upper-level community and learn to live like their well-to-do neighbors. They bought a car and remodeled the entire house with gleaming redwood floors, marble tiles, fancy lighting, modern kitchen appliances, and luxury furniture. She stopped working outside in order to devote all her time to her husband and toddler son even though they already had a full-time nanny. Her sense of readiness for community membership was closely tied to her family's ability to demonstrate a certain level of consuming power and to make the "right" choices in everyday life.

Like Liang, many other middle-class urban residents I met also feel that they must engage in proper consumption to validate their status and gain respect from their neighbors. But since everyone was learning to become a member of an emerging jieceng, what was considered proper and suitable was shifting and unclear. Oftentimes, there existed competing notions of suitable consumption, which could generate anxieties among the practitioners. They watched and compared themselves with their neighbors' activities in order to get a better sense of what and how to consume. Joining the exclusive, fee-based clubhouse (*huisuo*) within the community was also a way to gain prestige.

Another domain that has become the focus of China's new middle-class life and aspirations is the investment in their children's future. There is a growing interest among middle-class parents in cultivating their children's suzhi by sending them to various expensive personal skill and lifestyle training courses. A *New York Times* article, "Chinese Children Learn Class, Minus the Struggle," describes vividly how affluent parents in Shanghai seek "ways to cement their children's place in a fast-emerging elite" (French 2006). They start the race of class early by enrolling their kids in a range of courses and private lessons including golf, ballet, horseback riding, ice-skating, piano, skiing, polo, and so on. Some even attend finishing schools such as a special etiquette program run by a Japanese woman in a five-star hotel who teaches refined manners and how to be proper ladies and gentlemen. The article suggests that this new trend "speaks not just to parent's concern for their children's futures but also to a general sense of social insecurity among China's newly rich" because "these people are rich economically but lacking in basic manners, and they are not very fond of their own reputation."

Kunming's well-to-do parents might not yet demand finishing schools, but the urge to prepare their children early for a successful life in a highly competitive society was palpable. Most of the middle- and upper-middle-income families I interviewed were willing to spend a good portion of their income on children's extracurricular activities. They affirmed to me that this was a very important investment and would prove to be worthwhile because their kids would eventually stand out among others. Xiao Fang was a twelve-year-old girl whom I talked to several times. Her mother was a university professor and her father was a lawyer. She told me that there was a lot of pressure on her to achieve a good academic performance and in addition she had been taking private piano lessons for five years. I asked whether she enjoyed playing piano. "Not really, but my Mom said that I must have some special skills," she replied. "Otherwise, I will fall behind and no one will notice me." Physical appearance was also an important indicator of not only beauty but also of class. Xiao Fang's mother was concerned about her daughter's teeth and made sure she wore braces for two years even though orthopedic work was costly. Her mother was also worried about Xiao Fang's slightly hunched shoulders and spent ten thousand yuan on therapeutic massage for a year hoping that this would correct her posture. What is so striking to me is that the sense of class anxiety and fear of falling behind is clearly displaced onto the children. This anxiety is heightened by the fact that most children in urban China are singletons and thus the "only hope" of their families (Fong 2004).

In the newly formed *zhongchan jieceng* communities, there have emerged several new yet controversial consumption trends. Some see them as a sign of civility, good taste, and a leisure class lifestyle; others view them as a sign of uncivil behavior and poor taste. Here I would like to focus on two issues: pet dogs and new leisure activities that cater to women in the relatively affluent communities.

Pet dogs have become part of the new middle-class domestic life, which is relatively new in Chinese cities. During Mao's years and the early days of economic reforms, it was not unusual for urban families to raise their own chickens, ducks, and geese. But these were not considered "pets" in the Western sense, but were meant to be consumed by the family due to the meager food supply. Keeping pet dogs was seen as a public health problem and a sign of unrefined behavior. In fact, there were strict ordinances against keeping dogs in most cities (see Tomba 2004). The Kunming municipal government passed a specific ordinance in 1996 to limit the possession of dogs. Although it allows adult individuals to raise small pet dogs, owners must get approval from the local public security bureau and obtain the official health and immunization certifications. There were a number of stringent rules regarding dogs' presence in public space and fines for violations. Despite such rulings, the possession of pet dogs in recent years has been increasing rapidly and most owners do not register their dogs and ignore the official regulations. If one walks into a middle- or upper-level housing compound today, he or she is almost certain to run into pet dogs. Some are on a leash, but most run loose, bark at people, and poop wherever they want. Most owners do not bother picking up after their dogs because they think it is the responsibility of the cleaning workers to keep their community clean.

The dog trouble has become one of the most contentious issues in many communities. In the compound where I stayed, residents were deeply divided and defended their own positions passionately. Those who owned or would like to own a pet dog insisted that it was their individual right to have a pet and that it was a purely private matter. Thus, others should not interfere with their choice and lifestyle. By contrast, those who did not own or did not want to have a pet dog believed that their normal life was violated by pet dogs that created constant noise, messed up the environment, and sometimes even harmed pedestrians. They viewed the spread of pet dogs as a vulgar fashion and an uncivil, selfish behavior because it enhanced one's own pleasure at the price of making others miserable. They argued that keeping pet dogs did not fit the local living environment because most urban families lived in apartments without a private yard and consequently dogs were often let out to roam in communal space without adequate supervision. One evening as my daughter was playing with her friends within the compound, I ran into a couple who were taking a walk with their small white dog. The woman who lived in the same building with me picked up her dog to show me how cute her pet was and was trying to convince me to get one for my daughter. She said that life was so much more enjoyable with a dog and she loved the companionship, particularly as their son was growing up fast and becoming independent. She walked away contentedly with her dog running behind her. Meanwhile, I heard an elderly couple nearby whispering to each other: "It is annoying to have to deal with these dogs. She is just trying to imitate Westerners."

In the summer of 2007 when I was there, a group of residents in the compound organized a campaign against the spread of pet dogs. They posted several newspaper articles that criticized dog possession and asked the property management to post the city's ordinance on dog possession on the community bulletin board. Some of articles contained pictures of dogs attacking pedestrians as evidence of the potential danger of keeping dogs in the community. One resident, a university professor, wrote and posted an article, "A Dog's Conduct Reveals the Owner's Conduct," in which he condemned what he saw as the "lack of civility" (*buwenmin*) among many dog owners who did not train their pets well and failed to clean up after them. He claimed that it was the owner's responsibility to keep their dogs clean, healthy, and well behaved, and that if the owner failed to do so, he or she did not deserve to have a pet. He concluded that a dog's manner reflected the owner's suzhi. Several residents who were reading the article on the bulletin board praised the author's insight and his courage in expressing his thoughts. They agreed that the presence of untrained and unsupervised dogs in the community space was an irresponsible act and could even be a public hazard.

At first, I was a bit surprised by the strong emotions that this seemingly minor matter had evoked. For a while, I did not want to pay much attention to it nor did I intend to write about it. After all, in my eyes this issue was not an important aspect of middle-class making that would affect one's livelihood. Secretly I viewed the whole dog issue as merely a form of middle-class groan and moan. But over time I began to realize that this seemingly trivial matter was not insignificant as it touched the nerve of an emerging middle-class life and consciousness. For both proponents and opponents, individual freedom and the rights of private property owners figured centrally in their arguments. The proponents felt that it was their right to own a pet and take it into the communal space that they jointly owned. The opponents argued that the communal space was being invaded by unauthorized dogs. They further invoked the notion of civility or a lack of civility in an effort to shame the dog owners. The conflict thus derived from their different understandings of their entitlement to the communal space and what constitutes good taste and a desirable lifestyle. Given the steady increase in pet dogs, the Kunming municipal government announced the draft of a more lenient decree in September 2007, which eliminated such harsh phrases as *xianzhi* ("restraining"), which was used in the previous ordinance, replacing it with the relatively neutral phrase *guanli* ("regulation").[12] Its goal was to encourage registration and more effective regulation, rather than suppression. It also called for "raising dogs in a civil manner" (*wenmin yanggou*).

Another controversial trend in middle-class consumption that I observed is the emergence of sites catering to a small group of "leisure women." Although the majority of urban Chinese households today are still based on two incomes, some women from well-to-do families have quit their jobs to stay home and thus have plenty of leisure time. Since their husbands are usually preoccupied by businesses away from home, these lonely women frequently seek such leisure activities as hair styling, manicuring, and facial treatment that have flourished in the wealthy xiaoqu. The upscale places often offer a membership that ranges from several hundred yuan to over one thousand yuan a year. Some high-end, imported facial and hair treatment products alone can cost two thousand yuan per package.

One of the leisure activities for men and women with disposable income is to frequent "feet-soaking entertainment centers" (*xijiao cheng*). These are small specialized salons where customers can soak their feet in warm baths made of special Chinese herbal medicines and then receive a foot massage. Many of them are covert sites for sexual services. Such salons tend to be concentrated in the new private neighborhoods where the residents have both the time and the money to spend. Because of the illicit services they offer and the high cost, these sites are seen by many citizens (especially the older generation) as decadent spots or in bad taste. One luxury chain store set up a beauty salon right outside the large middle-class compound where I stayed. It offered hair and facial treatments, saunas, massages, and feet soaking in a quiet, private setting. But due to the high cost, not many residents there could afford it. Some did not want to be associated with it due to concerns about their reputation. As one female resident in her late forties told me, "I predict that it will run out of business because its price range does not match the income of the nearby residents. I usually go to other cheaper places to get my facial and massage. Even if I can afford it here, I will not want to go because my neighbors and friends might see me and wonder what other things I might be doing there."

Advertising Jieceng

The making of *zhongchan jieceng* goes beyond the spatial reconfiguration of communities and consumption practices. It is also realized through another closely related domain—mass advertising for new homes. Real estate developers not only manufacture homes, they also construct and spread new notions of *zhongchan jieceng* and a distinct set of ideas, values, and desires. Through the powerful tool of advertising, these widely circulated ideas and images become a primary source of social imagination through which the urban public comes to conceive what it means to be middle class and how its members should live. Advertisements for private housing frequently make explicit linkages between a particular lifestyle (embodied foremost in one's housing choices), a set of dispositions, and one's class location. At a press conference, a Kunming-based developer once declared that its ultimate goal was to "target the professional elites and create a utopian community for this special group of people to converge and develop into a clearly defined jieceng so that they can live an integrated, pure upper-class life." Thus, developers do not simply sell the material products (houses); they also sell the cultural packages and symbolic meanings. Yet, as Pierre Bourdieu (2005, 23–24) has convincingly argued, the power of home advertising lies in its ability to evoke dormant consumer desires and render them hypervisible by creating an aura around the commodity object. This is a dialogic process, rather than a one-way invention: "We know that, like all symbolic action, advertising is most successful when it plays on, stimulates or arouses pre-existing dispositions, which it expresses and provides with an opportunity for acknowledgement and fulfillment" (Bourdieu 2005, 55).

Let us take a closer look at one of the advertisements published in a major newspaper, *Yunnan Information Daily*. The advertisement was titled "Town Houses Are Really Coming!" and it took up an entire page of the newspaper. It was sponsored by a real estate corporation that was building a large residential community. The lower half of the page is a picture of a smiling young Chinese woman embracing rosy flower petals while at the seashore. The caption below reads: "The platform of the middle-class's top quality life: although not villas, the Sunshine Coast Town Houses are a special, tasteful living zone that specifically belongs to the city's middle-class." The upper half of the page is a carefully crafted narrative on what town houses are, where they come from, and what they stand for. Because most Chinese people are unfamiliar with the history of town houses and their social index in the West, developers can easily manipulate the symbolic importance of this kind of housing. The opening section of the article identifies town houses as a preferred way of life for new middle-class

Figure 14. "Town Houses Are Really Coming!" A newspaper advertisement for a newly built town-house community sells the concept of the new middle class.

families: "In the year 2000, a brand new living space called 'town house' ignited the buying zeal of China's middle class. From Beijing and Tianjin to Shanghai, Guangzhou, and Shenzhen, town houses have caught the eyes of all urban middle-class people and have become their top choice in reforming their lifestyles.... Town houses signify the beginning of a truly new way of life in China." It further claims that "town houses are extremely popular in Europe and North America, and are becoming the classical form of residential space for the middle class.... They can foster unprecedented 'community culture' and a strong sense of belonging among a distinct group of residents."

Such claims suggest that if one can afford this type of home and lifestyle, one will automatically become part of China's new middle classes as well as a privileged global social class marked by Euro-American modernity. More important, it also seeks to summon the past experiences of Chinese people's life and their desires for a better life through the charm of words and images. What is so appealing about town houses to Chinese is that they offer not only private property ownership but also extended private space (such as a small private garden) beyond the limit of "bird cage"–like danwei housing. Developers thus can market town houses (including small private gardens) as a "perfect, independent space that allows one to touch the sky and the earth." The connection between private space and personal freedom is important here. Owning one's own home, spatially and socially detached from the danwei and from the neighbors, is taken as a form of true liberation because it enables one to break away from various social constraints and surveillance. The crux of this advertisement is that buying a home is buying class status, and that community membership is all about class membership.

Some developers may not use the term *zhongchan jieceng* directly, but the message they attempt to send out is loud and clear: buying a home/ choosing a community is all about belonging to a class. For example, one advertisement for a newly constructed community was written on large banners that were hung over several major commercial streets: "For Urban Noble White Collars Only. A Social Circle of 500 White Collar People." In the Chinese context today, "white collar" is used to refer to the relatively wealthy, not necessarily professionals. In another grand advertising campaign launched by the developer of Sunshine Garden (Haoyuan), a massive new housing complex in the western suburb of Kunming, the advertisement, which reached almost every household in the city, highlights the centrality of community in the formation of a class milieu:

> Haoyuan is the noble residential community specifically designed for successful people and societal elites only. The current homeowners are all

successful people, cultural celebrities, famous doctors, lawyers, artists, high-level intellectuals, and returned overseas Chinese. Haoyuan is the ideal living place for those who pursue high-class lifestyles and tastes and for those who seek success in their life. Remember the story of "Mother Meng Choosing Her Neighbors." Having a common living space shared by responsible, career-oriented societal elites is crucial for the creation of a first-rate cultural milieu and an opportunity for your further career success.

This narrative appropriates a well-known, age-old, moral story about how Mencius's mother moved three times until she finally found a decent neighborhood to ensure that her son would only receive positive influences from their neighbors. Her effort eventually paid off as Mencius later turned out to be one of the greatest men in Chinese history. This morally loaded story is used to convince today's home buyers that there is a proven linkage between one's living environment, class status, and future success. According to this cultural logic, residential communities are not simply a place to live; they provide the "cultural milieu" necessary for sustaining a distinct social group and the success of their future generations. An advertising slogan clearly states that "to choose a house means to choose a lifestyle" (see Fleischer 2007).

Ironically, I have discovered during my fieldwork that a large portion of the residents in the luxury communities were not the so-called noble high class or cultural elites, but mostly private entrepreneurs and merchants who had accumulated quick personal wealth outside the state system. These people tended to be regarded by the society as having little cultural capital. But my point here is not that this advertisement makes a false representation of the community; such housing advertisements, true or not, play a powerful part in reorienting the urban public's understanding of class by linking it directly to distinct community forms and consumer lifestyles. The insecurity resulting from one's lack of social status can reinforce the desire to turn toward the material index of class.

"Masters" and "Servants"

While residential communities have become highly differentiated by wealth, a sharp class division is also emerging within the upper- and middle-level community. The most visible disparity takes place between the relatively well-to-do homeowners/residents, who see themselves as "masters" (*zhuren*) entitled to be served, and the low-paid community and domestic service staff, who are treated as "servants." The latter includes a wide range of people who perform physical and affective labor: security guards, hourly wage cleaners, gardeners, domestic workers, repairmen, movers, and remodeling workers hired by individual families. Their work is crucial to keeping the community safe and clean and to ensuring the quality of middle-class domestic life and well-being, yet they remain invisible and criminalized because most of them are migrants and seen as being untrustworthy "outsiders" with low suzhi.[13] There is a love/hate relationship between the two social groups. On the one hand, service workers are an indispensable part of middle-class family and communal life; on the other, their presence causes anxiety and is cited as a source of crime.

Most community service workers in Kunming lived outside the housing enclaves and came to work during the day. According to the urban residents, these workers could be easily identified by the kinds of clothes they wore and the activities they engaged in. There was a clear gender division of labor among service workers. The majority of gardeners and cleaning workers I encountered were women who were paid poorly (a few hundred yuan per month) because their work was considered low skill and manual. They were responsible for keeping the communal space clean. Typically they would sweep the streets, pick up trash, and mop the stairways in each building every day. Sometimes they would spend hours gathering on the lawns to pull weeds. According to my long-term observation, residents in the communities where I stayed rarely paid attention to the workers, let alone greeted them. Residents walked by and greeted others as if these workers did not exist. Some cleaning women brought their children with them because no one else could look after them at home. These children, typically age three to six, were left on their own in the compound without any adult supervision. They hung out at the playground for hours and sometime occupied the swings (there were only two for the entire complex) for a long time, making some residents very unhappy because their kids could not use the swings. There was also a potential danger of drowning and traffic accidents due to the presence of a man-made pond and frequent moving vehicles within the community. A three-year-old boy of a migrant couple was run over by a car just outside the gate because his parents were preoccupied with their work and did not notice that he had run into the street.

Movers and furniture delivery crews, although run by urban bosses, are made up of rural migrant men who undertake the most strenuous physical labor at extremely low wages. Because most Chinese residential communities do not have elevators installed in the buildings (up to seven stories) except for the high-rises, workers have to carry heavy furniture and appliances on their back and climb up several floors on foot. This is backbreaking and sometimes dangerous. One day on the stairway to my apartment I saw a thin man, less than five feet six inches tall, carrying a huge refrigerator on his back with a thick rope. I was afraid that he would be crushed by the refrigerator and was holding my breath as I watched him trying to get up to the sixth floor. Slowly he made it to his destination—the floor where I stood. Big drops of sweat were running down his head. For a trip like this, a worker would only earn 20–30 yuan. If he was injured, he had to pay for the medical costs and risked the possibility of losing his capacity to work. Sadness engulfed me when I compared his hard work and meager earnings with the fact that a middle-class teenager could easily spend five hundred yuan on a pair of Nike shoes or two thousand yuan on an iPod.

Security guards, who also were largely young rural migrant men, tend to have a slightly higher status than other service workers. But their role is somewhat ambivalent: on the one hand, they represent a form of local authority to reinforce order, security, and traffic rules; on the other hand, they are not respected by most urban residents who treat them merely as hired servants. One day I encountered a security guard trying to enforce a parking rule by asking a homeowner to remove his car from the restricted area. The driver became irritated and shouted at the guard: "You just want to give me trouble! I only want to park here for a while. Who do you think you are? This is my home and I am the master here." The guard replied: "Well, I am sorry but I am just doing my duty." The driver grudgingly moved his Audi and continued to curse the guard as he drove away. Sometimes, security guards have to perform potentially dangerous jobs. In the event that they get injured or die, there is no life or medical insurance to cover their loss. During the summer of 2004 when I returned to visit my parents, they told me the heartbreaking story of a young security guard, Xiao Liu, who was severely injured while helping a family within their residential compound. One day a woman who lived on the fifth floor accidentally locked herself out. A young guard volunteered to climb up to the fifth floor in order to get into the house from the window to unlock the door. He did not think it would be very difficult, but somehow he slipped and fell hard onto the ground. He became paralyzed and was eventually sent back to his parents in the countryside. Some families in the compound (including my parents) raised about two thousand yuan and gave it to him before he returned home. I had met Xiao Liu a few times before this incident during my previous stay with my parents. Thus, I felt distraught and could not help but wonder what his life might be like afterward. The head of the security guard team refused to tell me what compensation Xiao Liu might have received and how he was doing back home.

Domestic workers, including baomu (young female live-in nannies and caregivers) and *xiaoshigong* (hourly wage workers), are another vital part of the workforce that supports the middle-class lifestyle. The former group is composed of young migrant women in their late teens or early twenties who engage in physical and affective labor through cooking, cleaning, and taking care of the children or elderly of middle-class families. The care they provide is corporeal, yet the products are "intangible, a feeling of ease, well-being, satisfaction." (Hardt and Negri 2000, 293). Young domestic workers in Kunming were isolated from one another and did not have any social ties with the outside world. At best, baomu were "intimate strangers" (Sun 2009) in urban homes with few rights and no social recognition. On the rhetorical level, baomu are considered part of the employer's families because of the spatial intimacy they share, and are expected to act like loyal, docile, and dutiful daughters (see Gaetano 2004). In reality, there is a great deal of tension and distrust between domestic workers and their master families. The urban residents I interviewed frequently cited stories about unreliable baomu running away with money and stolen household belongings, and emphasized the need to scrutinize their daily activities and social interaction with others. A maid was usually given a house key and a magnetic card to open the communal gate, but the fact that they had the keys made their "masters" rather anxious. It was a common practice for the employers to hold their baomu's identification card and even bank deposit booklet to prevent them from leaving before the end of the contract.

The distrust was also expressed in urban employers' frustration with the presence of domestic workers in their home, which could infringe on their sense of privacy. As Wanning Sun explains, "The seemingly paradoxical process of wanting to outsource housework, on the one hand, and not wanting the domestic worker to intrude on one's private space on the other, has engendered a profound anxiety about the home, a feeling of always being 'not quite at home'" (2009, 15). One retired elderly women complained to me repeatedly that what she disliked most about having a baomu in the house was that she could not talk freely about certain issues with her family members: "Sometimes I had to close my bedroom door in order to talk to my husband about some private matters. But a few times when I came out of the room suddenly, I found my baomu standing close to the door to listen to our conversation. This is very annoying! She should know where her proper place is in this household." On the other hand, employers felt that they had the right to know everything about their baomu in the name of paternalistic protection: how they had spent their time while outside, whom they had talked to over the phone, why they talked to that person...some even demanded to read the letters baomu wrote to their parents.

Maintaining the distinction between the "masters" and the "servants" in everyday life was also important to some young urban women I interviewed.[14] They were appalled by the possibility of being mistaken for a baomu by others. One woman told me that one day she was so humiliated when she went out in casual clothes with her elderly parents and ran into an acquaintance of her parents who thought she was their baomu. Ever since then she has been very careful about her appearance. "At least I have to be above the dressing level of *xiao baomu,* which means I have to pick out a better quality and style of clothing to wear. Now I usually put makeup on and wear nice earrings when I go out. It is simply embarrassing to be mistaken for a baomu," she affirmed. Another woman said that she felt more authoritative in front of her maid when she was properly dressed up because her appearance would remind the migrant woman who was the boss. "If you appear to be on the same level with them, they will not respect you and listen to you," she noted. Thus, the daily act of dressing and putting makeup on has become a way of marking social difference, maintaining status, and asserting authority.

The varieties of service workers I have depicted here occupy an uneasy, paradoxical position in the new order of private urban life. They are wanted and despised, depended upon and distrusted, physically visible and socially invisible. Without them, the urbane, comfortable lifestyle that middle-class families are pursuing would not be possible, yet the private paradise does not belong to the workers. Instead, they are merely laborers who are called to serve the "masters" and at the same time are treated as "the moral other" in the production of postsocialist urban civility (Pow 2007).

THE cultural politics of class in the postsocialist period has a specific contour and requires a closer look at the interplay of property, space-making, and consumption practices. Although the shop-floor experience is still central to the formation of a working-class identity and class consciousness among factory workers, many laid-off state employees, and many migrant workers, this is not the case for the emerging upper- and middle-class subjects.[15] Once spatially dispersed under the public housing regime and the danwei system, urbanites could not easily be identified as distinct social classes. Today, under the new property regime individuals who have acquired private wealth are able to converge in stratified, private residential communities. Such emerging living space offers a tangible location for a new jieceng to materialize itself through spatial exclusion, cultural differentiation, and distinct lifestyle practices. In this process of space-making, consumption practices have become central to the performance of class and distinction and the creation of a class milieu.[16] Some scholars have suggested that consumption practices in the Chinese context are not necessarily about asserting individuality, but are intended to mark out one's success and membership through what is regarded as a correct choice (Dutton 1998, 274; see also Schein 2002). I would not go so far as to suggest that consumption choice in contemporary Chinese society is a mere refashioning of a deeper, unconscious commitment to the notion of collectivism. Rather, I see the emphasis on consumption practice as a pathway to a new class membership based on distinction and exclusivity.

The way jieceng is spatialized and performed in Chinese cities echoes a global trend toward the privatization of space, security, and lifestyle. Increasingly upper- and middle-class families in North America and Latin America, for example, are drawn into what Teresa Caldeira (2000) calls "fortified enclaves"—privatized, enclosed, and monitored residential spaces—to pursue comfort, happiness, and security (see also Low 2004; McKenzie 1994). As people retreat behind gates, walls, security guards, and surveillance cameras, spatial segregation and social exclusion are intensified. Mike Davis describes this kind of spatial politics and conflict as expressed in Los Angeles as a "new class war at the level of the built environment" (1992, 228). Neil Smith calls such divided urban geography "the revanchist city," in which struggles between the middle classes and squatters and homeless people will only intensify (1996, 47). How the inherent tensions and contradictions in the increasingly polarized urban environment will play out in the Chinese context is not yet clear. It is troubling to note that the emerging class-based spatial and social order is often seen by the Chinese public as a natural and progressive move away from Maoist absolute egalitarianism. The pursuit of private paradises, privacy, and personal happiness are thus justified even if they are at the expense of equality, public space, and the rights of the poor.

5

Accumulation by Displacement

It was a cloudy summer morning after a rainstorm. Mrs. Fong, a seventy-year-old long-term resident of Kunming, and her younger son, Fong Nian, who had been recently laid off from a factory, took me to see their house, which had been passed down to them by her mother-in-law but was soon to be demolished to make way for a new commercial development. The house was part of a large century-old residential courtyard situated in a small yet lively old neighborhood in a prime district of the city. The Fong family has long been close friends with my parents and I had visited them there many times before. But when we arrived at the house this time, I could not believe what was in front of my eyes: most of the courtyard had been torn down except for the northeast corner where the Fongs' home was located. We carefully walked through broken bricks, tiles, and wooden beams, and climbed up a squeaking stair that was about to crumble. Fong Nian unlocked the door and told me that he and his wife had lived there for several years, but recently they had moved out to stay with his parents because it was no longer safe to stay there. I noticed that some simple furniture was still inside and a picture of his grandmother was still hanging on the wall. Dust had gathered everywhere. As he was wiping the picture with his sleeve, he said to me: "This is my grandma and this used to be her house. She gave it to my brother and me when she passed away. But now it is going to be gone."

The Fong family had been in an intense dispute with a development agency for more than three months regarding its scheduled demolition and their subsequent resettlement. They were threatened with eviction if they refused to move out by the deadline. The elder son, Fong Ming, who was in his early forties, acted as the family negotiator and was outraged by what he deemed to be an abuse of power by the development company. He responded with a suicide threat. The Fong case is just one of numerous conflicts over eviction, property rights, and relocation that have occurred during the spatial and social restructuring of Chinese cities. Although this process has been going on for two decades, the pivotal point of change for each city was different. The preparation for the 2008 Olympic Games, for instance, led to massive evictions of Beijing residents to make space for new freeways, stadiums, shopping malls, hotels, and other facilities. In Kunming, it was the preparation for the 1999 International Horticulture Expo that led to the largest demolition of the old central city neighborhoods and the formation of the new geographic pattern.

Far from being a smooth process, *chaiqian* ("demolition and relocation") has generated countless disputes and growing grass-roots resistance from those whose property rights have been violated by encroaching powerful commercial interests that are backed by the local government. Contestation over chaiqian has become one of the most pressing social problems facing Chinese authorities. At the center of this new "land war" or "bloodless revolution" (Pomfret 2003) is the struggle over property rights, compensation, and the way chaiqian is carried out. Various forms of civic activism have emerged among the displaced residents who seek to protest their rights as homeowners and challenge the ferocious power of government-backed developers.[1]

The rapid expansion of the real estate industry and the rise of the new middle classes is not simply a matter of successful entrepreneurial endeavors or innocent consumption practices. It is also a matter of remaking urban spatial order and cultural distinctions between the relatively affluent and the less affluent through massive displacement. The glamorous new central financial district and private residential paradise for the new middle classes is built on the ruins of millions of demolished homes of long-term ordinary residents who have been forced out of the urban core, a process that often involves violent acts and fierce contestation. In unraveling this unpleasant story of land development and spatial restructuring, I show that forced evictions and unprecedented displacement are essential to "postsocialist primitive accumulation," propelled by the newly formed pro-growth coalitions between local governments and developers. Further, the rise of the middle-class lifestyle is made possible by displacing lower-income families to the periphery of urban areas. I characterize this pattern of urban development as "accumulation by displacement" to accentuate the centrality of space in political and economic reconfigurations.

Meanwhile, property-related conflicts have generated a new form of civic activism and play a critical role in the development of a popular consciousness of rights.[2] This form of activism has an important class dimension because it is often the property rights of a certain class of citizens that are abused. Lower-income families without any institutional backing tend to receive little or no compensation and are pushed into the undesirable outskirts of the cities.[3] But these displaced residents also adopt multiple strategies of resistance, including legal action, to advance their interests. What is particularly salient in this new wave of grassroots civic activism is the rise of a popular consciousness centered on property rights, and how this new language of rights has become a vital basis for Chinese citizens' individual and collective action.[4] The focal point of my account is the Fong family's struggle because it vividly illustrates the lived experiences of many displaced families and their resistance strategies.[5] I will also highlight the collective struggle of a Hui ethnic minority neighborhood in downtown Kunming and the politics of ethnic solidarity and urban development. In order to provide a better sense of the range of struggles that Chinese citizens engage in, I also draw from secondary accounts of several prominent cases of civic activism, especially collective and legal actions, that have occurred in other cities.

Chaiqian: A Violent Prelude

One of the key symbols marking China's contemporary development craze and the search for spatial modernity is the word *chai* or *chaiqian*, which means "tearing down" or "demolishing and relocating." In Chinese cities today, one frequently sees houses, buildings, or entire city blocks and neighborhoods marked with a giant word *chai*. This word is usually painted on the wall in black or red paint, announcing to the owner and the public that the property is to be demolished soon. The sign conveys a sense of physical and symbolic violence as most demolition involves physical destruction, noise from heavy bulldozers, and the collapse of buildings and walls. Sometime, it is accompanied by crying residents who refuse to leave when their homes are brought down forcefully. *Chai* has become a despicable sign, a violent prelude to urban redevelopment.

I remember clearly that in the late 1990s Kunming was covered by the white character *chai*. Many locals were fearful that this sign might show up on their house one day when they woke up. Rumors went around about which neighborhood would become the next victim. In the three years before the Horticultural Expo, over 90 percent of the old neighborhoods were destroyed; tens of thousands of residents were forced out of the city. This was a major government-orchestrated event and individual families had little chance to resist. Zhao Wei's family was one of the many pushed out of their home. His family had owned a courtyard house in the central business district and had lived there for four generations. Two of the rooms facing a busy street were rented out as stores. In 1996 his family was told that the entire neighborhood would be demolished for renewal projects sponsored by the government and that they had no choice but to obey the relocation plan. Zhao recalled:

> We were basically ordered to leave and had very little say in where to go and what kind of housing we would be put in. My family was assigned to Zhenhe Xiaoqu, a poorly constructed relocation community in the middle of nowhere. When it rained, the roads turned muddy. There was no bus line connecting us to the city at that time. We had to bike for nearly an hour to get to where we worked. People call such resettlement communities *nanminying* (refuge).

Chaiqian can be a highly disturbing event to those who witness the physical destruction of neighborhoods that had long been part of the familiar local cityscape. A high school teacher described to me a demolition scene he saw in November 1997, which was now deeply engraved in his memory:

> My friends and I went to see the demolition of Wucheng Road and Jinbi Road, the two main streets and largest traditional commercial and residential areas. Even when we were still far away from the site, we could see the dust flying everywhere in the air. When we got there, I saw house after house crumbling to the ground. The scene was incredible. You know some of those houses had beautifully carved and painted wooden beams, window frames, and door panels. Some people rushed in and tried to drag some pieces out. You could also buy them in a lump sum for very little money. Nowadays they are considered antiques because it is hard to find them anymore.

There are two types of land clearing involved. One targets the urban core for extremely profitable redevelopment projects, which involves the expulsion of the families who have lived there for decades; the other aims at taking over suburban farmland for metropolitan expansion authorized by the municipal government. My account focuses on the former but I would like to make a brief note of the latter. According to You-Tien Hsing's study (2009b), suburban villagers in northern Chinese regions tend to be displaced completely without the possibility of holding on to their existing homes, but villagers in southeastern regions with strong lineage organizations are able to retain their relatively small residential lots (known as "villages in the city") even though they are forced to give up their collectively held agricultural land. In Kunming, I have observed both processes at work depending on the negotiation and power dynamics between the developer and the villagers.

The demolition and relocation of the densely populated inner-city neighborhoods has become one of the toughest problems facing development agencies and local governments across Chinese cities since the mid-1980s. Given this situation, two kinds of entities came into being. One is a government branch office called the "demolition and relocation bureau" (*chaiqian ban*) that persuades families to leave and arranges resettlement. The task facing this office is very difficult and time consuming as the staff often encounters angry residents who are being forced to relocate. But the work can also become lucrative as developers who want to speed up the clearing process to start the construction are willing to bribe officials. The other agency is a highly profitable commercial entity called the "demolition and relocation company" (*chaiqian gongsi*) that does the demolition work. The majority of developers in Kunming try to avoid this potentially hostile situation by subcontracting the demolition work to these tough, specialized chaiqian companies that do not hesitate to use violent force when necessary. On the ground, residents often see the demolition crew as the "running dog" of the developer and do not really differentiate between the two. Indeed, the two entities work very closely together to produce the desired result as quickly as possible. I made several attempts to interview some officials and crew members working in the demolition business, but they all declined to speak to me. One cadre told me I should leave them alone and that what they did was necessary in order to modernize the city: "If we do not demolish the old, how can we build a new world?" The demolition workers I met on-site told me that they were not allowed to speak to anyone and that they were simply following orders. Once, during an interview with a deputy manager of a large real estate firm, I had the opportunity to ask him about chaiqian-related issues. He was reluctant to talk about it, but gradually he opened up and admitted that this was one of the toughest challenges facing his firm:

Do you think we like to do this? No! But we have no other choice. We need land for construction. Without government support, we would not have been able to take the inner-city residents out. The suburban villagers are tough in a different way. If you do not leave enough residential lots for them to build houses to rent out, they will come to fight with their fists and shovels. We understand their anger. After all, they will lose the farmland that has been their only means of production. So it is natural that they want to get their share.

For a long time between the 1980s and the 1990s there were no specific government regulations concerning the procedures for chaiqian, leaving ample room for abuses of power, rampant corruption, and violations of residents' property rights. It was not until June 2001 that the State Council finally passed the "Regulations Regarding the Demolition and Relocation of Urban Structures." Although these rulings provide some guidelines about negotiation procedures, compensation, relocation arrangements, and legal mediation in case of disputes, it is far from adequate. But as I will show in the next section, this new regulation largely favors the interests of developers; there also remains a huge gap between the law and its enforcement.

Negotiating Property Rights and Compensation

The demolition of millions of inner-city homes is usually carried out in the name of economic development and urban modernization. Two types of structures are involved: residential homes and nonresidential buildings owned by work units. Because the demolition of the latter is negotiated between two institutional entities, there have been fewer disputes. Most clashes take place in the attempt to remove residential homes, especially privately owned homes of long-term city residents such as the Fong family. Although multiple agencies and individual actors are involved, there are three major players: local government, developers and demolition companies, and homeowners. Most homeowners are not organized and thus must defend their rights on an individual basis in confronting corporate power. Developers and demolition companies want to increase their profit margin by significantly reducing or holding back the amount of compensation for displaced families, or even by threatening and physically forcing reluctant residents out of their homes. Although city and district governments are supposed to oversee the entire process and mediate disputes to ensure that displaced residents are properly compensated and relocated, in reality it is often developers' interests that are served. Many local government officials have extensive clientelist ties with developers and profit from new development projects. As such, corruption is deeply embedded in the operation of the entire real estate industry. It is increasingly difficult to disentangle corporate interests from bureaucratic power, leaving individual homeowners little room to seek justice.

What are the key sources of conflict in relocation? Why are some residents unwilling to move? First, some families have lived in those neighborhoods for several generations and have developed strong sentimental ties to these localities. Moving into new suburban multistory buildings also means that there will be fewer chances to interact with the neighbors and the loss of a close-knit social fabric as well as loss of businesses and schools. Second, the focal point of the clashes between residents and developers/demolition companies is over compensation and the relocation site. During my research I found that most families were actually willing to give up their current place in exchange for a new home, but they were extremely dissatisfied with the compensation offered to them. Compensation is often provided in two forms—cash or resettlement housing. The specific terms are usually negotiated between the developers and the families. But determining the cash value of the current housing structure and agreeing on a comparable housing unit elsewhere is a complicated and contested issue.[6] According to the state ruling, provincial and city governments should provide specific criteria to determine the appropriate cash compensation according to the following factors: location, type of usage, and the size of the structure to be demolished. The calculation should be based on the market price. For noncash housing transfers, the difference in value between the old and the new property can be made by cash payment. But in reality this valuation process is full of problems and uncertainties. Most evicted families in Kunming were pushed out of the city core to underdeveloped suburban communities far away from their workplaces, schools, hospitals, and stores. The quality of life thus decreased dramatically even though some of them had acquired a larger, new flat. Many residents claimed that developers and demolition companies simply embezzled funds and gave only partial compensation money to evicted families. In the worst cases, the money never reached the evicted families. In order to provide a deeper understanding of what was at stake and how the negotiations over compensation worked, I shall now turn to a closer account of the Fong family.

I had known the Fongs for years. One day while I stayed with my parents during my summer research trip back to Kunming, we had an unexpected visit from Mrs. Fong. As soon as she walked in the door, she began to weep as she said to my mother:

A terrible thing is happening. They [the demolition team] are going to tear down the house in which Fong Nian [her second son] and his wife live. Fong Ming [her eldest son] got very angry and argued with the company heatedly over compensation. He said he will kill himself in front of them if they do not give us a reasonable settlement deal. You have to help me and do his thought work (*sixiang gongzuo*) to prevent him from taking such foolish action. Although the deal they offer us is really not fair, it is not worth my son's life.

Mrs. Fong and my mother have been close friends for decades and that is why whenever she has difficult personal or family problems she rushes to my parents' house. I brought her a cup of green tea to calm her down. That day she spent almost two hours with me and my mother talking over the situation her family was facing. The Fong family had lived in Kunming for four generations. Fong Nian's paternal grandmother was the wife of a civil servant in the provincial government. When he died in the late 1940s, Fong Nian's grandmother inherited the family property—a large two-story courtyard house in a densely populated neighborhood in Wuhua District (one of the four core districts in Kunming). This house had a wood structure and a dark blue tile roof. The courtyard was paved with stones and had a deep well in the center. At that time this ten-room house was considered a fairly nice property. Four of the rooms were rented out for income. But with the Communist takeover came the nationalization campaign by the socialist regime. In 1955 government officials visited Grandma Fong and told her that she could only retain two smaller units (a total of four rooms) for herself and her younger son who still lived with her at that time; the rest of the house was to be confiscated by the city government housing bureau and rented out to those who desperately needed a place to live. At first, she was promised a small amount of compensation each year, but it lasted less than three years. Grandma Fong, who had bound feet, had never worked outside the home and thus had no income of her own. Her sons had to support her financially since she had lost the rental income. During the Cultural Revolution, the Red Guards harassed her because of her "unclean" family background as a small landlord. When she died in the early 1980s, the ownership of the two housing units (forty square meters and twenty square meters, respectively) was transferred to Fong Nian and Fong Ming because they were her only grandsons. At that time, they were both teenagers living with their parents in a college housing compound where their father taught. Thus, the two units were rented out for a few years.

In 1995 the Fong brothers moved into the two units. Fong Ming, a doctor trained in Chinese medicine, worked at a state factory clinic for several years. Because his salary was extremely low (200–300 yuan per month) and the factory performed poorly, he eventually quit his job and became a retail agent. This new job was highly unstable as he no longer had the "iron rice bowl" and could not predict his monthly income. But at least he had a place of his own to stay. His younger brother, Fong Nian, who had a minor mental condition, worked as a manual laborer loading heavy bags of lead at a local factory. The work was physically demanding, dirty, and potentially harmful to his health, but the pay was not bad (900–1000 yuan per month) and the benefits were attractive. He later married a migrant woman from a remote county in Yunnan Province. Yet, as a result of the second, more far-reaching wave of the state-owned enterprises reform, the factory was bought by a Hong Kong firm in 1999 and subsequently many workers were laid off. Fong Nian lost his job and was unable to find a new one. He and his wife struggled financially and had to rely on his parents for basic living expenses. That year his brother was engaged to a Kunming woman who taught at a local professional school. Because she had an apartment assigned by her work unit, Fong Ming moved out to live with her after they were married and was able to rent his two rooms to a migrant family that owned a small vegetable retailing business. The income was mostly used to subsidize his younger brother.

One day in July 2000, several people showed up on Fong Nian's doorstep and told him that he must get ready to leave within two weeks because a large market building was to be constructed on the site and the project had already been approved by the government. At first, these people claimed that they represented the city government. But later Fong Ming verified that they were not government agents at all; they simply had a piece of official paper authorizing the project. I asked Mrs. Fong which developer they were dealing with. She said that she did not know exactly because her family was only negotiating with the demolition company. I asked her which government agency was overseeing the process. She answered: "The government does not want to get involved directly. Once the developer has obtained a proper document and delegated a demolition company, this company has all the power to decide how much compensation to provide and where they want to relocate you." In Kunming there were over one hundred demolition companies, but only a dozen of them were state owned while the rest were privately owned. There were really no standards in deciding on compensation. Demolition firms would get a lump sum payment from the developer or local government to cover the demolition cost and the compensation to individual families. Thus, if they were able to reduce the amount of money paid to residents, their own profits would be larger. This is how Fong Ming described the strategies used by these firms to reach their goal:

These are tricky businesspeople who often use three steps in dealing with residents: threatening, cheating, and giving in. First, they threaten you by insisting that you must leave immediately according to the government order. If you are afraid of them and sign the agreement they provide, you will only get a small amount of money. If you do not take their word, they will cheat you by claiming that you are violating the law, or your house is not worth much in this area according to such and such calculation. If you do not know the law and policy well, you might just give up. Then they win. But if you insist on your terms and refuse to move out, they usually dare not touch your house. If they do that, you can sue them, which will delay the construction. That is not what they want even if they will win the case in the end. They want time. So in this situation, they are more likely to meet some of your demands.

From this point of view, the outcome of compensation depended on the attitude, knowledge, and negotiating skill of the residents. If one did not fight for it, he or she would get little compensation. Developers and demolition firms always tried to maximize their profit margin by using whatever means they could to limit compensation. In the Fong case, the demolition firm first offered them only sixty thousand yuan in cash to buy out their ownership of the two units (a total of sixty square meters). They immediately refused it because this calculation was based on a rate of one thousand yuan per square meter, which was significantly lower than the market rates for any commercially constructed housing located within the ring road. As Fong Ming argued, "With this price we will not be able to buy any housing within the ring road, let alone in this particular neighborhood as it is the center of local businesses." The property also had an added value because it was located right on a bustling market street and could easily be rented out for commercial use. But the firm did not consider this factor at all. Since Fong Ming was college educated and had two close friends working in real estate, he had a good sense of how to deal with demolition companies. He studied relevant government documents carefully and was well aware of his basic rights as a homeowner.

After arguing with the Fongs back and forth, the firm offered a better deal: to compensate the Fongs with ownership of two new apartments (a two-bedroom unit and a one-bedroom unit) in Liangyuan Xiaoqu, a recently developed lower-income community in the western suburbs. This deal appeared to be a good one because the Fong brothers would receive two new flats of a slightly larger square footage (about sixty-five square meters total). But there were several catches. First, the Fongs were asked to pay fifty thousand yuan in cash to make up the price difference calculated by the firm. Second, homeowners in the new communities were levied a steep comprehensive fee in order to have their water, electricity, gas, phone, and other services hooked up. In Liangyuan, the fee for each unit was twelve thousand yuan, and this fee was not included in the deal offered by the demolition firm to the Fongs. As a result, if the Fong brothers accepted the offer, they would have to pay a total of seventy-four thousand yuan in cash, which was far beyond their financial capability. Even with the help of their parents' life savings, they could not even come close to this amount of money. Fong Ming suspected that this was an intentional strategy by the firm to force them to accept the first cash settlement since they did not have the money to accept the second offer. Third, due to the inferior location of the relocation site, it would be quite inconvenient for Ming to go to work in the city every day and for Nian to get help from his parents (he and his wife frequently had their meals at his parents' house after he lost his job). If they decided to rent the new flats out, the Fongs would not get a good rent either.

Based on these considerations, Fong Ming went to the demolition firm again. This time he insisted that his family would accept the offer only if the additional fifty thousand yuan demanded was waived because he argued that the calculation was unfair. Further, he asked the firm to help pay for the comprehensive fee because his brother was unemployed and also had an official disability certificate. The firm rejected his demand and the case went into impasse. The conflict intensified every time Fong Ming or his mother spoke to the firm representatives. Mrs. Fong's blood pressure went up so high one time that she almost passed out during a heated argument. After that, Fong Ming became the sole negotiator for his family. But he often found himself overpowered by the firm and felt that justice could not be done. One day he became outraged and made a suicide threat while arguing with several men at the firm who treated him rudely. I asked him about the possibility of a lawsuit. He replied:

> The law only sounds good, but it is made to protect the interests of corporations and the rich in reality. First of all, I have no money to get a lawyer and no time to go to court. I have to work every day to survive. Second, I have no *guanxi* to bribe officials, but the firms do. They have political backing and money to make things happen. Eventually the court will rule against me. I am nobody. It is a waste of time and money.

Many residents like Fong Ming have little confidence in the legal system due to rampant corruption and the clientelist ties between developers and government officials. As a homeowner I interviewed put it: "Nowadays it is getting darker and darker. Officials and big developers wear the same pair of pants and protect each other's interests. The court is their court. Together they 'eat' ordinary people and push them far outside of the city.

At the same time, their pockets become full." It is worth noting that a lawsuit does not stop the demolition. According to the new state regulations, if a homeowner files a lawsuit, demolition does not need to be halted during the hearing period as long as some sort of compensation is provided. If the homeowner does not agree with the court ruling, the local legal bureau can order forced demolition. In such cases, homeowners do not have much say regarding the compensation and relocation arrangement.

While we walked through the debris in the almost crumbled courtyard, I asked Mrs. Fong what had happened to other families that had lived there. She replied, "They have already moved out. Because they are considered renters of public housing, not private owners like us, they do not have much leeway in the negotiation. They have to take whatever is offered to them by the demolition company and go." In this entire neighborhood, it was usually those who owned housing structures that rejected what they deemed as unfair compensations. They were then labeled "nail households" (*dingzi hu*), meaning that they resisted relocation firmly like nails in wood. Homeowners like the Fongs felt that they had been robbed twice in their lifetime: the first time was through the socialist nationalization during which they lost most of their properties to the new revolutionary state; the second time was through the development craze brought by the market reform as powerful developers were able to dispossess and displace them while the legal system provided little protection for ordinary citizens. "To me this place means more than just a place to live. It is a home filled with memories and it has the spirit of my grandma," said Fong Nian as he took his grandmother's picture down and carefully wrapped it up. He stood there for a while and locked the door before we left. But now the family was being forced to put a price tag on it. Even worse, they had no power to determine the price.

After two months of dispute and stalemate, the demolition company finally made a concession to waive the fifty thousand yuan they were going to charge the Fong brothers. But they insisted that the Fongs would be responsible for the twenty-four thousand yuan comprehensive service fee for the two new flats. The company gave in partially because it was under strong pressure from the developer who wanted to start construction soon. At the same time, the Fong family was also willing to accept the offer because they realized that time was running out for them, too. The remaining house was in danger of collapsing after other units had been torn down and with the rainy season approaching. Their house would not have stood for long after several storms. If it fell apart, they would have nothing to claim. But still they could not find enough money in time to pay for the required service fees in the new community. They quarreled with one another as they could not agree on a strategy to solve the problem. Finally, they did several things to raise money. Fong Ming took out all the savings he had and borrowed money from relatives and friends. For Fong Nian, his parents contributed their life savings. Mrs. Fong also fought with the factory that had laid off Fong Nian to get some two thousand yuan it owed him. They hope to rent the two apartments out and use the rent money to recuperate from the financial drain. Fong Nian's wife soon divorced him and he moved in with his parents. His mental condition worsened and he was put on constant medication. Fong Ming continued to live with his wife in a small apartment provided by her work unit on the outskirts of the city.

As Chinese cities embrace more commercial development and government-sponsored projects to remake metropolitan spaces, this new "land war" has intensified in recent years. It is often justified through the discourse of modernizing and beautifying the city and through neoliberal market rationality—that is, the highest and best use of the land.[7] As the Fongs' case shows, this battle is fought on an unequal ground. First, because many large development projects are backed up or partially funded by local governments, developers have prevailing power in determining the fate of citizens' homes. When developers fail to offer fair compensation, homeowners have little legal recourse. Second, political corruption allows ample room for the abuse of power, such as ignoring contracts with homeowners, holding back compensation funds, and even using violent means to force families out. The Fongs were able to reach a compromise after a persistent struggle, but in many other cases residents faced harsher treatment by tougher firms. Third, official compensation rates tend to be significantly lower than market rates because even though real estate prices have gone up quickly in recent years, the official rates remain the same. Thus, homeowners are caught between a fast-changing market and a slowly evolving bureaucratic machine.

Yet homeowners are not passive victims; they try to mobilize the resources they have to advance their interests. Particularly in recent years, as the post-Deng regime has given greater attention to protect private property and recently amended the constitution to recognize private property ownership as a legal right, Chinese citizens are more aware of their property rights and are willing to fight for their homes and place in the city in the face of eviction. Consequently, various forms of civic activism based on the notion of property rights have emerged.

Homegrown Urban Activism

Urban residents' battle over corporate developmental power is arguably becoming a very influential form of civic activism in reform China although it has not or may never develop into an organized, translocal social movement. According to a report by the Chinese Construction Ministry, among all 4,820 letters of complaint it received between January and August 2002, 28 percent were related to chaiqian; among the 1,730 formal appeals, 70 percent were related to chaiqian; among the 123 collective appeals, 83.7 percent were about chaiqian (Zhao 2003). But most of the popular resistance has been individually based or small-group oriented; only in recent years have more and more citizens begun to organize collective petitions and file lawsuits against developers and even local governments.

"Nail Households"

"Nail households" is a term commonly used in China to refer to those families that simply refuse to leave their homes due to compensation disputes or opposition to relocation. The situations facing these people are harsher because developers often do not offer the opportunity to rehouse them and the cash provided is inadequate to purchase any housing on the market. Some of these residents use stand-offs (refusing to move) as a strategy to gain time and leverage in the negotiation process. The several cases I present here took place in other cities and received national attention.

In 2003, some ten impoverished families in a lower-income neighborhood near downtown Nanjing utterly refused to leave because they simply had no other place to move.[8] A large economic and technological development corporation bought the land-use rights to their entire neighborhood for 623 million yuan. The compensation offered by the developer was only half the market rate. Even if some residents were willing to move out of the city, they still needed to come up with extra cash to buy lower-end economic housing. Several families lived in the middle of the ruins, as other homes around them had been bulldozed down. One of the "nail households" there was headed by Sun Changzhen who faced specific difficulties. He was laid off by his factory and was not able to find another job. His family of four relied on his wife's meager income and the three hundred yuan monthly rent to buy food, clothing, and other basics. If he lost this home and moved to a flat in the suburb, he would lose the three hundred yuan income as well, making it almost impossible for his family to survive. Further, even to buy a cheap flat in the suburb would require an additional forty thousand yuan, which his family did not have. So they demanded that the local government bureau in charge of demolition and relocation provide them with a comparable economical housing unit elsewhere, but the request was turned down. A month later, the water and electricity to his house were cut off. It was in July and the temperature reached 39 degrees Centigrade. The Suns had to fetch water from a nearby construction site and could not use any fans to cool the house down. The officials thought that such threats and hardships would simply force the Suns to give up, but they were wrong. The Suns continued to live there, hoping that the bureau would eventually increase the compensation fee. The bureau used different techniques such as persuasion and expressed a false willingness to negotiate. One day Sun Changzhen was called to the bureau. While he was away from home, a demolition team arrived at his house and told his family members that Sun had signed the agreement form at the office and that it was time to move out. His seventy-year-old mother did not trust these people and climbed onto the roof to prevent them from tearing down the house. Several days later, his family went out for a while. When they returned, the house had already been flattened and their belongings were buried in the ruins. Since the Suns had not signed any agreement form, this act clearly violated the rights of the homeowner according to the new law. But it was not clear from the report whether the Suns had sought further legal action or how they managed to survive after being forced out.

In 2007, a "nail household" in the city of Chongqing became a powerful icon in the struggle for the right to stay in China. This case, along with a striking picture of a single small building standing on a vulnerable island of mud in the middle of a huge construction site, was widely circulated on the Internet and in the international media. The owners who lived there and operated a restaurant there had engaged in two years of negotiation with the developer for fair compensation. They defied a court order to abandon their house and the woman declared: "I'm not stubborn or unruly. I'm just trying to protect my personal rights as a citizen. I will continue to the end."[9] A week later, after the report, partially due to the intense media pressure, a deal was reached that gave the owners satisfactory compensation and the house was demolished. Although this story had a relatively happy ending, the vast majority of ordinary people forced to make way for urban redevelopment face nightmarish experiences.

"Stand-off" or betting on time is the only viable choice many residents have in bargaining for a better resettlement deal. They know they will have to leave eventually, but they hope that the delay may put pressure on the development company, which is eager to clear the ground for construction. In some cases, such as the Fongs, this strategy worked to a certain degree in that residents were able to strike a better deal. But in other cases, such as the Suns, residents gained little but suffered throughout the stand-off period. In the end, lower-income families were displaced from the center of the city to its periphery, while the center was increasingly occupied by the wealthy and powerful groups.

Some residents threaten suicide when their livelihood is threatened by forced relocation and no proper compensation deal can be made. In most cases, it is a verbal threat coming out of a heated argument. But there have been a few incidents in which things have gone seriously wrong. In August 2003, a so-called self-immolation protest was widely reported in the media. This incident took place within the same Nanjing neighborhood I just described. Weng Biao, a member of the ten remaining "nail households," drenched himself with twenty liters of gasoline when he went to the relocation bureau for further negotiations on compensation. "Weng got into a heated argument with the office personnel and threatened to set himself on fire. Security guards tried to restrain him, but in the scuffle his lighter was somehow ignited. Both Weng and a guard were seriously burned. Weng died fifteen days after the incident" (*People's Daily*, September 17, 2003). Although no one knew for sure how the fire was set off, there was widespread speculation that it might not have been an accident as reported. Another attempted suicide took place in Beijing in September 2003. A forty-five-year-old man from Anhui Province set himself on fire in Tiananmen Square to protest the eviction of his family. He was rushed to the hospital by the police and saved by immediate medical treatment (Hwang 2004). But another Beijing resident burned himself to death in the same month because his family was violently forced out of their home by a new commercial development.[10] Such acts are significant because they tend to receive a lot of media attention and consequently make the upper-level government more aware of the plight facing ordinary residents caught in the development craze. Therefore, even though such tragic acts cannot change these individuals' fates, they have influenced the recent constitutional amendment to protect private property rights. Yet concrete regulations and local implementation are desperately needed in order to produce real, meaningful effects for the everyday lives of Chinese citizens.

Protests and Ethnic Solidarity

In more recent years there have been growing numbers of small-scale street protests, public petitions, and even legal action against developers in many Chinese cities. The two most prominent collective actions took place in February 2000 when some ten thousand evicted families filed a lawsuit at the Beijing Second Middle Court against a demolition company, and in February 2003 when nearly twenty-two thousand Beijing residents signed an open letter to President Hu protesting the eviction of their families

(Hwang 2004). Protestors in these controversies and others also turn to the new media to make their cases and gain moral support from a broader public. At first, most residents only demand fair compensation for their lost property. But after encountering various obstacles and mistreatment by developers and local authorities, they have begun to organize themselves to seek justice. What is particularly striking is a heightened awareness of property rights among urban citizens. They denounce their local government for being deeply corrupt and for letting profit-driven developers prevail over the law, and thus demand that the central government take prompt action to protect the interests of the people. The Internet makes it easier to share information and coordinate collective action in a timely manner. By contesting eviction through collective protests and through legal channels recently made available by the state, these homeowners are paving the way for rights-based collective action and possible political alliances in the future.

But public protests and demonstrations are still deemed highly risky in contemporary Chinese political culture. Although nominally Chinese citizens have the right to protest, they must get approval from authorities and such requests are almost always denied. As a result, their demonstrations are regarded as illegal; authorities can arrest and detain demonstrators. For example, on the eve of the National People's Congress in March 2004, Shanghai authorities tightened control over housing protestors by putting dozens of vocal activists under house arrest to prevent mounting anger among evicted residents from erupting into large-scale public demonstrations (Savadove 2004). In the same year, an old Beijing neighborhood that had existed for more than a century was torn down to make way for the construction of new skyscrapers (see Sillanp 2004). Two dozen local activists gathered at a small alleyway restaurant to plan for appeals and demonstrations in order to draw wider public attention. Their struggle was articulated in terms of fighting for property rights. As one activist put it, "The government is breaking its own laws. It is robbing people of their private property." But they were cautious about what kinds of actions to undertake as their activities were watched closely by plainclothes policemen, and the shadows of the Falun Gong repression and the 1989 Tiananmen event still lingered.

In Kunming, the eviction protests sometimes are intertwined with and complicated by ethnic politics. The fate of a Muslim ethnic neighborhood in particular highlights how ethnic politics, corporate commercial interests, and city planning collided and shaped the outcome of local collective action. Although more than twenty ethnic minorities reside in Kunming, they are spatially scattered. Shuncheng Jie was one of the oldest neighborhoods and the only spatially visible ethnic community in the city. Located at the very heart of the city's central business district, it was inhabited by approximately one thousand Muslims who belonged to the Hui ethnic minority. This neighborhood was initially established during the Qing dynasty, more than a hundred years ago, and became the home of several renowned traditional restaurants (*laozihao*) in the 1930s and 1940s. It was known as the first and most vibrant "Cuisine Street" and commercial center in old Kunming. During the Maoist years, Shuncheng Jie continued to exist but business was depressed. The post-Mao economic reform brought back the vitality of this old community as family-run restaurants and street vendors specializing in Muslim-style cuisine quickly flourished beginning in the 1980s.

Beginning in the mid-1990s, many real estate developers began to turn their attention toward this neighborhood due to its premier location. The potential profits from redeveloping this area were enormous, but the high concentration of ethnic Hui families and businesses made land acquisition more difficult. The Hui had demonstrated strong group solidarity through a long history of uprisings and resistance to Han domination in Yunnan Province (see Armijo-Hussein 1997). The city and provincial governments intended to replace this old ethnic neighborhood with modern and glamorous commercial buildings for two reasons. In some officials' eyes, this crowded, rundown residential and business quarter only blemished the new metropolitan image Kunming was striving to project.[11] Further, this ethnic enclave was seen as a potential unruly place where collective resistance might take place during times when Han-Hui tensions ran high. Several attempts to demolish and relocate this community by the municipal government had failed in the 1990s. In 1997, as part of the grand city makeover to prepare for the 1999 Expo, Shuncheng Jie once again became a major target. An official notice was delivered to the community urging residents to move out immediately. It was justified as part of the citywide makeover for public benefit. Hundreds of Muslims from this neighborhood and other parts of the city gathered in front of the city hall and staged a sit-down protest. Deeply concerned about the potential for social instability as a result of ethnic Hui discontent, the city government eventually backed down and left this neighborhood alone while the surrounding non-Hui neighborhoods were largely demolished.[12] Most Kunming residents I interviewed believed that the Muslim status of the residents and the ethnic solidarity demonstrated in their well-organized collective action played a critical role in saving this community from demolition. As a local taxi driver put it, "Who dares to demolish Shuncheng Jie? This is where the Muslims live and the houses are their private property. If you dare to touch them, they will immediately mobilize and unite. Even their fellow Muslims living outside the city are willing to come and fight for them. It is just the way they are. They have wide connections much beyond this community and their action gets international attention."

But the story did not end there. With the ever-mounting pressure to redevelop and the scarcity of land in prime urban core, Shuncheng Jie, the last undeveloped "frontier" in the central business district, could not escape demolition in the end. In 2004, it was slated for a major 2.5 billion yuan mixed-use commercial development project undertaken by the Sailun Real Estate Corporation. Eleven high-rises including five luxury residential buildings and two world-class office buildings designed by an American architectural firm were to be built and were expected to become signature landmarks of a globalizing Kunming. The toughest job was to clear all the existing houses and relocate the Hui families. When the residents were notified of the plan, they were furious and refused to leave. To prevent large-scale ethnic protests and collective resistance from erupting, the Wuhua District government directly helped create a relatively attractive compensation package and oversaw the entire demolition process. This time the homeowners were promised the option of moving back into two of the new buildings on-site specifically constructed for them, or they could opt for cash compensation at a rate that was almost double what was offered to other displaced residents.[13] The developer reluctantly agreed to build two low-cost residential towers to house the families that had lost their homes. Those who agreed to cooperate and moved out in the early phases were given extra cash bonuses. However, several "nail households" refused to leave because they had lived there for over fifty years and had deep social and emotional ties to the place. The demolition crew threatened them by throwing bricks at their windows at night and by cutting off their utilities. Due to unyielding pressure from the government, a better compensation plan, and fear of violence, the Hui residents eventually moved out.

The collective negotiations and ethnic solidarity that Shuncheng Jie residents engaged in were effective to a certain extent because they helped secure a much better compensation package for the residents and allowed the eventual return of many homeowners. Even if the Hui ethnic group did not stage any large-scale collective resistance this time, the official and popular recollections of their past uprisings and audacity in resisting oppression played a critical role in the government's decision to supervise the negotiation and demolition. But in some people's eyes, this was ultimately a story of helplessness and injustice because, after all, the community was wiped out despite relatively favorable compensation. In an article titled "The Last Shuncheng Jie," a sympathetic local intellectual lamented: "In

Figure 15. The old Shuncheng neighborhood being demolished in 2004.

this age that glorifies money and power, ordinary homeowners have long been ignored.... Time has deprived them of the right to speak out and given the victory to those in control of bulldozers" (Zhu 2005). As I revisited this area in the summer of 2008, the massive construction was well under way. A Canadian IMAX theater and possibly a Starbuck's would soon appear. As advertised, Shuncheng Jie would become a new paradise for the middle classes and the embodiment of Kunming modern.

Toward Legal Action?

A new trend in contesting urban development is the use of legal and administrative channels. In more recent years, the number of formal complaints and lawsuits filed against the local government and developers has skyrocketed in many cities. According to a report (J. Cai 2003), the national public complaints office received over 11,600 complaints from residents regarding relocation problems in the first eight months of 2003, up 50 percent from the same period the previous year. Filing complaints with the central government office is not new, but the surging numbers we see today are unprecedented. As new laws and regulations have been passed, more citizens are inclined to make use of what the government promotes—the rule of law—to fight for their rights. By taking legal action and staying within the parameters of what is officially defined as "civil" and "lawful," discontented residents seek justice while reducing potential political risks under an authoritarian regime. An important regional difference I have observed is worth noting. Affected residents in large metropolitan areas (Beijing, Shanghai, Guangzhou) under far-reaching global influences are more likely to engage in legal challenges or large-scale public protests. Kunming residents are less likely to engage in such actions.

In early 2003, six plaintiffs, representing some 2,150 tenants from the Jingan District, the heart of the largest redevelopment project in Shanghai, filed a lawsuit against one of the most prominent developers, Zhou Zheng-Yi (Verhovek 2003). They charged Zhou with illegally acquiring land in Jingan and subsequently evicting thousands of residents there. They demanded that Zhou's corporation provide greater compensation or rehouse the evicted families in the new housing complex to be built.[14] This was a tough battle as tycoon Zhou had close ties with the so-called Shanghai Gang, the power base of former president Jiang Zemin. Meanwhile, a Shanghai lawyer, Zheng Enchong, who had helped hundreds of eviction cases, was advising on this case. But in June, the Public Security Bureau suddenly detained Zheng and accused him of stealing state secrets. Although the authorities denied any connection between his detention and the Jingan lawsuit, many believed that his arrest was due to his role in the Jingan case, which had offended powerful local interests (Kahn 2003). In August, a district court rejected the residents' legal claim and ruled that tycoon Zhou had acted legally. The plaintiffs did not give up and appealed to a higher Shanghai court.

Later that year, the situation suddenly changed. Zhou was put under house arrest on charges of serious financial irregularities. It was speculated that this action was part of a symbolic move by the new Chinese leadership to demonstrate its willingness to curb serious financial fraud in the real estate and financial sectors. This case was carefully orchestrated, however. Zhou's political ties were not mentioned and the court hearing was closed to the public. In May 2004, Zhou was sentenced to only three years in jail. This extremely light sentence caused widespread public criticism, and many believed that Zhou's political ties had enabled him to receive such a short sentence (Lee 2004). At the same time, Zhou's development project in Jingan was put on hold. When I visited Shanghai in June 2004, I saw the ruins of the neighborhood but no signs of any construction.

The arrest of lawyer Zheng for developer Zhou sent a chilling message that it was highly risky for lawyers to work on behalf of individuals against powerful corporations. But the unprecedented number of disputes also created a potentially lucrative market for city lawyers. In response to this situation, the Shanghai Lawyers' Association announced that a team of 152 lawyers and eighty law firms would begin to offer legal assistance to residents in disputes with local governments or with developers (see J. Cai 2003). Some people hoped that the backing of a larger association might lend the lawyers more clout. But it is unclear to what degree these lawyers will be willing to challenge bureaucratic and corporate power as many of them have close personal ties with officialdom and the real estate industry. Also, their motivations for helping the residents are driven more by financial gain than by a sense of seeking justice.

How do we make sense of the above individual and collective property-related actions? How can we characterize this emerging form of urban activism in postsocialist China? It has been widely documented that urban homeowners and residents constitute a powerful source of civic activism and can mobilize a wide range of negotiation and resistance strategies depending on the specific situation. Some earlier studies (Logan and Molotch 1988; Marris 1974; Mollenkopf 1983; Palen and London 1984) show that intensive conflicts between developers, local governments, and residents occurred during the 1960s and 1970s when American cities were undergoing massive postindustrial urban restructuring. Inner-city middle-class homeowners and other residents who did not have absolute rights to the property were able to mobilize themselves in various ways (ranging from militant community activism, protests, and neighborhood revolts to invoking civil rights laws) in order to halt or alter the development plan. Black and other poor ethnic neighborhoods were particularly affected. Similar processes, seen more or less through the lens of "gentrification," have taken place since the 1980s in North America and Europe (see, for example, Herzfeld 2003, 2009; Ley 1996; N. Smith 1996). These different forms of activism have been largely characterized as "uncivil" in that they relied on direct, unruly confrontations and a rebellious spirit rather than legal battles over property rights. In some areas, local resistance produced limited gains in that the residents were not completely displaced or the redevelopment plans were modified to accommodate the existing community. More recently, Mike Davis (1992), Setha Low (2004), and others have depicted another kind of powerful urban and suburban social movement organized by middle-class and affluent homeowners who defend their property values and safety through NIMBYism, tax revolts, and private security protection. The actions they take to achieve their goals are often exclusionary, antidemocratic, and thus "uncivil."

In light of these discussions, I suggest that a more fruitful way to grasp China's urban activism is not through the "civil"/"uncivil" discourse, but through the notion of "situated civic action" specific to recent Chinese history. Civic action signifies its public and community-based nature (as opposed to state-initiated) against the predatory developers backed by local governments. It involves the appropriation of discourses on property rights and citizen rights as well as that of unruly behavior to confront illicit land appropriation. Some residents facing forced demolition in Shanghai also invoked the officially sanctioned revolutionary repertoire, such as waving the national red flag on their property and singing "The Internationale," during protests to demonstrate their solidarity and determination to fight injustice (Shao n.d.). These mixed strategies cannot be easily labeled as citizenship or class struggle, civil or uncivil practice, nor can their localized contestation be characterized as a "multi-class movement" across the urban society as defined by Castells (1984, 320). Rather they constitute a highly fractured and situated form of property activism contingent on locality, history, and the social and political resources available to those affected. In Chinese political culture, this tactic of staying local and addressing pragmatic issues entails less risk as it is more likely to be tolerated by the state than the effort to forge a translocal, sustained social movement.

Sanctioning *Wuquan*

In the process of reforming land use, privatizing housing, and developing a mixed economy, popular consciousness and official discourses on private property and property rights are changing. I would like to briefly trace how the official sanctioning of property rights (*wuquan*) took shape in recent years and its potential impact on chaiqian. The first major step taken by the state was the 2004 amendment to the Chinese Constitution, which acknowledged that "lawful private property is inviolable" and that the state encourages, supports, and guides the private economy. This amendment represented a significant departure from the previous socialist ideology and was the first time in the five decades of the PRC's history that the Chinese party-state had enshrined private ownership. In July 2005 the National People's Congress made another dramatic move by releasing the newly created "Draft Law on Property Rights" (*wuquan fa caoan*) and invited public debate and feedback. The draft law, posted on the NPC's website and widely circulated among the urban public, invoked a heated debate among economists, legal scholars, and intellectuals. Although applauded by those who saw the legal protection of property rights as a necessary condition for the expansion of the market economy, it was questioned and criticized by others. The most vocal opposition came from Gong Xiantian, a law professor at Beijing University, who accused the draft law of "offering equal protection to a rich man's car and a beggar man's stick" (Kahn 2006). He mocked the legal experts who drafted the law for "copying capitalist civil law like slaves." His view represented an undercurrent in Chinese society of discontent with uneven capital accumulation, rising inequality, and the dissolution of state responsibility for the welfare of its citizens.

The revised Property Law went into effect in October 2007.[15] It contains five parts and nineteen chapters concerning the creation, transfer, and ownership of property. The stated aim is to provide comprehensive protection to three basic kinds of property in the PRC—state, collective, and private. Three aspects are pertinent: chaiqian, homeowners' rights, and the politics of community governance. First, it places private ownership on an equal status with state and collective ownership. The 4th Clause of Chapter 1 clearly states that "state, collective, private, and other ownership rights are all protected by law. Any danwei or individual is prohibited from violating such rights." The 64th Clause of Chapter 5 further specifies the items protected under private ownership: "Private individuals have ownership rights to all legally obtained income, housing, daily use items, production tools and materials, and other movable and immovable capital." It assures urban homeowners that their property will no longer be at the mercy of changing state policies. This formal legal protection of private ownership is in itself a revolutionary act for a state that still claims to be socialist in its ideology. Second, the law specifically prohibits any unlawful demolition of private homes and forced relocation in the name of development. This is significant in the context of rising property-related conflicts and disputes caused by urban renewal and the expansion of commercial development into suburban areas. Third, the law specifies that communal space in the new commodity housing compounds belongs to the homeowners, and not to the developers. The 75th Clause also legalizes the organization of homeowners' associations and recognizes their power. This change has important implications for understanding the changing community governance that I will discuss in the last chapter.

The new property law has already begun to reshape the way Chinese people think about property, rights, class, and community. Yet, the very concept of *wuquan* remains a somewhat alien notion to most people, especially those who lived through socialism. Before and after the law was enacted, I was conducting field research in Kunming and thus had the opportunity to observe popular reactions. It was clear that the degree of concern and familiarity with *wuquan* was highly class specific. Large entrepreneurs, private business owners, intellectuals, and upper-middle-class homeowners were more attuned to this legal change because their interests were at stake. They also had better access to information and were interested in learning about this law. Some of them had downloaded and read the entire document from the NPC website and had participated in the online national debate. A law professor from a local university organized a public session at the provincial library to explicate the draft law to interested individuals. A self-made real estate developer told me bluntly: "I am very concerned about this law because I believe it is a progressive thing that will bring long-term stability and development to our society. Our society needs it; our future generations will benefit from it." By contrast, ordinary citizens who did not own much property were less interested because they were not sure how they would benefit from it. Instead, they believed that government policies were more important and would affect their immediate livelihood. In particular, lower-income workers, retirees, migrant workers, and street peddlers I spoke to said that they had never heard of the draft law and they were not interested in learning more about it. Only when involved in direct conflicts with developers did they want to know more about the law and how they could use it to protect their interests. However, the property law has opened up a new space for reconceiving property relations despite the enormous gap between law and practice. Although accumulation by displacement and dispossession will continue, the abuse of power might be somewhat restrained in the new legal climate.

As I have shown in the case of Kunming, China's amazing economic growth over the past thirty years has largely been built on an ambiguous regime of property rights that has allowed for such rapid and crude capital accumulation.[16] The reform regime faces a quandary: on the one hand, there is momentum both inside and outside the state to sanction property rights and protect private wealth; on the other hand, the rights of ordinary homeowners in everyday life are frequently violated by corporations and local governments in the name of development. In this unequal power triangle, government officials and powerful commercial interests have become deeply entangled in the name of economic development and urban renewal. Given the ambiguous property rights regime, developers and local governments can easily carry out large projects by displacing families on-site without bearing serious legal responsibility for such acts. In this context, I question a popular position that many scholars (especially economists) advocate: that clearly defined private property rights are key to economic development. For example, in an article titled "Property Rights—the Key to Economic Development," the authors claim that "prosperity and property rights are inextricably linked.... Nations prosper when private property rights are well defined and enforced" (O'Driscoll and Hoskins 2003, 1–2). It is problematic to assume any neat, one-dimensional correlation between exclusive private property rights and economic development. The pattern of dispossession displayed in China has its own characteristics, however. Although the scale of displacement has been very large and the methods used have been harsh, the Chinese government has also strived to keep registered urban residents under a roof, thus preventing massive homelessness or sustained protests about evictions. Local resistance often makes gains in terms of compensation, but it is rarely able to halt or alter the demolition of their community. Further, the unequal power relations between local governments, real estate corporations, and disfranchised residents signify the formation of a different political culture under intensified commercialization and privatization. With the rise of real estate development, what we see today is not just an enmeshing of state elements and private businesses or the breakdown of a rigid state-society dichotomy, as some scholars have observed (see Perry 1989, 1994; Rofel 1999; Shue 1988; Wank 1999; Yang 1994), but also how rising corporate power is transforming the way urban governing is imagined and conducted. Today, the making of a new spatial order and the restructuring of urban communities are increasingly carried out by the emerging coalition between corporate developers and government agencies. Their actions are guided by the market principle of profitability and commercial values. The primary social groups they strive to serve and profit are the rising new middle classes, while the lower-income masses become subject to displacement (spatially and socially) and dispossession.

6

Recasting Self-Worth

In traditional and socialist Chinese society, notions of selfhood and person-hood were deeply embedded in larger social relationships including family, kin, neighborhood, and danwei.[1] What it meant to be a socially recognized person in a local moral world was largely defined in interpersonal experiences through the practice of gift exchange (Kleinman and Kleinman 1991; Yan 1996, 14). Thus, the production of selfhood and persons was realized in a relational process of constantly producing and maintaining social ties and moral status as well as cultivating socially acceptable behaviors toward others (Pellow 1996, 113–14; Yang 1994, 192). Individualism that encourages personal desires and a discrete self as found in the West was relatively weak in prereform China. Rather, self-worth was closely intertwined with, if not completely subjugated to, the interests and needs of collective entities (from the family to the nation-state) and the moral judgment of others. This socially embedded nature of selfhood has been undergoing profound transformations over the past two decades, however, as China embraces privatization and globalization.

An NPR reporter has argued in a series of reports that Chinese society is becoming what he calls "a nation of individuals."[2] Others have also declared that the age of "We" is vanishing while the age of "I" is coming (Chen Jiu 2006). Although one can recognize that such dramatic characterizations are intended to create a shocking effect in order to accentuate the magnitude of recent changes, it would be too simplistic and naïve to declare that "We" has been erased by "I" in the reform era. What is emerging is a more complicated configuration, in which the social and the collective remain important despite the rise of individualism, yet at the same time the I/We contradiction is becoming more pronounced and playing out differently depending on gender, age, occupation, and other socioeconomic factors. This entangled form of emerging individualism is inseparable from the rise of mass consumerism, the privatization of housing, and the reinstitution of property law. Yet, it is also conditioned by history, locality, and the cultural milieu in which specific Chinese subjects live. In this context, I suggest that the notion of self-worth has become more individualized and materialized in recent years through the idiom of property possession. Love and marriage have also become increasingly measurable by tangible material possession.

The centrality of property transaction in marriage practice is not new or unique to China. Rubie Watson has pointed out that "marriage in Chinese society is about the movement of things as well as persons. Betrothal gifts, dowry, and presentations made by wife-givers or wife-takers are all part of the complex calculus of family life in Chinese society" (1991, 352). In the 1970s, watches, bicycles, and sewing machines were popular choices for "marriage-related consumption," and the 1980s brought color televisions, refrigerators, washers, and furniture (Ch'ien et al. 1988; Ocko 1991). Since the 1990s, houses and cars have risen to the top of the desired items. What makes this current trend striking is (1) it forms a sharp contrast with the high socialist era that utterly rejected any market logic in conceiving court-ship and marriage (at least in the public and official sphere); and (2) there is a significant shift in the desired objects from ordinary consumer goods to big-ticket items such as real estate and cars. Due to the increased cost of the investment, one can imagine the heightened intensity of disputes over property ownership in the event of divorce.[3]

In this chapter I seek to explore how self-worth, love, and the conjugal relationship are being revalorized with the increased importance of pri-vate property in Kunming's domestic life. I examine specifically how and why owning a private house has gradually become the decisive factor for the middle classes in considering whether to marry and a focal point of contention in dissolving that relationship. Yet, this trend does not suggest that notions of love and emotionality are disappearing or are of no impor-tance anymore. On the contrary, a new language of love and romance (as opposed to family obligation) is emerging and contending with increased concerns over property. It is this tension and articulation between love/emotion and property/material ownership that my ethnography seeks to grasp. The stories I will present in this chapter indicate that these two sets of concerns coexist and transform one another, thus generating new and often contradictory understandings of what love and marriage mean in a postsocialist market economy.

It is important to note that most Chinese cities today still reflect hetero-normative domestic arrangements even though public emergence of same-sex relationships and social spaces for gays and lesbians is increasing rapidly, especially in Beijing and Shanghai where more activists and institutions that promote same-sex rights are found (Engebretsen 2009; Rofel 2007). During my research in Kunming, however, I did not have the opportunity to interview any individuals from the same-sex community. Thus, I do not presume that my account here necessarily speaks to how the changing notions of self-worth, affective ties, and marriage articulate with property concerns among those of same-sex desire.[4] Within the urban heterosexual domain I studied, patrilocal residence is no longer the norm; the majority of young couples prefer to set up their own residence before or soon after they get married. The nuclear family has become a common domestic arrangement and a house of one's own is a principal indicator of an independent lifestyle, a measure of success, and a concrete embodiment of middle-class aspiration. At the same time, young couples maintain close ties with their kin and are expected to fulfill filial obligations to their parents through frequent visits.

Although there is an increased emphasis overall on material ownership in the social and intimate realm across the urban population, it is also important to call attention to the distinct gendered nature of this shift in personhood and situate it in Chinese history. What self-worth means and how it can be measured has varied greatly for Chinese men and women in different historical periods. In China, self-worth has long been closely intertwined with the distinct notions of masculinity and femininity whose meanings are culturally and historically constructed and class-specific (Brownell and Wasserstrom 2002). In traditional China, normative masculinity was formed around two sets of attributes known as *wen,* which referred to certain refined behaviors and scholarly achievement, and *wu,* which denoted physical strength expressed through martial prowess (Louie and Edwards 1994). Both sets of traits were not innate qualities but were achieved through purposeful cultivation of one's mind and body according to Confucian and Taoist cultural expectations. Femininity in premodern China was based on notions of filial piety, modesty, and domesticity, culminating in the practice of foot binding as a rite of passage into womanhood, which first started among the leisured elites and then spread to the peasantry in the seventeenth and eighteenth centuries (Ko 2001). In the Maoist era, state socialism attempted to erase gender and sexual desires in the public sphere as part of the liberation project. This effort led to "the masculinization of women's bodies" (Yang 1999, 40) and state promotion of the so-called iron girls—strong proletarian model workers who could perform men's work and "hold up half the sky" in building socialism (Honig 2000). Thus, gender differences became largely muted in public discourse and were replaced by a set of highly politicized, non-gender-specific characteristics, such as revolutionary fervor and selfless work (Chen 2002, 317).

Such erasure of gender difference not only failed to address the problem of gender inequality but also deprived Chinese men and women of their unique gender identity and public expression of their sexual desires.

In today's market economy and consumer culture, not only do we see the reemergence of gender difference and sexual desire in public spaces but we also witness a rapid commodification of the differentiated longings. For men, self-worth is tied to a form of masculinity manifested in one's ability to make money, possess desirable material goods, or gain political power.[5] The traditional *wen* and *wu* qualities and the passion for revolution have been eclipsed by material accumulation in the contemporary quest for a masculine self. For women, self-worth is deeply intertwined with the refeminization of their body, physical appearance, and conduct. There is a growing, intense interest among young and middle-aged urban women in fashion, cosmetic surgery, and etiquette training classes with the aim of cultivating refined femininity (see also Yang 1999). Responding to this market demand, there is a proliferation of clinics specialized in breast reconstruction, eye lifts, face-lifts, and other procedures to produce a beautiful and sexualized feminine body. In Kunming, such places are often swamped by middle-class women who wish to improve their body image and self-confidence, so as to become more desirable and valuable in the new market of dating and marriage. In a sense, their bodies and bodily images have become a form of valuable commodity that can be exchanged for material wealth and comfort. The intense interest in bodily investment among urban Chinese women and the material quest among Chinese men are a closely related dual process. As some researchers have suggested, the search for new masculine identities often requires new kinds of femininities because these two concepts only make sense in relation to each other (Gilmartin et al. 1994; Glosser 2002). Thus, the remasculinization of men demands the refemininization of women. This dual process is not only an effect of a raging market culture that seeks to harness consumer desires but also a reaction to the socialist erasure of gender that is seen by many Chinese today as having been dehumanizing.

Before I turn to detailed ethnographic cases, let me first analyze public debates on the relationship between housing, self, and marriage in the media as well as in newspaper advertisements on spouse-seeking. The bulk of the chapter is devoted to several stories of the families I met, which illustrate how the shifting notions of self-worth and modes of valuation reconfigure the intimate realm of heterosexual love and marriage under new circumstances. Their narratives also show that this reconfiguration is a rather complex and gendered process rather than a simple story of materiality trumping emotionality.

Of the Material Index

One day I was surfing one of the most popular Chinese Internet search engines, *Baidu,* and I typed in the following Chinese words: *fangzi* (housing), *hunyin* (marriage), and *ziwo jiazhi* (self worth), and then hit go. Numerous Web links that contained articles, reports, and blogs on these topics immediately appeared. I was curious and began to read them. Over time it has become clear to me that housing (or material possession in general) is becoming an important index of one's worth and happiness, and the most contested item of legal negotiation in settling a divorce. Let me begin with an article, "The Modern Men's Contest," which represents a strong critique of the troubling trend of materialization in Chinese society. The author begins by lamenting the loss of *benzhen* (roughly translated as "inner or spiritual qualities") in the age of materialism: "In this modern era, human beings are materialized (*wuzhihua*) to a large degree. A person's worth and status can be simply equated with the possession of houses, expensive cars, and other assets." The writer continues to describe the fierce material competition in China today with a witty tone: "Modern people like to greet others with such questions: 'Have you bought a house yet?' Or 'Have you upgraded your house?' Houses and cars have become their favorite assets because these two things in their eyes best represent one's material well-being and best exemplify their worth and social status." The term "modern men" is used in a cynical sense because the so-called modern people are lost in the blind contest over material possession while their spirituality is submerged by superficial external objects. This article is a powerful commentary on an ironic situation of emerging consumer alienation, in which people become possessed by their own material possessions.

In another article, "House and Marriage" (*Wenzhou Daily,* June 27, 2004), a school teacher, Xiang, remarks on the dismal reality facing himself and many other men—not owning a place to live is a major obstacle to getting married. He reflects on a fundamental change in what Chinese society valued before and now:

> In ancient times, marriage followed two basic principles—matching the status of the two families involved, and matching a man of talent with a woman of pleasant appearance (*langcai nümao*). But today, a man's *cai* [talent] has mutated into another kind of *cai* [material wealth]. If a man does not have talent or good looks today, it is not a problem. But if he does not have wealth, that will not work. And one of the most important reflections of his *cai* is home ownership.

Here Xiang is playing with homonyms to accentuate the radical change in values. The two Chinese characters, *cai* (talent) and *cai* (material wealth), have the same sound but mean entirely different things. The former highlights inner qualities and aptitudes that cannot necessarily be translated into the latter—measurable material goods. The shift from the first *cai* to the second *cai* in marriage considerations thus indicates a deeper and larger shift in societal valuation that underscores the importance of material wealth. Xiang notes his painful realization of the dilemma facing him: "Nowadays if one wants to find a wife, he must have a house. This is an extremely important prerequisite or shall I say capital....But for ordinary people like me who only have a modest income, buying commodity housing is as difficult as climbing up the sky."

This teacher's narrative reflects what I found during my conversations with many Kunming residents about their dating and marriage choices. Homeownership has undeniably become one of the primary concerns in their decision making and how they assess the worth of a potential spouse. This is particularly true for men who are largely held responsible for providing a place to live. A special column in the popular Kunming newspaper *Metropolitan Times* (*Dushi Shibao*, August 31, 2004) epitomizes this sentiment by featuring a series of reports on the centrality of housing in marriage with a revealing title, "A House Is a Man's Dignity" (*Fangzi Shi Nanren de Zunyan*). I was struck to see this straightforward statement presented in a large, bold font, something unimaginable to many Chinese just a decade ago. The report tells the story of a young man, Chen Feng, who came to work in Kunming in 1999 from a nearby county. He worked hard, was able to stay in the city, and eventually fell in love with a local woman. But he did not have a house of his own. On the other hand, the bride's parents had a large house in the suburbs. So he agreed to move in to live with her parents after the wedding. This residential practice is called *daochamen*, which is rare and considered somewhat disgraceful to the groom in China. But some of his friends thought he was lucky because he had a wife and a place to live. Chen, however, did not see it that way; he felt awkward and inferior:

Every day when I come home, I have to eat with my parents-in-law and thus cannot talk about my work and life freely with my wife. After a while, I even feel uncomfortable walking in the house with my slippers. Eventually I become completely silent whenever they discuss issues related to this house because I constantly remind myself that I am only a guest in this house. Sometimes my wife and I argue over small things. I always keep my voice low and give in quickly because I realize that I live in a house of others.

Chen was extremely sensitive about the fact that he was not the owner of this house and thus felt inferior to other family members. Five years later he was able to purchase a modest private housing unit using a mortgage program. When his dream finally came true, he exclaimed to his friends: "I have bought a house of my own!" He described the profound change in his mood and his increased sense of manhood:

> The minute I paid the down payment I began to feel much better. Even though it took me a long time to save that much money and I have to pay over one thousand yuan a month for the next thirty years, I feel happy and relaxed. I have studied my feeling for a while and concluded that the reason I feel this way is because I now have status and respect (*zunyan*). Because I am a man, I must have a space created by myself. The property deed with one's own name on it means a great deal to a man.

Chen's narrative indicates that owning a private space/house is intrinsically linked to his sense of respect and self-worth, which is the foundation for his manhood. For him, to be a real man is to own property and be the main breadwinner in the family. The inability to provide a place for his family is seen as a failure of his manhood—the source of his insecurity. Such understanding is clearly reflected in the second article in this column, "I Do Not Want to Live in Her House." The male author criticizes some women who want to own their own house and claims that he does not understand why they want to do so: "I believe that buying a house is a man's business or at most a project of a man and a woman's joint effort. But it is certainly not a woman's business." He even feels pity for those women who work hard to pay mortgages instead of enjoying their youth and beauty. For him, women owning a house could potentially threaten his manhood: "If I look for a girlfriend, I do not like to find one with her own housing. Simply put, if I live with her in her house, I will never be able to raise my back up (*yaoban zhibuqilai*). If I cannot raise my back up, how can I make a good lover?"[6] For this man, the lack of home ownership has weakened the basis of his manhood, making it difficult for him to act confidently.

The title of the third story is also very telling: "How Can One Talk about Marriage without Owning a House?" Ai Ning, 28, split up with her boyfriend after five years of dating. The reason is that he does not have a house even if he is a nice man. It is not an easy decision as they are both in love with each other. But she is resentful of sharing a small room with her parents and sisters and longs for her own space. Since her boyfriend is too poor to provide the space she desires, she decides to end the relationship despite their feelings. Ai Ning told the reporter at the end that her mother's friend had introduced her to a new man who owned a two-bedroom condo, but she had no idea whether they would get along. Home ownership appeared to be a crucial factor in deciding whether a courtship was worth developing, yet it was unclear to what extent this factor would ultimately trump her romantic feelings.

The increasing centrality of property ownership in dating and conjugal relationships is vividly portrayed in a cartoon featured in this column. A man and a woman hold hands together and face each other as if they are exchanging vows. Their heads and upper bodies are framed by a house with a smoking chimney. I see this cartoon as a vivid reflection of an emerging mentality among many urban Chinese that home ownership has become a necessary condition for men to talk about love and marriage, as well as demonstrating their manhood and *zunyan*.

The increased salience of property ownership and gendered understandings of marriageability is further reflected in spouse-seeking advertisements (*zhenghun guangkao*) in local newspapers. This section, similar to what is known as the "love connection" in the United States, usually takes up an entire page of a daily newspaper. I have surveyed several hundred advertisements posted in two major local newspapers—*Metropolitan Times* (*Dushi Shibao*) and *Spring City Evening Daily* (*Chuncheng Wanbao*)—between June and August 2007. In the majority of such brief personal narratives, which run about one hundred words each, private home and car ownership is often highlighted after a brief listing of age, height, degree of education, and occupation. The emphasis on material well-being is particularly evident in men's ads, coupled with a short narrative of one's longing for emotion and love. A typical posting reads:

> A Successful Gentleman [in bold and large font]: 39, 1.74 meters, bachelor's degree, a short previous marriage, no child. Mature and well-cultivated, honest, handsome, with a sizable income. I own several apartments in the city and a high-quality car. My material wealth, however, cannot replace the loneliness of my heart. I am a sincere person longing for a lady who is honest and kind like me, someone who wishes to spend the rest of her life with me (open to any location and marital history). (*Dushi Shibao*, July 25, 2007)

A typical phrase used in most ads to denote one's financial status is "*bei chefang*," meaning "equipped with a car and a house." This Chinese expression does not clearly indicate the quantity and the quality of what one owns. For example, *fang* can be a small apartment, a larger condominium, or a single detached house. *Che* can be a cheap, used domestic car or a luxury imported car. But the very fact that one owns a home and/or a car already puts one in a different category of people. Some advertisements choose more specific phrases, such as *bieshu* (villa), *haozhai* (mansion), and *mingche* (renowned car), to indicate the higher level of possessions.

There are also group postings that are brief and inexpensive. For example, one of them titled "A Special Edition of Excellent Unmarried Gentlemen" lists twelve men with their age, height, degree, and occupation. Each one ends with *bei chefang*. Clearly, home and car ownership is a key factor in marking one's class status and marketing one's social worth. By contrast, another group posting, "A Special Edition of Excellent Unmarried Ladies," consists of similar information about six women, but skips the information about their *chefang* ownership status. Instead, all of the candidates add remarks about their physical appearance and figure by using such words as "white skin," "beautiful and fashionable," "model-like body," "elegant," and so on. Such gendered conceptions of self-worth are not absolute, however. Some personal ads by women also use such straightforward phrases as *nü fushang* ("wealthy female merchant") to highlight their financial status to attract readers' attention, but it is a less important factor in their marketing scheme. For women, wealth is a plus but must be accompanied by a desirable figure and pleasant feminine looks. Otherwise, their material possessions may not be so valuable or can even become potentially threatening to men who cannot measure up. Some women I spoke to felt that reshaping their body into a sexy, feminine, and desired object is more rewarding. I once asked a friend why she was willing to spend two thousand yuan (more than a half of an ordinary Kunming household's monthly income) on a set of special, imported facial products. She replied frankly: "It is worth the investment to prolong my youthful appearance. I am already into my forties. If I do not take care of how I look, my husband might look for other younger women."

The shift toward a property-centered perspective of worth represents a deep rupture in the construction of gendered selfhood and the understanding of love, marriage, and domestic relations. Yet, this shift is never complete, but is conditioned by the constant presence of human feelings and emotions as well as history and locality. In other words, market logic cannot simply devour the affective dimensions of life; rather, it transforms them (Stewart 2007). The ethnographic portraits I will present next show how this rupture in valuation plays out and reshapes gendered selfhood and intimate relationships in ways that are not always neat or predictable.

Villa Love

Ms. Su was in her late forties when I first met her in 2004. Even though she had been financially, socially, and emotionally separated from her husband, Mr. Jiang, for a few years, they lived in the same apartment they purchased from her work unit because he had no other place to go. She and their son occupied a separate part of the apartment and did not share any meals with Jiang. But they could not avoid running into each other every day in such a small space. "We live under the same roof, but we are like strangers as we both prefer not to talk to each other," said Su. I asked why they did not seek a divorce for several years. She said that it would be too complicated since they had to deal with the division of the property and he had no other place to go: "I cannot just throw him out of the door even though this apartment is under my own name. Sometimes, I feel sorry for him because he is a very smart man, yet he is not highly motivated and lacks good luck. He writes good novels and paints well, but no one recognizes his talent. Then he just gives up and stays home. I cannot support him. Someday, when I have a serious relationship, I will push for a divorce." I could sense that she still had some feelings or at least sympathy toward him even though there was little love left. She had dated several men but none of the relationships lasted.

Ms. Su was attractive but insecure about herself. She believed that the most important capital (*caifu*) a woman could possess was a beautiful physical appearance and feminine demeanor, which could be improved through technological intervention and personal cultivation. Therefore, she underwent several cosmetic surgeries to change the shape of her nose, eyes, and chin. She had several Botox treatments to reduce her facial wrinkles and was also on a special diet and vigorous exercise program to stay slim. The only thing she could not change was her height. She believed she was too short and thus only wore high heels. In her view, all these efforts not only would make her look younger and thus more attractive to men but also give her more self-confidence.

In 2005, she met a Chinese American man, Mr. Zhao, who had returned to Kunming to look for his cultural roots. He was born into a wealthy family that enjoyed high social and political status in Yunnan Province before the Communist revolution. His family later emigrated to the United States when he was still a child. He had been divorced three times but was considered well-to-do because of his successful family business. Zhao and Su met in Kunming through a mutual friend and soon started to date even though he was twelve years older than she was—an age difference that most Chinese today would consider improper. Su was very pleased with his family background and his financial well-being. She pointed out to me several times how eminent his family had been in the province and how much money he was willing to spend on her. He bought a new car and hired a domestic worker for her. A year later, she finally filed divorce papers and helped her ex-husband move into a small apartment. She said that Jiang was very manly and proud, and did not ask for anything from her, not even the apartment. She was touched and felt sorry for him as he did not have much income.

Meanwhile, as her love affair developed, she gradually realized that she had found her Mr. Right. Zhao was caring toward her emotional needs and was generous financially. But one thing bothered her greatly: he did not propose to marry her and was instead content with their relationship as lovers. She was deeply disturbed at first as she interpreted this act as a sign that commitment was lacking on his part. He explained that he really loved her but was afraid of marriage because of his previous experiences. He reasoned that real love did not need to be confirmed by legal papers. But Su was not convinced and felt that she needed some evidence of love beyond words. "How can I know for sure that he loves me and how can I explain to my friends if there is nothing tangible there to prove his love? Besides, people will think I am just another fool. How do I introduce him to my friends? You know marriage is still important in our society," Su said.

Then one day Zhao gave her a big surprise: he decided to buy a piece of farmland in the rural suburb of Kunming and build a Western-style villa on it. He hoped that this secret villa would be their little paradise and a way of showing his commitment to the relationship. Su was very touched and excited about this plan. For about a year, they worked hard to oversee all the details of the architectural design, construction, and interior modeling and decoration. The total cost was close to one million yuan, a significant investment based on prices in Kunming's real estate market.

Su was proud of this villa, so she offered to take me there for a tour. One sunny afternoon in July she picked me up in her new car. We had a lot of time to chat on the road since it took about forty minutes to get there. As our car left the crowded city and turned onto the winding mountain road, I asked her: "How often do you guys come here?" She replied: "Actually not very often because we each have a place in the city. But whenever we come to spend the weekend, it is truly relaxing. Look at the natural scenery here. You just cannot find it in the busy, noisy city. This is our dream come true." "What about the marriage? Does it still bother you?" I asked carefully. "Well, I do not think it is going to happen soon," she said. "But that is OK for now. I think he is very serious about me. Maybe he is just scared." "Do you think this house really makes a difference?" I asked boldly. "Yes, of course," she replied. "First of all, I feel that we have a real home together now. I also know that he loves me and wants to spend his life (or at least many years) with me. Only a fool would throw away such a large amount of money quickly. Don't you think so?" Then she paused and said, "Even if someday he ends up leaving me, I would still have gained a lot. How many Chinese men here can buy me the villa of my dreams?" She used a local term, *huadelai,* to describe this relationship as if it was a business transaction. *Huadelai* is commonly used in the Kunming dialect to mean lucrative or gainful based on a careful calculation.

Did Su really believe that his love was as real as the villa? Or was this the next best thing she could have? As I was pondering this question, the road in front of us suddenly became narrow and bumpy. Occasionally we had to stop the car for wandering cows and sheep. I looked around and saw that we were surrounded by boundless golden sunflower fields. Finally, we arrived at the gate of a courtyard hidden among a patch of fruit trees. "Here it is!" Su said as she stopped the engine. From the outside, the court-yard looked just like one of the nearby farmhouses. But as we entered the gate, a spacious, Western-style, two-story villa stood in front of us. It was strikingly different from the houses in this area in terms of its architectural design, color, and construction materials. It had a brownish stone face, a large brick chimney and large balcony, large white grid glass windows, and white French doors. All of these features were distinctly foreign or Western in the eyes of most local people. Only in movies and popular magazines imported from the West and a few new luxury villa communities could one find such homes. The interior of the house was tastefully decorated with large Italian-style floor tiles and hardwood floors, a fireplace, luxury light-ing fixtures, and very ornate furniture and bedding that most local people would consider "classical European style." Above the fireplace in the high-ceiling living room hung a huge oil painting of Su standing by the seashore. This painting (and its primary location) was important as it indicated Su's status as the master of this house so that no visitors would mistake it. This house, which was over three hundred square meters plus a huge yard, was a mansion by Chinese standards.

As she was picking some plums and apples from the trees in the back-yard, Su said: "We go out together in public now. I usually call him *laogong* in front of others. No one has ever asked whether we have a marriage license. My friends know that we have this house together." *Laogong* is a relatively new term that mainland people have borrowed from Hong Kong and Taiwan to refer to one's husband, but it is somewhat vague as it does not necessarily mean an officially sanctioned marriage. I pushed her a bit further: "So whose name is actually on the property deed?" She hesitated for a few seconds and replied: "No one's. Let me tell you what happened. This piece of land is actually a farmer's own family residential space, which is prohibited by the government to be sold and used for other purposes. So we never got the official deed but only signed a private contract with the original owner to lease the land for forty years. Even though this is considered illegal, it is a common practice in China today. Many government officials and rich businesspeople do it." The villa meant several things to Su. It was a way of validating their relationship because the financial investment in this house had almost overridden the significance of a marriage license. Even though this situation was not ideal, the villa at least alleviated some of her anxiety. The villa also served as a potential compensation for her time and emotional investment if the romance eventually failed. At least, her dream of attaining affluence and a high-class lifestyle had been realized.

Despite such rational justifications, anxiety and unease continued to seep in from time to time. I was struck by the disjuncture Su was experiencing: on the one hand, she was very frank about equating the villa with a pledge of love, materiality with emotionality; on the other, it was never that easy and simple. Sometimes, she was not sure whether the relationship would last and how she would feel if she ended up with a big empty villa without love and a lifelong commitment. Sometimes, she wondered whether she could separate her romantic feelings from her longing for material well-being, as they appeared to be deeply intertwined. At times, she was also irritated by her parents' probing of their unconventional relationship, which they considered problematic, if not disgraceful. Su was aware that she lived in a judgmental society, in which other people's opinions and perceptions mattered. Once an elderly woman who knew Su's situation said to me in a disapproving tone: "In essence she is selling her body in exchange for his wealth. What a shame to maintain a relationship like that!" She precluded any possibility of love in this relationship and viewed it as a matter of pure financial calculation. But not everyone thought this way. When two of my high school friends heard about this story, they thought it was *huadelai* because Su had gained something real and valuable. They also underscored the quantity of money invested and believed that it indicated a degree of seriousness. As one of them put it, "It is not difficult for a man to buy you a nice dress, take you to a fancy dinner, or even buy you a car. But it is different when he buys you a house of over a million yuan. It means something."

The story of Su represents a different way of thinking about love, marriage, and property in an increasingly commodified society. Tangible materiality and intangible feelings and emotionality can now be brought onto the same scale. I do not suggest that such thinking and equations were absent in Chinese society before.[7] However, the valorization of private property after several decades of Maoism has reached a new intensity and is of far-reaching significance for reconceptualizing romance and domestic relations.

Settling Divorces

If owning a house has become a crucial factor for entering dating and marital relationships, it has also become a central issue in settling divorces. Many couples seeking a divorce fight fiercely over home ownership and the way property is to be divided. In most cases I studied, the trigger for the separation was extramarital affairs.[8] The one who felt betrayed by his or her spouse tended to seek revenge by holding on to the dying marriage and thus denying the other party the freedom to remarry, or they used this opportunity for leverage to demand a better settlement to compensate for his or her emotional damage. The one who wished to exit the relationship for the "third person" (*disanzhe*) was more likely to give in during the negotiations over the division of property. Loss of home ownership was often taken as the ultimate price one must pay for infidelity that had caused emotional damage to the other party.

I was introduced to Dr. Liu Dong in 2001 at a friends' dinner gathering. We became good friends and had been in touch with each other since then. He was in his late thirties and was considered a popular doctor at a local hospital. When I first met him, he seemed to have a wonderful family that many people would envy. His wife was an attractive woman and a professor at a local university and they had a lovely eight-year-old daughter. But soon rumors spread that Liu was having an affair with a divorced professional woman. He first denied it categorically, but three years later the affair became public. He began to bring his lover to friends' gatherings and declared that he was in love with her and the relationship was serious.

After discovering the affair, Liu's wife was heartbroken and swore to refuse any proposal of divorce from her husband. She wanted to save the marriage and protect their daughter from the pain of a broken family. She told him that she would be willing to forgive him as long as he would end the affair quickly. However, Liu was determined to pursue the new relationship. Facing his adamant attitude, his wife had gradually grown cold and practical. They fought frequently and eventually began to negotiate over a divorce. Her condition was simple and firm: she would receive the full ownership of the three-bedroom apartment they purchased from his work unit several years ago. She also demanded the custody of their only child and full financial support for her from Liu. Although this apartment was not as nice as the new commodity housing, it was worth more than two hundred thousand yuan due to its nice location within the second ring road. They had also invested a lot of time and money in remodeling the home. Thus, her demand was not a small matter, but involved the largest asset they had at that time. Liu hesitated and hoped to negotiate for a better deal, but his wife would not give in. She was also hoping that her demand for home ownership might make him change his mind eventually. After a year of negotiation, he decided to meet her conditions and filed for divorce.[9] In a way, her demand was almost like a ransom, or a compensation for the years she had spent with him.

After the divorce, Liu worked hard in order to earn enough money for a down payment on a new apartment. Two years later he bought a new home in a private commodity housing compound far away from his work unit. Liu moved into the new apartment with the woman he loved, but it was never clear to me whether they were married as they never held a wedding ceremony for friends and relatives. Even though he had to commute to work every day, he preferred this arrangement because he was tired of the gossip and did not want to run into his ex-wife and co-workers. As he explained to me, "This is much better for us. In this new community, our neighbors are strangers to each other. They do not know and would not bother asking about my family history. I need a private space and privacy even if it means I have to pay more and live far from work. Within the old work unit living space, I could never start a new life."

Settling property disputes in the event of divorce can be emotionally exhausting. Women often find themselves in a disadvantageous position due to the male-centered housing arrangement under the danwei system. Professor Zhong Ping taught at a local university; her husband, Pan Cheng, was also a professor at a local science university. They lived in a small apartment assigned by his university. They had been married for about fifteen years, during which Pan went to Europe to study for his doctoral degree for four years in the late 1980s and then took a postdoctoral position for two more years. Over the six years they only saw each other briefly two times during summer breaks. During this long separation, they encountered various marital problems and gradually grew estranged with each other. They each had extramarital affairs but never confronted each other. After his return, their relationship deteriorated as they found it extremely difficult to communicate and thus argued constantly. Zhong had an active social life and liked to go out with friends; Pan by contrast was very introverted and liked to stay home. He became jealous about her social activities and felt insecure about himself. He first became abusive verbally during arguments, and then physically violent. One night they had an argument and he kicked her in the legs. She was shocked and left the home in anger with their daughter. Under familial pressure from both sides and for the sake of their young child, they did not seek a divorce but lived apart for several years. She and their daughter stayed with her parents until her university allocated her a small apartment. Zhong and Pan occasionally met at family gatherings but rarely spoke to each other. She also lost almost all the savings to Pan because he was the one who handled most of the financial matters and normally put the deposits under his name.[10]

Then in 1999, Pan's university built several new and heavily subsidized apartment buildings for the faculty. But there were not enough units for everyone who wanted one. Pan was entitled to purchase one unit because of his increased academic position and family status. On their household registration booklet he was still officially considered a married man with a child even though his wife and child did not live with him. If he had been divorced at that time, he would not have been eligible for the new housing. He purchased a large apartment of 120 square meters on the campus for less than one hundred thousand yuan, although its market value was at least twice or three times that. He was able to pay off the entire cost of the apartment plus the extra fifty thousand yuan for interior modeling and home furnishing.

That year Zhong fell in love with another man and wanted to end the marriage formally despite familial pressure. She was hoping to dissolve the marriage through private negotiation (*xieyi lihun*), a common and simpler practice that most Chinese prefer if the two parties can reach an agreement about property division and child custody. This way one would avoid the trouble and disgrace of going to court. But things did not go as smoothly as Zhong had hoped:

> I called him first and told him my intention. He sounded very cold but said OK. He asked me not to tell his parents because he did not want to worry them, and not to tell his danwei because he had just got the new apartment based on his family status. Then we set up an appointment to discuss property- and child-related issues. I was afraid of discussing anything with him by myself face to face, so I brought my sister with me. When we arrived at his new home and knocked on the door, he opened the metal security door and greeted us with a reluctant smile. His apartment was nicely furnished with modern fixtures and comfortable new furniture. We were like strangers at a business meeting. As soon as we sat down, he asked: "So what do you want on the agreement form?" "First of all,

I want the custody of our child. There is no room for negotiation about this." "You can have her," he replied quickly and coldly. He seemed to be anticipating a battle and knew it would be on the house and money. I said frankly: "I will not ask for this house you live in nor the car you just bought, but I need some compensation in the form of cash. I will have to buy my own place someday and have no other financial resources as a single mother." He asked quickly: "How much do you want?" I said: "One hundred thousand yuan!"

I actually had no idea how much to ask for, but before the meeting I had consulted a few friends who suggested a much larger amount [at least two hundred thousand yuan]. They said that this was the only time I would get anything from him and that he had saved a lot of money over the years from his overseas trips and sideline research projects. When he came back from Europe, he showed me the savings, which was more than one hundred thousand yuan already, but he quickly deposited the money in the bank under his name. I did not think about it much because I thought he was my husband and it did not matter whose name was used. Further, during the time we lived apart, he was also not paying for the cost of raising our daughter but only bought small things for her occasionally. But I knew he was stingy and would not give me that much money. I wanted to end the marriage soon and thus asked for a smaller amount. As I had expected, he replied: "No, that is too much. I do not have that much savings." Then he went on and on to talk about how difficult it was for him to raise the money to pay for this apartment, and that he was not in a hurry to end the marriage and would be willing to delay the divorce. But I knew that he had just bought a car. However, I had no way to trace his savings. In China people can easily hide their money by transferring it under a relative's name, and banks do not have to give you any information. I felt sick negotiating over money with him, and we were on the edge of another fight. So I backed down and suggested eighty thousand yuan, which he reluctantly agreed to. When it came to child support, he bargained again, which made me feel very sad. I settled on whatever he offered and left his place.

According to Zhong's rough calculations, eighty thousand yuan was probably one fifth of their common assets (house, car, savings, and other valuables). But she wanted to end the marriage so that she could begin to heal her emotional wounds. She wanted to feel free inside and start a new life even if it meant a financial loss. Also, she could not stand the emotional pain and humiliation caused by the bargaining. Pan knew her well and did not hesitate to take advantage of it. Even though he had no love left for her, he was willing to hold on to the empty relationship because he could benefit from it (such as being qualified for a new and larger housing unit). He exploited her eagerness to leave and used it as leverage to protect his assets. He had been waiting for her to propose the divorce because in China the initiator tended to get less sympathy from the public and to lose out financially. Public opinion still mattered to one's reputation and social life and it was particularly true for someone such as Pan who had political ambitions to rise in the university's administrative hierarchy. Three years later, Pan was promoted to the chair of his department and then to the dean of his college. He dated other women but remained single. He was doing extremely well financially: he bought two more private apartments on the commodity housing market as investments and upgraded his car to a brand-new BMW. He refused to increase the alimony to his daughter even though the cost of living had increased significantly in Kunming.

Zhong's new relationship with another man did not last long, but she was much happier. She worked hard and saved enough money to purchase a new three-bedroom apartment through her university. "Even though many of my friends think that I should have stuck with him because of his financial and social status, I have no regrets that I left him," she told me. "Only after the divorce did I began to feel that I am finally able to move out of his shadow. Of course, there are times I am envious of his houses and cars, and envious of two-income families. As a single mother I have to work harder than other people and save more carefully in order to pay for the new house and my child's education." Zhong sometimes bemoaned her difficulty in finding another suitable man as she felt that she was getting old. In contemporary China, divorced women are still in a relatively disadvantaged position due to persistent gender bias. A divorced man with wealth can easily marry a younger woman, but it is far more difficult for a divorced woman to find a suitable partner if she has already lost her youth. This gendered way of evaluating marriage eligibility is certainly not new, but the turn to a market economy and consumer culture has reinforced such thinking and the commodification of intimate relationships.

The Shadow of Doubt

Financial considerations affect not only dating, marriage, and divorce but also whether one should get married again. If a woman manages to secure a handsome settlement from her ex-husband, marrying another man whose economic status is significantly lower than hers is potentially risky. Even though in reality the situation is never black and white, there is always the shadow of doubt about his true motivation: Is it love or greed?

If the second marriage falls apart and the division of the property takes place, it would mean a big financial loss to her. Several women in this situation whom I interviewed were cautious about their next move and felt ambivalent about entering another marriage.

Xie Yun is a single mother of a six-year-old boy. I have known her since high school. When I reconnected with her in the summer of 2004, she was married to a wealthy entrepreneur. She never told me explicitly what his business was, but only indicated that he was highly successful. They bought a luxury apartment in one of the upscale housing compounds in a very desirable downtown area. Their son attended an expensive private nursery and had his own nanny. But over time the existence of her husband became mysterious. We visited each other many times because our kids liked to play together, but I never met her husband. She only said that he was extremely busy and that his branch offices were in several other cities. I noticed that there was not a single picture of her husband in their home. One day in 2006 as we were watching our kids riding bikes and talking about an unexpected divorce of a mutual friend, she suddenly let out a sigh and said:

> Men just cannot get rich. As soon as they have money, they want to chase younger women. I do not know about American men, but this is the reality here. Chinese women are very pitiful because when their husbands cheat on them, they have to put up with it if they want to save the marriage even though his heart has changed. I cannot do that, so I let my husband go. Actually I have been divorced for almost three years. He fell in love with another young woman and was with her most of the time. He pushed me so hard for a divorce that I just could not stand the emotional torture. My son does not know his Dad well because he was only three when his Dad left. But he gives our son whatever he asks for and they talk briefly over the phone once a month.

As part of the settlement, Xie Yun got the luxury apartment and a new car. Her ex-husband also agreed to pay for all their living expenses and the son's private school education. Recently, her ex-husband upgraded her car to a brand-new silver Audi and bought her a larger apartment in the same compound. She was letting her relatives stay in the old one for now and planned to rent it out in the future. The total cash value of the two apartments and the car easily approached three million yuan, not counting a generous annual alimony and education expenses (including private piano, hockey, chess, and swimming lessons). As a result, Xie Yun no longer needed to work outside the home and could live a comfortable life.

Under Maoist socialism, being a housewife was deemed shameful and was compared to being a social parasite. But popular attitudes toward women staying home have been changing in recent years. Some begin to see it as an indicator of one's affluence. A mutual friend of ours once commented on Xie's situation by saying that "she probably is very much hurt inside, but she is doing much better than other women. She does not have to worry about supporting herself and her son for the rest of her life. One has to sacrifice in one area or another. You just cannot have all."

I asked Xie Yun whether she was dating or had considered marrying another man. She said she wasn't because "it was too difficult to find a good, honest man with a successful career. "If he is successful, the same story will repeat [itself]. If not, I have to deal with the property issue. It is just too complicated. Also, this new man will not feel so comfortable coming to live in a house paid for by my ex-husband. It injures his self-esteem. I think once a man knows my situation, he will back down. It happened before." She often felt suspicious about the motives of men interested in her. She could not be certain and the doubt made her anxious. So she decided to remain single at least for now and focus on raising her son. Her parents moved in with them and the son was undoubtedly the center of their world. Xie characterized herself as conservative and indicated that dating without the prospect of marriage was just not her cup of tea.

Ms. Deng Mei, another divorced woman whom I met, had developed a very different lifestyle and approach to romantic relationships. In her late forties, Deng was the owner and manager of a small yet successful company that exported fertilizers to many countries overseas. Her company had generated a profit of one to two million yuan in a row over the past several years. We met through a friend in 2000 and I have stayed in touch with her since then. She had already been divorced for a few years and her daughter was a freshman in college. One day she invited me and the friend who introduced us to her house for dinner. The residential compound where she lived did not look fancy, but her condo was spacious and tastefully remodeled and furnished. The kitchen was very modern, and all the cabinets were made of expensive hardwoods, which is not common in Chinese households. After she finished cooking four delicious dishes, we sat down at her beautiful dining table and started to chat while enjoying the food. She told us that she had no intention of getting married again but was very happy with a long-term affair with a married man, a reporter for the municipal television station. "We have been seeing each other for almost three years. He comes often and spends a lot of time with me. I am happy about this arrangement as it simplifies everything. No financial issues are involved. It is just pure feelings and emotions. And I know he stays with me because he loves me, not because he wants my money," said Deng Mei.

"But are you lonely sometimes or do you worry about your lover leaving you because of his family obligations?" I asked. "Not really because I like to have my own space and you know I am very busy with my business. I also have a lot of friends. If he has to leave someday, then let it be. As for now, we are very much devoted to each other, more than many married couples. But when we see each other, it is because we want to, not because we have to," she replied with confidence. Then, our conversation turned to cosmetics. She showed us her special antiaging facial products and makeup techniques. She assured me that it was very important for her to spend time and money on keeping up her elegant appearance.

Deng's attitude is not a common one among Kunming women, but the number of middle-aged professional women who choose such independent lifestyles is increasing. Because they already own a house and have a secure income, they do not rely on the conjugal relationship for financial stability. Rather, they prefer to develop unconventional affective relationships to satisfy their emotional needs. In Xie's and Deng's cases, material well-being has reshaped their attitudes toward and choices regarding personal autonomy, affective ties, and marriage. While Xie would rather hold on to the exclusive ownership of the property by eliminating the possibility of re-marrying, Deng chooses to enjoy her own financial and personal freedom by engaging in a long-term romantic relationship outside the institution of marriage.

The Inadequacy Complex

Those who lack basic material ownership are increasingly considered undesirable, devalued, or seriously flawed in a market-driven society. This is particularly true for men who are expected to be the primary breadwinner of the family. If they cannot fulfill this expectation, they have a difficult time finding a potential spouse. If they manage to get married, they tend to have a lower status within the family and suffer from what I call the "inadequacy complex," which is caused by an acute awareness of their inability to provide financially. This feeling of lack extends from the financial realm to the perception of manhood and social worth. Masculinity, as some researchers have shown, is a highly unstable social construct fraught with anxiety over a perceived lack, whether material and/or sexual.[11] Several men I interviewed in Kunming were trapped in this situation and felt inferior within the household.

Fan Wen was a friend I had grown up with. He received a bachelor's degree in medicine but ten years ago quit his poorly paid job as a factory-employed doctor. He began to sell life and catastrophic insurance policies by mobilizing his social networks to recruit customers. The business went well for the first several years, during which he earned about two to three thousand yuan per month based on the commissions. But insurance is a tough business in China, because most people simply do not feel comfortable about paying for death benefits and are not used to the idea of putting money away for unforeseen illnesses and accidents. Soon Fan Wen used up all the social connections he had and could not recruit more new clients. His income dropped considerably, to less than five hundred yuan a month. To survive, he took on temporary low-paying jobs delivering receipts for a car insurance company and selling Chinese herbal medicines for a drug company. But none of these jobs lasted very long. He made only a few yuan per delivery and had to pay for the gasoline for his motorcycle and cell phone bills for frequent contacts with customers. The health products were expensive and difficult to sell. When he could not meet the sales quota, he was fired.

Such financial pressures caused a great deal of stress in Fan Wen's marriage. His wife was a teacher at a high school with a limited income. When they got married in the late 1990s, he had a decent income—definitely more than hers. They had hoped to buy a modest apartment after saving enough money for a down payment. But now their dream of home ownership was fading because they could barely make ends meet. A few years ago, they had an opportunity to buy privatized public housing from her school, which was significantly cheaper than commodity housing on the market, but they could not assemble enough money for that. For years, they had lived in a small apartment rented by her school. She became more and more resentful about their financial situation and felt ashamed in front of their friends and relatives. The tension in their marriage was growing. Fan Wen told me that they used to be polite and respectful to each other, but now they argued all the time. She criticized him for being lazy and incapable and they fought over small things. In their household, she was the primary decision maker regarding what to buy and what to do. His smoking habit became another point of contention because in her eyes this addiction was too much to support in a financial crunch. But he simply could not quit and wanted more tobacco to make him feel better. She pushed him to go out and get a "real" job, and asked him to prepare for the certification exam held annually by the government in order to obtain a medical license. In our conversation, Fan Wen talked about his dilemma and his feelings:

> Sometimes, I do not even want to return home because I know I have to face her nagging. I do not want to fight either because I feel I do not have the right to fight. I am a man and I cannot provide for the family. On what

grounds do I defend myself? Things are getting worse now. Sometimes, she can argue and scold me over the phone for thirty minutes. I just listen. I know she is angry at me and she has a good reason because I have to depend on her for housing and food. She has not left me because I think she still hopes that I will find something better with my medical background. Also, she does not want to have a child and I have not made a big deal out of it. Most men would divorce her, you know.[12]

Fan Wen's narrative reveals his complicated feelings toward his family situation. He understood his wife's frustration because they live in a market society, in which material well-being has become an important indicator for success and happiness. He felt strongly that it was his responsibility to provide for the family. Yet, he could not do so and felt that his manhood and dignity were in question. He found it hard to talk about self-worth and manhood when his financial capability diminished. This sense of failure and humiliation was reinforced by his wife's bitterness, anxiety, and constant disparaging remarks. He felt trapped and depressed. When he needed money badly, he occasionally turned to his relatively successful relatives for help. But that was only a temporary relief and the very act of asking for help was embarrassing, further underscoring his inferiority. By contrast, a wealthy man I talked to felt that he had the right to cheat on his wife because he provided everything for the family and thus deserved some fun in short-term affairs.

Fan Wen's quandary and distress are not unique. In an increasingly hypermaterialistic society, a new life orientation is emerging and what it means to be a man is shifting. As anthropologist Liu Xin puts it in his observations about the rise of a "new man" in China: "This new man, as a reincarnation of an old spirit, keeps his eyes wide open, both at work and at home, checking and examining how everyone around him—his neighbors, colleagues, and friends—manage their lives. Life has become a management of material things, comparable to and measurable in terms of other people's possessions" (2009, 176–77). Men must now contend even harder than women in the race for material gain in order to claim their manhood (see also Hird 2008). Masculinity in postsocialist China is increasingly being defined by one's entrepreneurial ability and the power to provide and consume.

THE heightened concerns over material possessions and consuming power are transforming love, marriage, and kin relations, yet they cannot completely override other social logics and reasoning. What I have learned from men and women in Kunming is that rational calculations of material gains, personal emotions, cultural expectations, and social obligations articulate with one another in ways that cannot be predetermined. Further, the tension that exists among these factors does not always work itself out, thus generating a sense of bewilderment and frustration among those who must navigate these forces. Although the language of love, romance, and emotionality has penetrated the urban realm of dating and marriage today, the conjugal bond is nevertheless deeply linked to concerns about property as my ethnographic account reveals. It is true that most urban Chinese now rarely use such terms as "dowry" explicitly, but a new form of calculating one's worth and desirability in market terms is at work. Now, self-worth and marriageability become objectifiable through men's material wealth and women's physical attractiveness.[13] Although women are active participants in the exchange, their own bodies have become increasingly commodified and objectified as a form of quasi property.[14]

Changing marriage choices also reflect the beginning of a deep shift in the conception and construction of self-worth from a socially and morally based one to a materially oriented one. Mayfair Yang once observed that "Chinese personhood and personal identity are not given in the abstract as something intrinsic to and fixed in human nature, but are constantly being created, altered, and dismantled in particular social relationships" (1994, 192). After three decades of economic reform, the sense of social embeddedness that was once at the core of the Chinese moral economy is being partially eclipsed by an individualistic and materialistic determinism. I use the word "eclipsed" rather than "replaced" because the socially embedded understanding of personhood and self-worth continues to be relevant in the Chinese social world. Thus, what constitutes a gendered self for Chinese men and women in the new culture of consumerism is a process full of tension and contradiction.

7

Privatizing Community Governing and Its Limits

The proliferation of private residential communities in Chinese cities raises an important question of how these emerging spaces can be governed effectively without putting further demands on already stretched municipal governments. This is a particularly urgent matter in the frontier areas of real estate development where local government offices, such as police stations and street-level offices, are either absent or too small to accommodate the rapidly expanding population. In Kunming, most commercial housing developments created as part of the metropolitan expansion into the rural suburbs face this situation. Who should take the primary responsibility for managing the newly formed communities? How should the policing of social order among the middle-class residents be carried out? What are the larger implications of the shift in postsocialist urban governance when the state no longer takes direct responsibility of managing the new residential space?

In this chapter, I trace the shift from direct state penetration into urban communities to a new mode of community governance, carried out primarily by real estate agencies that are not part the of state bureaucracy yet take on many government-like functions. This new form of authority, centered on market-driven developers and property managers, has become a powerful force in administering local affairs, keeping social order, and recasting citizens into a new kind of subject in Kunming. But because these agents are commonly regarded as commercial entities, their political nature is often overshadowed by their market role and commercial interests. My ethnography seeks to demonstrate that the rise of this privatized local governance should not be understood as a retreat of state power or the opening of civil society; rather, it signifies the emergence of a distinctive

187

mode of postsocialist governance that draws upon nonstate actors and combines neoliberal techniques of rule and the use of violence. This alternative mode of privatized local governance does not necessarily replace but coexists with other forms of urban governance that rely more on local state agents and administrative measures.

The notion of neoliberal governmentality that has been much debated is useful yet limiting to my inquiry of what is happening in Kunming. Governmentality, Foucault explains, concerns "how to govern oneself, how to be governed, how to govern others, by whom the people will accept being governed, how to become the best possible governor" (1991, 87). From this perspective, governmentality includes a wide range of institutions, procedures, and tactics, both inside and outside the state, that enable a certain kind of power to be exercised (Gordon 1991; Gupta 1998). This broader conception of governance allows one to discern how power operates in those domains that appear beyond the control of state bureaucracy and regulation. Some scholars have argued that under neoliberalism a distinctive technology of government that appropriates a quasi-entrepreneurial model and competitive market logic is thriving in advanced capitalist societies and beyond (Barry, Osborne, and Rose 1996; Brown 2003; Burchell 1996; Ferguson and Gupta 2002). The "degovernmentalization of the State" is far from a lessening of government, however, nor does it represent a diminished will to rule. Rather, the neoliberal political project seeks a form of politics "beyond the State" by relying on "a form of government that combines action by political and non-political authorities, communities and individuals" (Barry, Osborne, and Rose 1996, 2).

My ethnography reveals that what is taking place in Kunming's new housing regime is not just another example of neoliberal governmentality at work. What we encounter is a much more complicated terrain of power dynamics. On one level, the story I am about to tell seems to fit the global neoliberal trend of "governing at a distance" (Rose 1996), as more and more government responsibility and accountability have been transferred to semiautonomous entities, the private sector, the community, the family, and individuals in the name of consumer choice and personal development (see also Hoffman 2006; Ku and Pun 2004).[1] Thus, a new kind of politics, which governs through the market, private forces, and entrepreneurial activities, has become a preferred way of managing urban communities and citizens.[2] Yet, if we look more deeply into the emerging power dynamics, "governing at a distance" does not always work out smoothly but can produce unintended consequences. The mounting power of private authorities in local governance has engendered vigorous contestations between homeowners and real estate developers and managers across other

Chinese cities. In the absence of direct government scrutiny, real estate authorities are not deterred from using violence and illicit forces to intimidate disgruntled homeowners and stifle opposition. Their actions are often shielded by the culture of pervasive corruption and their entrenched alliances with local bureaucracy. When the conflicts escalate, the municipal government is compelled to step in to help settle the disputes. Such strife between middle-class homeowners and property developers/managers is viewed by the party-state as a potential threat to social stability. In more recent years, new legal measures have been created in order to ease the tensions and to better regulate the new private residential space.[3]

The Rise of Real Estate Authorities

The responsibility of real estate developers in China does not end with the construction or the sale of housing units. In the 1990s, according to a state policy called "whoever develops must manage," developers were required to take direct responsibility for managing the residential communities they had built. Later on, a new policy termed Property Regulation Rulings (2003) stipulated that, during the early stage of community formation, developers must create or subcontract a property management agency for each housing compound they construct; during the later stage, homeowners could form their own association and select a management firm of their choice.

Commercial property management (*wuye guanli*) is relatively new in China. Under socialist rule, it was mostly *juweihui* (residents' committees) and danwei that provided urban communities with basic social services and regulation (see Dutton 1998; Lu and Perry 1997; Parish and Whyte 1984; Walder 1986; White 1991). *Juweihui* is a unique type of mass organization created and closely controlled by the Communist party-state. It is responsible for carrying out state policies, mediating local affairs, and providing basic community services and social surveillance.[4] The regulation and services provided by *juweihui* and danwei are not profit-driven; they are regarded as part of the administrative responsibility conferred by the state. During the economic reform, there has been a new trend of professionalization and entrepreneurialization of residents' committees and community services (see Wu 2002).[5]

Although the first Chinese property management company was established in Shenzhen in March 1981, property management as a commercial industry began to develop in China only in the 1990s as a response to the rapidly expanding private communities (see He, Lo, and Wang 1999). The

Chinese Ministry of Construction issued a new ruling in 1994, "Regulation Methods for New Urban Residential Communities," formally promoting the commercialization and professionalization of community management. In 2001, the number of property management companies exceeded twenty thousand, with over two million employees nationwide (*Beijing Evening Daily*, October 20, 2001). But as a whole this industry is still immature and lacks adequate legal regulation and rules of operation. Most problematically, it is closely tied to real estate companies that have no prior experience in managing residential communities. In Kunming, because most new private housing is established on formerly suburban farmland, there are no preexisting street-level government offices, urban residents' committees, or police ready to incorporate the new communities into the city. The city government is deeply concerned about these places turning into "power vacuums," yet it is not able to extend its control into these mushrooming suburban communities.[6] The strategy used to deal with this situation was to require that housing developers create their own auxiliary property management agencies. According to a local newspaper report, 95 percent of the 260 property management agencies in Kunming were auxiliaries of developers (*Chuncheng Evening Daily*, March 15, 2002). These commercially driven agencies have become a powerful source of authority and control in shaping middle-class community and domestic life.

The property management companies I encountered took charge of an array of issues, which could be roughly divided into two categories: "hardware matters" and "software matters." The former included the provision of basic community services such as plumbing and electrical maintenance, home security, water and electricity bill collection for the city bureaus, and maintaining the common green space. The latter was relatively unclear, involving mediating disputes among the residents, organizing public activities, and assisting such government actions as conducting the census, overseeing family planning, and conducting criminal investigations. In a way, management companies assumed a role similar to that of the *juweihui* and even the police. Thus, even though they were not part of the government, they acted like state agents. Ms. Huang, a female manager who worked for the Golden Garden, a large, upscale, fortified private housing compound in Kunming, saw the change this way: "In my eyes we are equivalent to *juweihui* because we have to take care of all the big and small matters just like them. For example, we would get called if so-and-so's dog shit in front of someone else's door, or if some families made too much noise at night playing mahjong. I do not see much difference except that we are expected to do more and to provide better professional community services." Ms. Huang had been working in this housing compound for about three years and claimed that she knew at least three hundred out of the thousand families living there. She showed me a thick book that was used by the company to keep detailed information about each household, including its current members and their age, gender, identification card number, and household registration status; family-owned cars; and even temporary visitors. The property was patrolled around the clock by private security guards. But unlike *juweihui* and the police, her company was a profit-seeking commercial entity created by the Guandu Real Estate Corporation only a few years ago. The managers and staff had no previous experience in property management. According to Huang, the management had encountered a great deal of financial difficulty and had been subsidized by the parent firm to prevent bankruptcy.

Property management agencies often play an ambivalent dual role. They are commercial enterprises whose purpose is to supply services and seek profits, but they are also a form of local authority in maintaining social order. Existing outside the formal governmental structure, they lack the political clout necessary to buttress their regulatory activities. But at the same time, precisely because they are private firms outside officialdom, they have more latitude to set their own rules and practices according to their own preferences. For example, all property agencies levy a "comprehensive service and regulation fee" (*zonghe guanli fei*) on residents once a year in the private communities. Although this fee is supposed to be determined by using the city pricing bureau's criteria in accordance with the level of service provided, developers and managers are notorious for bribing city officials in order to manipulate the rules and standards to qualify for a higher fee. At the same time, their promise to deliver quality services, safety, and a superior environment is often not kept, infuriating the residents, who subsequently refuse to pay the fees altogether. A disgruntled homeowner gave me an example of the poor service she received: "One day the water pipe in my bathroom was leaking. So I called the management office. They did send someone to me the same day, but he did not know much about plumbing because he was a local farmer hired by the developer as part of the agreement to use the village's land. He meddled with the pipe for a while and left without fixing the problem. I had to call my plumber friend to come help."

The management and homeowners in Kunming had very different perceptions and interpretations of the situation and the power dynamics in which they were situated. The conflict was framed in terms of service versus regulation. Most homeowners believed they were exploited by the management agencies and accused them of demanding unreasonably large fees for poor services. A young female resident complained that "all they [property management firms] know is to collect the regulation fees but they do not deliver promised services. They act like government officials and operate with an old socialist mentality of control and regulation, instead of thinking about how to serve the residents wholeheartedly." Living in a consumer culture, homeowners tended to see their relationship with management agencies as one of "masters" versus "servants." Because they had paid a considerable amount of money for their home and a steep fee for property management, they felt that they deserved first-rate service and full attention from the staff. This heightened sense of entitlement and awareness of consumer rights was clearly articulated by this male homeowner: "We consumers are like gods. They [management staff] should please us in any way they can. It is just like how it works in other service sectors." Rather than focusing on improving the services, the management was more interested in controlling their lives and conduct, according to some residents. Government officials were supposed to oversee the activities of the management firms, but they were often bought off by these firms and would not voice the concerns of the people. Since the majority of private residential communities in Kunming did not have a homeowner association before 2005, unorganized homeowners were left in a vulnerable position.

The management staff, however, painted a very different picture for me. Almost everyone I interviewed insisted that their firm was not making any profit and had to be subsidized by the developers. They claimed that the residents simply had no idea how costly it was to maintain a housing compound. Ironically, they insisted that it was the homeowners that held on to the old socialist welfare mentality, which should be obsolete in a market economy. "They only demand good services but are not willing to pay necessary fees," said Mr. Cheng, the manager of a large, lower-income residential community. He spent thirty minutes explaining to me in great detail all the managing work they had to do and the expenses involved. In the end, he did some calculation on a blackboard and came up with a number indicating the discrepancy between what his firm needed to do the job and the fees collected. If the firm was not making any profit, I asked, why did they stay in the business? He explained:

Even if it is a big headache, we have to do it because the government requires all developers to manage their xiaoqu. This is the so-called whoever develops must manage policy. There is no way out and the developers will continue to subsidize us. But last year we lost four hundred thousand yuan in property management. The only way to reach a balance is to increase the service fee, but residents are going to revolt. Some years we could not even collect fees from 70 percent of the households.

But Cheng also admitted that in this particular area some residents who were recently laid off from state factories were struggling to survive, let alone being able to pay the fees. This dilemma made his job even more challenging.

Conflicts over regulation fees and the quality of services between property management agencies and homeowners were widespread in Kunming as well as in other Chinese cities. On September 1, 2002, a popular local newspaper featured a special report titled "Endless Cross-fires in the Battle of Kunming's Property Management," which showed that lawsuits against property agencies were increasing dramatically, and 90 percent of the residents in the new private communities were unhappy with the services they received. In some places, the conflict had reached the point where more than half of the residents in a given housing compound refused to pay the annual regulation fees. As a threat and punishment, management firms simply abandoned the compound and cut off the electrical and water supply, causing serious disruption in thousands of residents' daily lives. Qingcheng Xiaoqu was one of the communities caught in the battle with management agencies. In February 2002, over one hundred families in Qingcheng refused to pay any fees because they were deeply dissatisfied with the service. The management cut off the electricity, water, and gas as well as garbage collection. As a result, residents had no drinking water and could not cook or flush their toilets. Elevators stopped working and hallways were too dark to walk through. Everyone had to carry a flashlight. Garbage was piling up and attracting flies and mosquitoes. Under such circumstances, the city pricing bureau and the construction bureau stepped in to mediate the dispute. They pressured the management agency to resume the basic services to the community and at the same time urged the residents to pay a reduced fee that had been adjusted by the pricing bureau. But the relationship between the management agency and residents remained antagonistic.

In some cities, there have been violent incidents caused by such conflicts. According to a report in *Beijing Youth Daily* (January 17, 2002), several unidentified "men in black" entered a housing compound (Peng Run Garden) in Beijing one day and beat up a homeowner who was an activist in organizing the residents' opposition against the management. The thugs were said to have been sent by the property management agency to punish and threaten those who dared to voice their discontent and mobilize others. During my fieldwork in Kunming, I had also heard speculation that some real estate firms, to bolster their local control, were deeply connected with the underworld, although no hard evidence was provided.

Private governance relies heavily on private security forces in the new housing regime where the police are not responsible for maintaining public security and thus rarely interact with the residents. Security guards are hired by the property management agency to take charge of everyday safety issues and community order. Their main task is to prevent theft and robbery by keeping strangers out of the walled compound and by patrolling the property around the clock. New homes and residential compounds are typically equipped with what is perceived by Chinese people as "high-tech" security devices such as alarm systems and surveillance cameras. Security guards can question anybody who appears suspicious, detain intruders, and hand them over to the nearest police for further action. The security guards working in Kunming mostly come from Henan, Shandong, and Sichuan provinces and rural regions of Yunnan. After minimum training they are given a uniform and expected to perform the role. Homeowners find out later that these guards are not professionally trained as promised by the developers in the sale advertisements, and their function is more on a symbolic level. As one resident observed, "They are not so different from the old retirees sent by the *juweihui* to patrol the streets in other neighborhoods, except that they wear a special uniform and they do not know the residents as well as the retirees did." Security guards in many housing compounds wear a special green or navy blue uniform that looks very much like the Chinese military or police uniform. Some Kunming residents find it hard to tell the difference between security guards and police officers. Some speculated that this mimicking of state authority through clothing and appearance is an intentional act to give the guards more power and legitimacy by blurring the symbolic boundary between official and nonofficial authorities. Because security guards are not allowed to carry guns, one of them told me that he felt more confident in the uniform as it gave him a certain status and an illusion of being a police officer.

As tensions between homeowners and developer/property management grew nationwide in recent years, dissatisfied property owners began to organize themselves in order to protect their interests against corporate power. A crucial step was to push for the legalization of homeowner associations as a counterweight to the rise of real estate authority, although grassroots mobilization among Kunming homeowners was slower and more fragmented than in other larger cities in China.

The Politics of Homeowner Self-Organizing

In Western capitalist societies, private homeowners have the right to form their own associations to protect their property values and interests. In recent years, there has been a global trend of middle-class homeowners in various localities mobilizing to defend their lifestyle by promoting new forms of spatial and social exclusion (see also Blakely and Snyder 1997; Caldeira 2000; Holston 1989; Low 2004).[7] In China, such grassroots organizations and social movements initiated by property owners were virtually absent under socialism and only began to emerge in more recent years (see Read 2003; Tomba 2005; Zhang 2006). For more than a decade since the beginning of massive private housing construction in the early 1990s, there was no law or clear state policy authorizing the official establishment of homeowners' associations. It was not until 2003 that Property Regulation Rulings (*Wuye Guanli Tiaoli*) were issued by the State Council and later revised in 2007. This official ruling grants Chinese homeowners the right to form their own associations (*yezhu dahui*) through democratic elections and recognizes the legal status of such organizations. Although the rulings signify an important step by the Chinese state to regulate emerging private communities, there still exists a huge gap between what is granted in official documents and actual practice on the ground. The conditions for legalizing a homeowner association specified by the rulings are very stringent and unrealistic. The association must elect a steering committee (*yezhu weiyuanhui*) with the approval of at least half of the homeowners in a given residential community. Any major decisions regarding changes in community structure and facilities require the approval of at least two thirds of the homeowners. The election and approval require voting that involves a significant amount of money and time on the part of the residents, many of whom are reluctant to make such commitments. As a result, most new communities still have not formed associations. The development of homeowners' self-organizing is also uneven across different localities. Residents of Beijing, Shanghai, and Guangzhou are better organized and more active than those in smaller cities and inland areas (such as Kunming).[8]

When I first began my fieldwork in Kunming in 2000 and 2001, disputes and battles over property management and regulation fees were already rampant, yet there were no official guidelines for whether and how homeowners could organize themselves to confront developers and management agencies. District officials that I spoke to generally discouraged grassroots organizing, citing concerns over societal stability. Most homeowners I interviewed had heard about the possibility of a new law authorizing their self-organizing, but they were not interested in any immediate action. In Chinese political culture, "organizing" without official sanction carries a great deal of risk. Thus, some residents were cautious about pursuing such activities without explicit state authorization. When facing pressing problems with the developers or management, some communities formed small informal groupings for collective action. But once the immediate conflict was resolved, the will to organize dwindled quickly.

A common mentality I encountered among Kunming residents could be summarized by the two phrases uttered by a homeowner during our conversation: "Let us see what happens" and "Let others do the work for me." If a management agency did an acceptable job, residents felt it wasn't necessary to form their own association. The lack of enthusiasm was related to two factors. First, the majority of residents in the new communities were businesspeople with demanding and unpredictable schedules. They regarded self-organizing as time-consuming and unappealing political activism that invited trouble but no material rewards. Second, they tended to aim at solving immediate practical problems, and thus once their pressing demands were met they saw no need to devote more time and effort to sustain such collective action. Mr. Liu, in his late thirties, was a branch manager of a commercial bank. He had just bought a luxury condominium in an upscale private community. He was savvy about property law and consumer rights, yet when I asked him whether he planned to participate in any homeowner organization's activities in the near future, he answered firmly: "No. If the service is OK and the fees are reasonable, I will not bother with homeowners' organizing because I have no time. Of course, if they [management] want to raise the fees and if the service does not meet the standard they promised, I will stand up to fight. Under that circumstance, I am sure that I will not be the only one; most residents in the compound will band together." Given the prevalence of such attitudes and political concerns, Kunming homeowners' organizations in the private communities were underdeveloped up to 2005 and the bulk of the actual work of mobilizing was carried out by a small group of activists willing to sacrifice their time and risk retaliation from the firm.

Xinfeng Xiaoqu ("New Wind Residential Community") is a lower-middle-class private residential neighborhood with over fifty-three hundred households that was established in the early 1990s. As in many other xiaoqu, the management was initially assumed by a regulation committee established by the developer on a three-year term. After the contract expired in 1997, the committee continued to function as the de facto management agent for several years, during which time numerous problems appeared. Some residents claimed that the management charged unreasonably high fees, delivered poor services, and never publicized its budget and expenses. In the summer of 2000, a proposal titled "Property Owners Are the Masters of *Xiaoqu*—the Undeniable Need for Planning to Establish the Xinfeng Xiaoqu Property Owners' Committee" was delivered to the doors of the residents. It specifically invoked the notion of protecting one's rights as a consumer and called for organizing a planning committee by "those who are passionately willing to serve the common interest of the masses" in order to establish a homeowners' association. The ultimate goal, stated clearly in the flyer, was to "stir fry" (*chao diao,* meaning "do away with") the current management company so as to hire a new one chosen by the homeowners to serve their best interests. The proposal received an enthusiastic response from many residents and quickly gained momentum.

Yet this move was viewed by the existing regulation committee as a subversive act of "a few people who want to disrupt the current system." Mr. Luo, the head of the committee, claimed that his agency had been appointed by the local district government, and thus represented the government in regulating this community. He further declared: "Although it is the general trend in xiaoqu management to hold property owners' meetings and establish property owners' committees, it is not practical to hold such a meeting currently in this particular area because many residents are not willing to participate in such voluntary activities." The regulation committee headed by Mr. Luo was indeed backed by the local district government, but the firm that carried out management work was purely a profit-driven commercial firm. Yet these two entities were "virtually one body of people under two different shop signs" (*yitao banzi, liangkuai zhaopai*). The threat of firing the management company was seen as a repudiation of the regulation committee as well. It was precisely in such an unclear situation that the regulation committee saw the proposal as a threat to its vested interests and very existence. It thus sought to denounce and criminalize the homeowners' attempt to self-organize. Mr. Luo's rhetoric also revealed a typical strategy used by many management firms. On the one hand, they acknowledged the trend of homeowners forming their own associations; on the other hand, when such efforts began to emerge they quickly sought to discourage and undermine them by claiming that conditions were not ripe and the residents were not ready to form their own organization. The regulation committee of Xinfeng even reported the "flyers incident" to the district police as a way to intimidate the activists, but it later claimed that it would not pursue further charges against any residents "who simply did not know the truth but were misled by a few troublemakers." In the end, the residents' mobilization was aborted and the management also agreed to improve their service.

Another strategy that avoids hostile confrontation is worth examining. Instead of appearing as antagonistic, some larger developers with more resources actively help establish homeowners' committees by playing a leading role in choosing the potential candidates, setting the terms of organizational rules, and organizing communal activities. In so doing, they cast themselves as being in a supportive, friendly alliance with homeowners, and are able to manipulate and monitor the activities of such associations. The management firm of Jiangbian Huayuan ("Riverside Garden"), a typical middle-class new neighborhood, operated in this way. It enjoyed a good reputation for delivering quality service at a reasonable price. It appointed a temporary steering committee of homeowners to function as a mediating organ. But Ms. Dong, a resident who had lived there for two years, told me that "although we appear to have a homeowners' committee, it only exists in form because the members are all appointed by the management. They suggested the names and asked us to choose from the list. I do not know any of them. As an ordinary resident, I do not know what the homeowners' committee should do for us, or what the proper procedure is for representing us." She was concerned that the committee members would not be able to fight for the interests of residents because they were chosen by and had close personal ties with the management. In this situation, the committee was already in a compromised position due to the deep involvement of the management. It could preempt the political potential of discontented homeowners by channeling their attention to other nonessential issues and by promoting dialogues to diffuse hostility. This strategy proved to be somewhat effective as long as there was no strong dissatisfaction about the existing management and the agency had the resources and willingness to meet some of the residents' demands. Homeowners' committees created under such circumstances tend to disseminate information but shy away from representing the residents in bargaining with the management. Further, the existence of such an organization can also enhance the developer's symbolic capital, for it gives the public an impression that this developer is open-minded and thus likely to treat customers fairly. This reputation may be appealing to potential home buyers and make the future sale of property developed by this developer easier.

The central and local governments are ambiguous toward urban homeowners' self-organizing but their attitudes are changing. They have recognized over time that residents in the new housing regime are atomized and need to organize themselves in order to counterbalance the increasing power of real estate management firms. Without a legalized channel to do so, more spontaneous, unpredictable disputes and conflicts will occur, and such popular unrest might lead to the destabilization of the current urban regime. Yet, the empowerment of private property owners can also turn them into a powerful social force to be mobilized under certain circumstances beyond defending their economic interests. This fear of going too far and losing control has held government officials back for many years from endorsing the legal right of homeowners to self-organize. Major progress took place in 2003 when the State Council issued the Property Regulation Rulings. As I discussed earlier, although this law gives Chinese homeowners the right to organize their own associations, hold meetings, and collaborate with the management agencies, it also contains some hurdles. More important, local officials that I spoke to in Kunming were still apprehensive about homeowners' organizing and thus tended to delay or deny the official authorization of newly established associations.

By 2006, when I returned to visit the several communities where I had done research, over half had already formed their own homeowners' associations. Most did not go through the required election process and were not formally approved by the district government. I was told that activism was largely confined to the steering committee, composed of seven to ten residents, while the participation of other residents was very limited. It is hard to gauge to what extent China's homeowners' associations will lead to what Putnam (2000) has envisioned as the establishment of long-term, progressive civic organizations that not only defend the rights of consumers and property owners but also tackle issues of citizenship and political participation.[9]

Weiquan: "Stop Selling the Land Twice"

In addition to the conflicts over community service and regulation fees, there exists another kind of fierce battle over the appropriation of communal space in the new residential compounds. In order to maximize profits, some developers attempt to construct additional commodity housing buildings on the common land within a xiaoqu. The existing families believe that such an act is a breach of the contract they signed with the developer and thus a violation of their property rights and their entitlement to the communal space they commonly hold. Therefore, they come together to challenge the predatory developers by engaging in protests, legal action, and other oppositional behaviors to block what they see as an illicit appropriation of their land. This new trend of activism, which has been called *weiquan yundong* ("rights protection movement"), is becoming a powerful social phenomenon in the Chinese cities. Sometimes, the confrontation turns violent when outraged homeowners clash with the illicit forces deployed by developers. The two cases I present below provide a glimpse into this form of prevalent conflict and the complexity of the social forces involved. They further illuminate a major problem that comes with "governing at a distance" in that the struggle for social justice can be easily tampered with by powerful real estate authorities.

Violence in Spring Garden

Spring Garden was built and is managed by the Dragon Development Group and located in the northern part of Kunming. This part of the city has become a new popular residential development zone, locally dubbed as the "big bedroom community." I first visited Spring Garden in the summer of 2005 because a family I interviewed lived there. It was a typical midlevel private housing compound consisting of dozens of seven-story condo complexes with green lawns and gardens in-between. But I discovered during the interview that only two months ago a violent confrontation had occurred in this seemingly tranquil place. It started with a dispute over the use of the land near the entrance of the compound. According to the residents, when they purchased their houses they were promised by the developer that no buildings taller than seven stories would be built on this land so that they could see the adjacent open fields and would not feel too cramped. But a year ago the developer broke its promise and began to construct two high-rises that were nineteen and twenty-five stories tall. The residents were kept in the dark about the plans and not consulted about them. When they found out about them, they felt betrayed. They immediately formed a temporary homeowners' association to halt what they saw as an infringement on their property rights. But the developer refused to stop the construction or to discuss the issue with the association leaders. After the two buildings were completed, the units were quickly sold to private individuals. The residents then found out that the families moving into the two new buildings would also share the use of the common space in Spring Garden. They were outraged because "this is equivalent to selling the same piece of land twice," as one resident put it. Ms. Chen, the woman I came to interview, recalled a violent encounter that had completely disturbed her vision of the new residence as a private paradise:

> The residents held a general assembly to discuss possible counterstrategies and decided to block the gate with steel bars to prevent the new residents in the two high-rises from entering their compound. The developer immediately hired three hundred security guards temporarily and sent them to crack down on us. They wore military-like camouflaged uniforms and broke through the blocked metal gate. They started to beat up protesting residents. I could see blood running on the ground from my window. We were frightened and called the police for help. But they would not come because they had been bought off by the developer.

"What do you mean that they would not come? What was their excuse for not coming?" I asked. Ms. Chen continued:

At first, they simply did not answer the phone. Then, a police car arrived very late and did nothing to stop the security guards. Eventually they fired two shots in the air to quiet things down. It was so terrifying. Most people returned home and the security guards disappeared. We heard later that the police station was in the process of investigating this case, but there is no result even until now. We believe that the developer has connections with the underworld and a lot of political clout too. So no justice will be done.

Violent incidents like this one are not unusual. Real estate developers are known to be extremely powerful given the amount of economic and social capital they have accumulated. Their connections to officialdom and the underworld make it possible for them to engage in acts such as using private security guards or thugs to threaten and beat up the activists without suffering any serious consequences. Some developers who breached their contracts even sued the resident activists for damaging their firm's reputation. The next case illustrates how a real estate firm in Kunming appropriated violence and the legal system to eradicate what they perceived as "obstacles" in order to reach their goal.

Riverside Battle over Green Space

I first heard about the "Riverside *weiquan* incident" or the "Riverside battle over green space" from a casual conversation with a friend in August 2004. I soon located reports from five major local newspapers from June 2004. Three of them stated that the development firm had just filed a lawsuit against several resident activists. I called one of the reporters and found out the names of the two lawyers working on behalf of the activists. When I contacted them and told them about my research, they agreed to meet with me and introduce me to some of the residents involved. At a meeting in the law office to discuss their next move, I met the two lawyers and four homeowners, two women and two men.

Riverside Garden was developed by the Dragon Development Group (the same parent company as that of Spring Garden), and the focal point of conflict was the use of communal space already designated as the green space within the community. In 1997, before the housing construction was finished, the apartments were already on the market for sale at a price of about twenty-one hundred yuan per square meter. At that time, this property was considered upper-middle-level housing. One of the factors that attracted many buyers was the developer's promise that nearly half of the development was committed to green communal space—a number much higher than most of the existing residential communities in the city. The developer promised to create a dreamlike living environment with ample lawns, trees, flowers, and strolling areas. Ms. Liu Jin told me how appealing this feature was to her: "The developer purposely used this green space as the selling point to allure us. If I knew that the green coverage would be significantly reduced and there would be high-rises built on our property later, I would not have bought my two units. But they lied to us." According to several newspaper reports and my own interviews, the sales agents indeed verbally promised all the buyers that there would be a large, open green space in their community, but this was not clearly written in the contract. Liu Jin, who planned to buy two apartments there, wanted to make sure that the promise was real. She called the municipal planning office and they assured her that no construction of any high-rises within the community would be approved. The residential units there were sold quickly within a year.

For the first five years, the residents enjoyed the large green space in their community, which had become a popular space for kids to play, the elderly to gather, and others to stroll and exercise. But the situation suddenly began to change in late May 2005. One day a group of construction workers arrived at Riverside Garden and started to cut down trees and remove light posts and benches. The noise of big trucks hauling away things disturbed the residents. They initially thought that perhaps the developer wanted to do some new landscaping work but then found it suspicious because they were not notified about it. Soon they discovered that this green field of twenty *mu* (about 1.33 hectares) would no longer belong to them and two new high-rises would be built on the site. The residents became furious at the developer. On June 2, they launched the "battle to defend the green field" (*lüdi baohuzhan*). Here is a brief account of the incident by Liu Jin:

> On the evening of June 1st, the road to our xiaoqu was blocked by dozens of homeowners because they heard that heavy construction machinery was about to move in. Initially we were told that the top leaders of the real estate firm would come to have a dialog with us. So we waited there. But no one showed up to meet with us. On June 2nd, when I came back from work at noon, I saw some five hundred men hired by the developer forming a circle hand by hand around the green space to prohibit anyone from

entering. There were still a few elderly people taking a walk within who refused to leave. They were simply carried out forcefully by the hired men. At that moment, a bulldozer was moving in. I jumped out and tried to stop them, but the driver would not listen to me. As some of the residents pushed into the green space, their men began to beat us. Many residents were injured and eight of them with more serious injuries were sent to the hospital. We have video to prove all this.

According to several newspaper reports, angry residents also injured several construction workers and broke the windows of the trucks and bulldozers. That afternoon, three to four hundred infuriated residents marched to the street and blocked traffic on the busy second ring road. They held large banners with such slogans as "Return Our Garden, Return Our Green Space," "The Dragon Real Estate Firm Is a Swindler," and "Riverside Garden Property Owners' Interests Cannot Be Violated." Local government officials and the police came out to persuade the protestors to return home. After a couple of hours, they finally left the street and decided to hang the banners from their home windows. To gain wider public attention, a group of activists printed and posted flyers about their struggle throughout the streets in the nearby area and ask residents in the community to display the slogans on their car windows.

The violent confrontation and protest temporarily halted the construction. The developer began to use other means to terrorize the residents. Mr. Ma, a middle-aged man that I met at the meeting, gave me the following account of a mysterious incident:

On June 11 an attempted homicide occurred. A female homeowner who was an activist drove to a nearby supermarket. When she stopped at a red light, two strangers suddenly came up and broke her car window and tried to stab her. She quickly jumped to the other seat and the knife cut her leg. The men vanished into the crowd. Luckily the injury was not life-threatening, but the incident terrified Riverside's residents. For a while our community was in the shadow of "dark terror," as some people phrased it. Since that incident, I have been afraid to go out alone at night. The management also installed seven surveillance cameras around the green field, not to protect us but to watch our activities. It also replaced all the security guards with a new crew we did not know. We think they are their thugs. They even followed some of our leaders. We can no longer feel safe at home even if the green field is saved. The developer has connections with the underworld and can hire thugs to bully us while denying any involvement. The police will not come to defend us either because they are bribed by the developer.

Even though the residents could not prove that the man who stabbed the woman was hired by the developer, they believed that it was not accidental and that she was clearly targeted, not for her money but to intimidate her. The timing of the incident was also telling as it occurred during the height of the conflict. I visited Riverside in July and the green space was almost destroyed but no construction was going on. When I took out my camera to take pictures of the site, a man who appeared to be a private security guard ran toward me and questioned why I was there and what the pictures were for. I said I was visiting a friend. He told me that no photography was allowed because this was private property, and that if I did not leave immediately, I might be detained.

The developer later told some newspaper reporters that they regretted not having communicated better with the residents and understood their emotional reaction, but they could not forgive the damage inflicted on the company's reputation by their protest. As a result, the firm filed a lawsuit against six activists at the local district court on June 10 and demanded that the defendants immediately "stop all the destructive action," clear the negative influence by making a public apology, and each pay two hundred thousand yuan for damage to the firm's reputation. The six residents simply could not believe that the firm had turned things upside down. As Liu Jin put it, "It was the firm that broke the contract, cheated on us, and exercised violence on us. But now it acts as if the developer is the victim demanding justice. Unbelievable!" Even though the defendants had photos, videos, and eyewitness accounts of the violence imposed on them during the encounter, they had little confidence in the legal system and were deeply worried about their fate. Individuals fighting against a powerful developer rarely had a positive outcome. According to Mr. Ma, when the incident had just taken place, the developer had already leaked word that if the residents dared to hire any lawyers to file charges against the firm, his people would make sure that the lawyers would face serious trouble. Then, on the first day of the hearing, the representatives of the firm made some threatening remarks, saying that if the defendants won, they would use their clout to make sure that the judge of the case would lose his job in the near future. "They act as if they rule this district. They do not even take the judge seriously. How can they take us ordinary citizens seriously?" said Ma.

The homeowners who were dragged into this litigation finally found two lawyers who were willing to take their case. I asked why they accepted the case even when they knew it was an uphill battle, and I wanted to know whether they were concerned for their safety. They told me that the foremost reason they took the case was that several residents living there were their friends who pleaded for help. Second, after studying the case, they felt strongly that the residents were mistreated and that it was their professional responsibility to help the weak seek justice. Third, the residents preserved ample evidence of the developer's wrongdoing, which could be used in their defense. The case was widely reported by major local news papers except for one whose major advertiser was Dragon Real Estate (and thus a main source of income). "We could in turn file a lawsuit against the developer, charging him with breaching the contract and the illegal use of violence. If they dare to touch us, their involvement will be too obvious and draw attention from higher authorities beyond their district. Chinese people's awareness of rights protection is increasing greatly. Hopefully we will get support from the media, the public, and higher-level officials who are not directly tied to the developer," explained one lawyer. Another reason they took the case, which they did not mention, was the legal fee they charged, eighteen thousand yuan, which was not a small amount.

In the law office I was allowed to read a set of litigation documents including the contract of purchase and four pages of detailed arguments repudiating the charges. They asked whether I had any connection with major foreign news agencies and hoped I could perhaps write a report on this case. Exposure in the international press is usually beneficial to the weak and powerless in such battles. When I told them that I had no such connections and could only document this case in my own publications later, they were a bit disappointed, but they were still pleased by my attention to their struggle. Curious about the role of the government in this clash, I asked whether they had considered seeking help from the district or city government." One of the women replied quickly:

Yes, we did pay a collective visit to the city government, but [it was] no use. One hundred to two hundred of us showed up at the city government building, but we were blocked by some ten security guards. None of the top officials came out to meet with us. Only a lower-level cadre from the Bureau of Popular Appeals came to talk to us briefly and dismissed us. We initially thought that the government would speak for justice on behalf of ordinary people because our rights were obviously violated. But that turned out to be an illusion. We are on our own.

Their situation is not a unique one. Local governments tend to take a hands-off approach by staying out of a dispute unless the situation gets out of control. The official rhetoric today is to let citizens seek justice from the legal system. This system is supposed to be relatively independent from politics, but in reality it is heavily permeated by political and corporate power. I heard an anecdote that encapsulates this troubling condition. A young reporter asked the head of the planning division of Dragon Real Estate: "Do you think in our country today it is *quan* (political power) that rules over the law or vice versa?" The director replied: "None of these. I tell you that it is *money* that rules over everything today."

Although the lawyers were somewhat confident about winning the case, the defendants were still deeply concerned because after all they were fighting against a powerful corporation. The two hundred thousand yuan suit against them each was not a small amount. Meanwhile, they were worried about the safety of their families as they were followed and watched by thugs sent by the developer. One of them said: "We sometimes feel like members of an underground party since we have to change our meeting places all the time. We cannot meet at home within the compound as it is under surveillance. We cannot call each other from home as we believe that our phones are tapped." Despite the obstacles, Riverside residents eventually won the green land battle on two fronts. First, the developer eventually withdrew the litigation after two rounds of court hearings due to lack of evidence. This was a big relief for the six charged residents. Second, over three hundred Riverside homeowners collectively filed a lawsuit at the municipal middle court in mid-August of the same year against the city planning bureau for wrongly issuing the Dragon Real Estate a license to develop commodity housing on the green space. They claimed that this common space belonged to them collectively according to the newly passed Property Regulation Rulings. They demanded that the city government cancel the land development license and formally transfer use rights to the disputed land to the residents. Two weeks later, the Kunming Municipal Planning Bureau announced that it would withdraw its approval for housing development on the disputed site and put this land under the category of "public green project" (*gonggong lühuadi*). It was speculated that the city government was under pressure from higher authorities to prevent this highly publicized conflict from escalating into larger civil unrest. On the evening of August 24, several hundred Riverside residents gathered in the communal garden and celebrated their victory with firecrackers and fireworks. In an interview with a newspaper reporter, a female resident exclaimed: "This decision is great news to our property owners. We believed that the government would eventually stand up for the people and protect the interests and rights of the masses." This discourse can be interpreted as a plea for greater government intervention in residents' battles against corporate infringement on their rights.

Disputes over the use of communal space for new construction are widespread across Chinese cities. Similar conflicts have been reported in Beijing,

Shanghai, Hunan, Guangzhou, and so on. Perhaps the largest grassroots movement of this kind was the Maizi Dian Green Land Battle, which took place in the Chaoyang District of Beijing in 2003. The case was very similar to that of Riverside Garden, but the residents of Maizi Dian were more organized and able to invoke the law and rally the intervention of their local district and municipal government officials. They created a special website called *Chengshi Lüdi Wang* ("Urban Green Land Network") for collective mobilization and to publicize their struggle to the larger world. The website kept track of all the important encounters and struggles, published numerous social commentaries, and posted relevant legal documents that property owners could utilize.[10] It also included over one hundred pictures showing the destruction of the green field, the construction of a luxury apartment complex (with units selling at the extremely high price of eighty-eight hundred yuan per square meter), and the defacing of massive advertisement banners for the new complex by resisters. One article signed by Maizi Dian residents was titled "Who Is the Law Enforcement Agent? The Masses Are Protecting the Dignity of the Law," which invoked government urban planning rulings to demonstrate the illegality of the new construction. It concluded that "the battle over the green land by the masses is not only to protect our own interests but also to protect the dignity of law, the image of the party, and the legal system." It urged the Beijing municipal government to step forward to protect the interests of the people by calling off the construction and returning the land to the residents. Under this mounting pressure from the several thousand residents, the municipal government eventually ruled that the construction must stop and wait for further investigation and consultation with the residents.

What might be the social, political, and psychological impact of the surging rights protection mobilization in urban areas? On the individual level, those who engage in *weiquan* pay a heavy price. Many property owners reported that during the several months of intense conflict they could not focus on their work or business, and thus suffered varying degrees of financial loss. For instance, Ms. Liu from Riverside Garden told me that ever since she was drawn into the lawsuit she had spent most of her time reading relevant legal documents, meeting with lawyers and other affected residents, and attending court hearings. As a result, she had to close down her hair salon for two months. Further, the value of their property was dropping due to the widely publicized confrontation. Some homeowners within the compound no longer felt safe and wanted to sell their homes at half the price they had paid so as to move to another community. But few people were willing to buy the property and move into this troubled place. Perhaps the greater loss was to their emotional and psychological well-being. One male resident in Riverside made a suicide threat, claiming that he would jump off his residential building to protest the developer's action and social injustice. Distressed residents often used such bleak images as "prison" and "surveillance camp" to describe their own community. When one could not feel relaxed and peaceful in one's own residential community, they felt that their home was no longer a true home. Ms. Liu articulated the impact on her family this way:

> Ever since June 2, I asked my husband and my son to live outside [Riverside Garden] temporarily and not return home because I was actively involved. I stayed home because I had to fight. I am especially worried about our child because he was not aware of the potential danger. If they hurt me, I could handle it. But I could not let that happen to my child. We have been living apart for over two months. I feel exhausted now. Look at the financial and psychological damage they [the developer and his thugs] have done to us!

On the collective level, *weiquan* has brought about several positive changes. The actual participation in collective activism brought previously isolated individuals closer and resulted in a stronger sense of group solidarity. As Ms. Liu pointed out:

> Prior to this incident everyone in the neighborhood seemed to be busy with their own things. We rushed out to work and rushed back home, hiding in our own private space and not wanting to talk to each other. I did not know my neighbors after living there for six years. But now because of the incident we all know each other and have more interaction. This is a good thing. This Autumn Festival the residents in our compound have decided to celebrate together by each contributing a moon cake. This is unprecedented.

Weiquan struggles also motivate homeowners to get organized on a more permanent basis. For example, during the months of confrontation Riverside residents began to discuss how to formally establish their own property owners' association and keep it as a permanent part of communal life. They hope that eventually they would be able to fire the current management company supplied by the developer. The experience of collective action has also enhanced the rights consciousness among the residents directly involved as well as other citizens who are the spectators of such events. The mass media and new information technologies provide a broader stage for such social dramas to unfold publicly. The residents in other communities I spoke to followed these events and lawsuits on the Internet and in newspapers. They applauded the actions of those who dared to defy the developers. Finally, property-based middle-class activism has become a driving force for important legal changes. As I have shown, the root cause of the "green land battles" is the greed of real estate developers who want to use land twice over for enormously lucrative new construction. The developers dare to do so because of the ambiguous and weak legal regime concerning property and the pervasive power of real estate firms. It is in this context of increasing property conflicts that the new property law was enacted. Yet it is far from certain whether and how the new law will make a significant difference in the near future in Chinese homeowners' quest for property rights and social justice.

As Chinese society undergoes profound privatization, both "state" and "society" need to be carefully unpacked in order to tease out the myriad forms of articulation and confrontation among different social elements that cannot be so neatly dichotomized (Anagnost 1997; Rofel 1999; Zhang 2001). In the post-Tiananmen period, greater emphasis has been placed on governing through market rationality and the idiom of self-governing by private entities and citizens. This move is an integral part of the post-socialist transformation that is seeking innovative and cost-effective ways to govern a rapidly changing and expanding urban society through desta-tization. This process involves changing "the whole orientation of state activity away from the welfare state" (Harvey 2003), or what Chinese people call "the marketization of community regulation." In so doing, the Chinese state hopes to preserve its financial resources and open up new avenues by drawing a variety of entities into local governing.

Despite diminished government financing and management of the private housing regime, homeowners are not necessarily granted more power nor do we see the growth of a robust civil society within these new residential spaces.[11] As private or semiprivate property agencies take on quasi-governmental functions and assume the role of managing and policing communities, middle-class residents are now subject to a different kind of authority, one that is formidable and at times oppressive. "Governing at a distance" in this context actually gives developers, property management agencies, and private security forces more power and room to maneuver against ordinary citizens. This situation differs from what Evan McKenzie has depicted as the rise of residential private government through home-owner associations in America's privatopia (1994). In the case of China, it is not homeowners, but developers and property managers, that have seized primary control of the community. Yet, this newly configured power

relationship is too often recast in apolitical terms, as merely a market relationship. Such depoliticization risks encompassing and rendering diverse
forms of politics and social life through the lens of market rationality and
consumer logic. My account of Kunming's emerging private housing regime is not about a teleological transition from authoritarian control to
individual freedom, but about how real estate privatization has produced
a different form of urban governance that draws from both authoritarian
and neoliberal repertoires of rule and generates inadvertent destabilizing
effects.

Epilogue

The post-Mao economic reforms have brought about unprecedented wealth and remarkable economic growth, yet rapid capital accumulation is a double-edged sword. On the one hand, the party-state can gain political capital and credibility from the impressive growth in the gross domestic product; on the other hand, wealth distribution is becoming increasingly unequal, engendering labor unrest, farmers' protests, and the middle-class property-based activism. A small group of the newly rich—private entrepreneurs, merchants, well-positioned government officials, and managers of large profitable corporations—is taking up an enormous share of the new wealth and cultivating a luxury lifestyle beyond the reach of ordinary Chinese citizens. At the same time, rural migrant laborers, urban laid-off workers, and other disfranchised citizens who are struggling to make ends meet have staged protests, appeals, and legal action to protect their rights and interests (see Lee 2000; Solinger 1999; Zhang 2002, 2006). Urban factory workers who have been laid off as the result of reforming state enterprises make moral demands on the state to take care of "the people"; migrant workers use labor insurgency to protest abuses and exploitation by their employers; rural villagers engage in "rightful resistance" to illicit land acquisition, heavy agricultural taxes, and other burdens imposed by a predatory local state (O'Brien and Li 2006). The activism and opposition among dislocated urban homeowners and middle-class homeowners who defend their property rights is part of these larger growing social conflicts. Altogether, these social groups have become a major destabilizing force for the current Chinese regime although their impact is not the same.

The escalating social inequality has been widely recognized as a chief problem facing the reform party-state. The most vocal criticism of this troubling trend comes from the "Chinese New Left" intellectuals. Led by its foremost thinker, Wang Hui, New Leftism is a critical response to a host of problems brought about by encroaching capitalism and neoliberal influence in the post-Tiananmen era. In particular, Wang (2003) sees the urban reform centered on the privatization of the state-owned enterprises and subsequent massive layoffs as an assault on the Chinese working class. The market expansion into many social and political realms has led to the erosion of social benefits for ordinary urbanites and the intensification of social injustice. New Left intellectuals maintain that they are not against reforms or globalization, but they call for an alternative to the neoliberal market economy in order to curtail market excesses, reduce the gap between the rich and the poor, and protect workers' rights and the environment. In an interview with *New Perspectives Quarterly* in 2005, Wang Hui explained his position: "Today China is caught between the two extremes of misguided socialism and crony capitalism, and suffering from the worst of both systems. We have to find an alternative way. This is the great mission of our generation. I am generally in favor of orienting the country toward market reforms, but China's development must be more equal, more balanced. We must not give total priority to GDP growth to the exclusion of workers' rights and the environment."[1] Although highly critical of the emerging social problems, members of the New Left (who prefer to call themselves "critical intellectuals") do not position themselves as dissidents against the regime; instead they see the current Hu Jintao leadership as a likely force for change and the agent to safeguard the interests of the poor in the face of rising corporate power. They praise the new leadership for taking equality, anticorruption, and the welfare of the working class more seriously than any previous reform leaders. Thus, the New Left critique is primarily directed at those liberal intellectuals (mostly economists) who demand more free market reforms and see the existing problems of social polarization as a necessary stage of development. The New Left intellectuals hope to maintain a critical, but not radically oppositional, position vis-à-vis the state and the market—that is, to accommodate marketization while correcting social problems through government intervention.[2] For them, leaving everything to the market alone is dangerous.

Given the heightened instability and insecurity, the current political regime has advocated a new vision of society through the ideology of "socialist harmony." At the 16th National Congress of the Chinese Communist Party in 2002, the central party-state proclaimed that building a socialist harmonious society is a critical step in strengthening the CCP's ability to govern. In a 2005 speech, "Improve the Ability to Build a Socialist Harmonious Society," addressed to provincial party leaders, President Hu Jintao gave an elaborate account of the centrality of harmony building and urged the leaders to take it seriously. He gave harmony an eminent position in constructing socialism with Chinese characteristics and presented it as the core of socialist material, political, and spiritual civilization. He also invoked several Confucian notions, such as *he wei gui* ("harmony is most precious") and *jian xiang ai* ("generous love for each other"), to illustrate that the principle of harmony is consistent with traditional Chinese values. In October 2006, the Hu leadership formally announced that its objective is to build a socialist harmonious society by 2020. The cardinal features of what the party envisions as "a socialist harmonious society" include democracy and the rule of law, equality and justice, trust and love, stability and order, and finally a harmonious coexistence between humans and nature.

Equality, managing social conflict, and governing are central issues in the harmony ideology. First, a harmonious society is not built on the principle of socialist egalitarianism; it allows and respects socioeconomic differences. Yet the differences must be kept at a tolerable level and adjusted through government intervention when necessary. It is unclear what a tolerable level would be, however. Second, a harmonious society should be able to accommodate social discord while solving conflicts in a peaceful, lawful way. Clearly the emphasis is placed on the latter, which discourages any direct confrontation or civil defiance such as protest. Acts of opposition and resistance can be easily rendered as detrimental to the making of a harmonious society and thus must be contained. Third, socialist harmony requires both appropriate government intervention and increased self-reliance and self-governing. Individuals and communities must rely on local resources and private funds to improve their suzhi and domestic relations while creating a safe and sound social environment. The cultivation of civility and self-governing at the individual, domestic, and communal levels is now seen as a private matter. Government intervention is necessary only when larger-scale social disruptions take place. It is worth noting that the final element—a harmonious coexistence between humans and nature—echoes the "humanistic" way of modern living advocated by the "new housing movement" that I discussed in chapter 3.

Over the past several years, the notion of "harmony" has become ubiquitous in local politics and is the most popular slogan in the city and the countryside.[3] Its impact on urban regimes is particularly palpable. Not only have all levels of the urban bureaucracy (provincial, municipal, district, and street) embraced this discourse but the majority of the residential communities, danwei, and enterprises also have adopted slogans such as "building a harmonious community," "building a harmonious enterprise," and "building a harmonious city." Private developers and property managements are quick to take on this new discourse in order to serve their own ends while demonstrating conformity with the goals of higher authorities. For example, the April 2005 issue of *Property Management* (the leading publication in the field of Chinese property management) featured a special forum on how to promote harmonious residential communities through modern property management techniques. One of the articles identified four essential elements of what it envisaged as a harmonious community: superb community service, the peaceful and friendly coexistence of neighbors, a sense of safety, and a moral culture of civility (Yun 2005). This idealized community life is vividly illustrated by a drawing of an imagined private housing enclave showing residents mingling with one another happily and private security guards attentively helping children and the elderly while patrolling public space. The author criticizes homeowners' activism against the developers for opposing the very principle of harmony. The article calls *weiquan* ("rights protection") an "irrational act" that is spreading like a virus and threatening the peace and harmony of communities (Yun 2005, 11).

Privileging harmony can potentially foreclose the field of contestation, thus delegitimizing and stigmatizing the social struggles of laid-off workers, migrants, peasants, and middle-class homeowners. Harmony is not always inherently good for democratic polity, as Judith Butler has argued, "for it is more valuable to preserve the field of contestation than to guarantee in advance its harmonious conclusion" (1993, 5). The danger I see in Chinese harmony politics is precisely the desire to foreclose social contestation and stifle opposition. As the *Economist* put it bluntly when commentating on the slogan "A harmonious society—a peaceful Olympics," which was posted in a Chinese city, "this is party-speak for 'do not make trouble'" (October 11, 2008). The harmony discourse has its appeal to certain social sectors given the recent history of the PRC, however. It forms a sharp contrast with the Maoist ideology of "class struggle as the principle," and offers a new departure from Deng's and Jiang's hyperdevelopmentalism. The attention to social peace strikes a chord with those who are averse to Maoist class struggle and those who are uncomfortable with a pure growth-centered regime. In particular, the ideology of harmony is seen by some new-middle-class urbanites as compatible with their search for a private paradise, comfort, and the good life. Yet, the party leaders know well that in order to create and maintain harmony and stability, they must grapple with the soaring inequality and unjust distribution of wealth so that the poor can be managed and contained. Premier Wen Jiabao and President Hu Jintao repeatedly assured the public of their commitment to improving social welfare and the livelihood of the poor, as well as curbing income polarization. But there is a great deal of resistance from local government officials and powerful business groups against the implementation of new policies that might better serve the interests of ordinary workers, farmers, and homeowners. Harmony and reconciliation are hard to embrace for those whose livelihoods are threatened, yet for whom there is little prospect for legal protection and justice.

In a very different cultural context, anthropologist Laura Nader argues that the use of harmony is intrinsically political and that the ideology of harmony has long served as a powerful tool in the making of the colonial and religious political order (1990, 2). One can identify some basic elements in the harmony ideology, such as "an emphasis on conciliation, recognition that resolution of conflict is inherently good and that its reverse—continued conflict or controversy—is bad or dysfunctional, a view of harmonious behavior as more civilized than disputing behavior, the belief that consensus is of greater survival value than controversy" (Nader 1990, 2). However, the notion of harmony is not one-dimensional and can be used by different social groups for different purposes. It can be used by those in power to orient suppressed or marginalized people toward conformity, or it can be used by the weak and subaltern to resist external control. In China, harmony ideology has been instigated by the party-state to divert social energy perceived to be dangerous to the established order. The very choice of the word *hexie* (harmony), as opposed to the popular Maoist notion of *douzheng* (struggle), is intended to depoliticize and signify the more humanistic approach of the new leadership, one that differentiates itself from the focus on political/ideological struggle (as with Mao) or the obsession with development (as with Deng and Jiang). Despite such careful wording, "building a harmonious society" is inherently a political project. It is also important to point out that this official discourse has been gradually adopted by the disfranchised and marginalized people for a different purpose. They use it to demand protection and assistance from higher government authorities in battles with a corrupt local state and predatory developers. Meanwhile, "against the law" (*weifa*), as C. K. Lee (2007) shows, has become the shared accusation or common idiom used by ordinary citizens in their quest for justice against the powerful who are not following the law.

The tension between capital accumulation and political legitimacy, growth and equity has long existed in the development of capitalism. What further complicates the Chinese situation is the attempt to combine economic liberalization, neoliberal thinking, and socialist authoritarian rule at once. The party-state still claims to be the ultimate guardian of "the people" but at the same time urges its citizens to "rely on one's self" (*kao ziji*) rather than "relying on the state" (*kao guojia*). Ironically, the old socialist expression, *zili gengsheng* ("self-reliance" or "regeneration through one's own effort"), so popularly advocated by Maoist nationalism to defy Western imperialism, has now been endowed with new meanings and finds a different salience in a neoliberal market climate. To be a good citizen today is to become self-reliant and self-enterprising, one who is able to navigate and thrive amid the turbulent social and economic changes.[4] In the national race for wealth and status, a new kind of self-managing, self-directing subject is emerging while the state is gradually shedding its accountability and moral responsibilities for taking care of its people (see Ong and Zhang 2008).

Although some China observers have located the rural areas as the main source of the accumulation/legitimation contradiction, citing predatory local state practices and insurgent peasant resistance (Friedman, Pickowicz, and Selden 2007; Mueggler 2001; O'Brien and Li 2006), my research demonstrates that urban areas have in recent years emerged as a new central site where this contradiction is intensified and negotiated (see also Chen Feng 2006; Hsing 2009b; Lee 2007). More recently, the international economic crisis that originated in U.S. financial and stock markets has had a direct impact on China. The Chinese stock market and housing prices have plunged and the economic growth that has stunned the world for the past ten years is slowing down. This big, sudden economic downturn makes many Chinese people nervous and angry as they see their investments plummeting and their livelihoods threatened. Middle-class homeowners in the cities were especially upset when their property values dropped by 10–20 percent in just a few months (*Economist,* October 25, 2008). This new economic downturn presents a tough challenge for the Chinese government whose legitimacy has largely rested on the nation's economic success. The $586 billion economic stimulus plan unveiled by China on November 9, 2008, is the first effort to ease the panic among the citizens. The state has also taken other measures such as cutting property taxes and reducing mortgage rates to help urban middle-class families and stabilize the housing market. Whether these new measures can work effectively is hard to predict, but it is clear at this moment that the party-state is experimenting with different strategies to prevent the economic recession and the contradictions within postsocialist development from evolving into a larger crisis of state legitimacy. In the midst of these unpredictable changes, the private paradise that the rising middle-class Chinese are pursuing and dreaming of may become a mirage, surrounded by emerging socioeconomic insecurities, anxieties, and class tensions.

Notes

Introduction

1. The numbers are from *The 2007 China Statistical Yearbook*.

2. In this book, I use the term "middle classes" rather than "middle class" to refer to this emerging heterogeneous social formation that includes diverse social groups.

3. My usage here is different from the original meaning of the term coined by Stephen Collier and Andrew Lakoff (2005).

4. Just how many people can be considered part of the middle classes in China is highly contested. The estimated numbers vary greatly from study to study. Some claimed that there were already eighty million people in this category by 2002 (Lu 2002). Some predicted an even bolder number of two hundred million people middle-class consumers by 2006 (*Xinxi Shibao* [Information Time] July 21, 2001). Most studies used income, the ability to consume, and lifestyles as the indicators. An article in *Foreign Policy* claimed that "by 2025, China will have the world's largest middle class" (Naim 2008).

5. Goodman and Zang use the term "new rich" to describe a broad social group that has acquired certain wealth during the reform and that is identified by Chinese loosely as part of the rising middle classes. They point out that "the new rich are not all by any means super rich," as this is a diverse social formation with its own hierarchies (2008, 3). But even so, the Chinese middle classes do not represent the considerably larger body of the population situated in the middle as in the case of the United States or Canada.

6. Weber differentiates classes from status groups in that the former is largely defined by production and the latter by consumption, but he also emphasizes that the two modes of group formation are closely linked through property ownership, which not only determines one's class situation but also serves as the basis for one's lifestyle. See the analysis by Anthony Giddens (1981).

7. It is also useful to revisit the notion of "productive consumption" provided by Karl Marx and Frederick Engels in *The German Ideology:* "production is at the same time consumption, and consumption is at the same time production" (1998, 131).

8. See also ethnographic accounts by Pow (2007) and Fleischer (2007) linking the choice of housing and lifestyle to class-making.

9. Michel de Certeau elaborates that "the trajectories trace out the ruses of other interests and desires that are neither determined nor captured by the systems in which they develop" (1984, xviii).

10. Hai Ren has argued that this ability to evade the law and take advantage of the gray economy is crucial for capital accumulation by China's entrepreneurs (Ren forthcoming). More broadly, the willingness to take risks and calculate gains against the potential danger of being caught is one of the fundamental traits that make up a neoliberal subject. I thank Ann Anagnost for bringing the relationship between risk-taking and neoliberal subjects to my attention.

11. The increased importance of consumption in post-Mao social life is clearly demonstrated by a series of studies. See Davis (1999), Hanser (2008), and Zheng (2009), for example.

12. NIMBYism is a form of grassroots movement commonly associated with contemporary middle-class politics to protect their home values and lifestyle by rejecting undesirable developments in their communities.

13. I borrow Hilary Cunningham's approach to globalization "as a phenomenon rooted in particular types of social activities and conditions, and as a process in which people come to imagine themselves and their practices in novel ways" (2000, 584).

14. Iván Szelényi (1996) points out that the making of a new class ("neo-bourgeoisie") is one of the major transformations in postsocialist cities. His own inquiry, however, is mainly concerned with the emerging political and economic elite class (see Szelényi and Glass 2003).

15. Daniel Miller (1995) has provided a useful account of the role of housing markets in class-making under capitalism. Fulong Wu's study of residential segregation in postreform Chinese cities suggests that "through market-oriented housing consumption, a new stratified sociospatial structure is in the making" (2008b, 404).

16. I borrow this concept from Paul Willis (1977) who originally referred to a set of distinct, localized cultural practices and beliefs associated with working-class youth culture in England.

17. See the special issue on "Rethinking Postsocialism" in *Anthropology News* (November 2008). The retreat of the state is a myth not only in postsocialist states but also in neoliberal capitalist societies. Scholars have noted the centrality of government in promoting and safeguarding free markets during neoliberal restructuring (see Maskovsky and Kingfisher 2001; Brown 2003; Sassen 1996).

18. For example, Judith Farquhar sees the 1990s as the beginning of a "postsocialist" era marked by an expansive and permissive reform economy and growing consumerism and individualism (2002, 3). Lisa Rofel argues that the 1990s witnessed a neoliberal formation in which a new kind of desiring subject, who "operate[s] through sexual, material, and affective self-interest," began to emerge in urban China (2007, 3). Ralph Litzinger also suggests that the 1990s present a very different space and time in China due to the influence of neoliberal globalization (2001).

19. Several scholars have begun to examine related issues from other disciplinary perspectives (see Davis 2002; Tomba 2004; Read 2003; Bray 2008; Wu 2005).

20. This process echoes what Wendy Brown (2003) has identified as one of the key characteristics of neoliberalism—market rationality permeating into virtually all social domains to structure human activities.

21. Since the mid-1990s, the Chinese government has launched a major campaign for "community building" (*shequ jianshe*), which takes the residential community (rather than the danwei) as the basic unit of urban governance, to promote self-regulation (see Bray 2008; Cho n.d.).

22. The civility project is not limited to the new urban housing regime. Ann Anagnost (1997) has shown that the reform state has actively appropriated the notion of civility in transforming rural communities as well.

23. Its isolation from other parts of China was due to the difficult physical terrain and historically underdeveloped ground transportation in this entire region (see Skinner 1977).

24. Yunnan is home to some twenty-five ethnic minority groups. Kunming is also known as the "spring city" due to its mild and pleasant weather all year around. These features attract a large number of tourists.

1. Farewell to Welfare Housing

1. The original Chinese saying is "*xinxin kuku sishinian, yizhao huidao jiefangqian.*" I thank Don Gibbs for bringing my attention to this popular rhyme.

2. In this chapter I focus on land resources. Another important form of such primitive accumulation is the devouring of state assets in the process of reforming state-owned enterprises (*guoyou qiye gaige*). As one U.S.-based economist, Lang Xianping, put it during a visit to mainland China, "The reform of the state-owned enterprises is in fact a grand banquet for devouring state assets." This statement ignited a heated debate about the state-owned assets reform in 2006 and aggravated those "mainstream" economists who had pushed for this reform (see Li 2006).

3. There is a large body of literature on the centrality of the *hukou* system in socialist China and on its continued significance in shaping the life of rural and urban residents during the reform period (see, for example, Cheng and Selden 1994; Zhang 2002; Solinger 1999).

4. According to Zhang (1998), in Beijing, for example, less than 24% of the buildings were publicly owned and most of them were for such nonresidential purposes as government offices, schools, and hospitals.

5. These numbers are from the *China Urban Construction Yearbook 1986–87*.

6. Similar practices for surviving a shortage economy were found in Russia as well (see Caldwell 2004).

7. The ultimate goal was to sell off all public housing, but the government also wanted to give low-income families the option to rent in order to avoid social unrest.

8. Married couples who are both eligible for the purchase must choose to buy from one of their employers.

9. In China teachers are compared to gardeners because they cultivate students in a way similar to gardeners cultivating plants.

10. All the official documents I refer to here can be found in *The Selected Collection of Law and Rulings regarding Housing Reform* (1998).

11. Before the reform, one would automatically get a housing assignment when hired by a state-owned entity.

12. This fund may only be used for buying, building, or improving homes. The contribution levels were set at between 5% and 8% of one's income.

13. Much research has shown that business-state clientalism has increased rather than decreased during the market economy era (Wank 1999; Pieke 1995).

14. See Hsing's article (2006) on the complicated negotiations among multiple actors: different levels and divisions of the government, developers, danwei, individual urban residents, and suburban farmers.

15. The information posted in general listings usually includes location (city), parcel number, size, specified usage, transaction type, base price, current highest bid, and starting and ending dates. When you click on the specific parcel, it will give you more detailed information such as the specific location, contact person, term, deposit, current landholder, and so on. To avoid redundancy, I sometimes drop the word "use rights" when referring to land transactions since in this entire book all such transactions in reform-era China only concern use rights.

16. See *Reports on China's and International Real Estates*, no. 6: 26, 1993.

17. The conversion rate from Chinese yuan to the U.S. dollar was roughly 8–1 before 2006, but it has dropped to 6.8–1 since then.

18. The cost of land use is one of the major factors in determining the total production cost, and thus has a significant affect on housing prices.

19. Elsewhere, I have provided a more detailed account of this problem as manifested in the politics of city planning in Kunming (Zhang 2006). See also Wang and Zhou (2004).

20. This practice was possible largely due to relatively good record keeping regarding property ownership before the socialist nationalization in East Germany. But restitution often caused conflicts between current occupants and the original owners.

21. A similar pattern of heavy public and employer subsidies in promoting homeownership rather than building rental apartments is also found in Taiwan and Hong Kong.

22. For example, the revised Romanian Land Law stipulates that the owner of a building also has ownership of the land on which the building is located. In Czechoslovakia and Poland, private individuals are generally allowed to acquire land with certain restrictions on foreign investors (Marcuse 1996).

23. This system is not applied to the rural areas where land is owned by the rural collectives and is not commercialized.

24. Such decisions are usually influenced by the rationale of the so-called highest and best use of land (see Derbes 1981; Blomley 2002).

25. "Traditional" or "century-old" neighborhoods and streets refer to what was built in the early twentieth century with distinct architectural styles. But many of them began to become dilapidated and have not been renovated.

26. The State Council has named a total of ninety-nine national-level "renowned historical-cultural cities" in China since 1982 and required these cities to follow stronger preservation measures.

2. Unlocking the Real Estate Machine

1. The ambiguous ownership forms I describe here are a common phenomenon in reform-era China. See Oi and Walder (1999) for a detailed discussion of blurred property rights in the context of rural township enterprises, and Tsai's notion of "adaptive informal institutions" created by private entrepreneurs to take advantage of the opportunities and to work around the constraints of formal institutions (2002). Alan Smart has raised the question of whether this messy character of the emerging property regime is a problem for further marketization or an innovative experiment that allows rapid capital accumulation (1998).

2. See Wank's (1999) and Pieke's (1995) extensive accounts of how the bureaucracy and the market have become inextricably linked during the reform years.

3. For detailed studies of the state-owned enterprise reform, see Jefferson and Singh (1999) and Hassard and Hassard (2007).

4. One exception is the Qinfeng Real Estate Development Co., Ltd., established by a group of young entrepreneurs in recent years. It has been growing rapidly and has acquired a sizable share of the commodity housing market in the city. Featuring a combination of modern architecture and traditional southern Chinese-style garden design, the Sunshine Garden residential community (containing some two thousand families) created by this firm is a huge success and has been praised by the Chinese Construction Ministry as an exemplary community for Chinese cities.

5. This type of housing is also considered commodity housing but the price is generally much lower than the regular market rate because the government subsidizes land acquisition fees and taxes. It is meant to meet the needs of lower-income families. A citizen must meet certain criteria to qualify for the purchase.

6. During my research I found out that it is not an uncommon practice for some private firms (especially the larger ones) to establish party organizations and use them as a way of

implementing certain state and firm policies, organizing moral activities, and reinforcing discipline in workplaces.

7. The reason firms from these places become the main source of new business practices is that they are the dominant foreign businesses in Kunming where locals can learn from directly.

8. *Mu* is a Chinese unit of area. One *mu* is equal to 0.0667 hectares or 2.47 acres.

9. Compare Zhang's (2001) account of Wenzhou migrants and Tsai's (2002) account of many innovative, informal financial arrangements created by China's small private entrepreneurs.

10. During the Cultural Revolution, millions of urban youth were sent to the countryside to participate in agricultural production and to be reeducated by peasants who were deemed morally superior.

11. Xuefei Ren's study (2008) shows, for instance, that local governments in Beijing were able to confiscate numerous urban homes and transfer the land to private developers in exchange for a sizable land-leasing fee as the major revenue.

12. ATM service was uncommon in China at that time. Only a few banks provided such service and the number of machines was limited. Thus, this was an attractive feature.

13. See also Xin Liu's discussion of this term (2002). The sexual connotation is reflected in a bizarre practice in many sales offices that when potential clients arrive at the door, the manager would yell at young female agents, "*Jieke*," a term specifically used to refer to the ritual of prostitutes greeting their customers.

14. See Hyde (2007) and Zhang (2000) for further discussion of the complex cultural connotations of this notion.

15. See a more detailed account in "Behind the Stories of *Shoulou Xiaojie*," *Yangzi Evening Daily,* June 30, 2004.

16. The connection between the need to sell personalities and the sense of alienation is also noted by C. Wright Mills (1951) in his study of the sales class in the United States.

17. Amy Hanser has argued that the sales counter in China is a prominent realm in which "entitlements are expressed and social distinctions are performed and legitimated" (2008, 3).

18. The three cases were reported in "Baogongtou Juanzou Mingong Xuehanqian Shiyuwan" (A Contractor Flees with over One Hundred Thousand Yuan of Peasant Workers' Blood and Sweat Money) on http://www.sina.com.cn 1/14/2004; "Shui lai Guanxin Zhexie Mingong?" (Who Would Come to Care for These Peasant Workers?), www.fyfz.cn 8/25/2006; and on http://www.soufun.com 9/7/2004. In addition, the Beijing Supreme People's Court reported that it received 25,987 cases involving defaults on peasant workers' payments in 2005 alone.

19. In November 2003 the China Central Television Station hosted a special program called "Peasant Brothers, How Well Do You Live?" that revealed the appalling living conditions of migrant construction workers.

20. The story of Zhen was reported by Henan Shichuang News on August 29, 2006, on http://www.hnsc.com.cn/news.

21. Using place of origin as the basis of social networks is a common strategy by rural migrants in Chinese cities (see Solinger 1999; Zhang 2001).

3. Emerging Landscapes of Living

1. I translate the Chinese term *juzhu* as "living" rather than "residence" or "abode" because it captures a more dynamic connotation of the original Chinese concept. Living refers to a way of life beyond the physical structure of housing.

2. The civic nature of this network is worth emphasizing as it demarcates this movement from other, state-orchestrated, movements.

3. It may appear perplexing to some readers why architects' creativity is mentioned in calling for a new business order. This act must be understood in the specific context of China where political and business interests almost always take precedence over the ideas of professionals. This call is an attempt to restore the rightful place of architects in urban design.

4. This idea was picked up later by the current political leadership to elaborate on how to build a harmonious society, which I will discuss in greater detail in the epilogue. There are other ideas about what constitutes new, modern, and desirable ways of living today.

5. The Chinese interpretation of Western residential styles as exotic forms an interesting contrast with the discourse of a "normal" life in the post-Soviet region, which sees the appropriation of a Western European level of material life as a way of restore a normal, good life that state socialism had deprived them of (Fehervary 2002).

6. Information about this debate can be found on www.people.com.cn, August 4, 2005.

7. In a different context, Jing Wang provides a fascinating study of how the new lifestyle culture and marketing strategies feed each other by analyzing an imaginary class of "bourgeois bohemians" in China (2005).

8. Zhen Zhang (2005) uses a similar term, "vernacular modernism," to describe the scenery of early Chinese cinema.

9. China officially recognizes fifty-six ethnic groups, among which the Han is the majority, making up about 91.5% of the total population.

10. It is not clear why the use of large blocks of lawns and open space is classified as the Continental European style (*oulu fengge*) by Chinese people, as this kind of design is widely found in many other cities throughout the world.

11. As part of a long, five-part series published in *Yunnan Daily,* one section offered a detailed account of the choice of architectural design and its logic as adopted by Sunshine Garden developers (see Zhang et al. 2000).

12. Deborah Davis (2005) has urged us to understand the emerging urban consumer culture in China in a way that is attentive to historical specificity and individual narratives.

13. Fears about crime are not limited to urban society but are also a salient issue for rural residents. However, what is so striking in the city is the way such fears are visibly projected onto urban architectural designs (such as the widespread use of walls, gates, and metal bars), new surveillance technologies, and private security forces.

14. These users are not responsible for the security guards' life insurance, injuries, and medical treatment. These costs are supposed to be paid by the supplying company, but in reality the guards rarely receive such benefits.

15. See Zhang (2001), Yan (2003), Anagnost (forthcoming), and Kipnis (2007) for further analysis of the cultural politics of suzhi, especially as it relates to rural migrants and the middle class.

4. Spatializing Class

1. According to Ling, there were only a few foreigners living there and the sign was used to create a cosmopolitan-like atmosphere.

2. This social group is not a structural continuation of the middle class that existed before the Communist takeover. It is a by-product of the recent privatization of home ownership, which was largely absent from the early 1950s to the late 1980s.

3. This is not to deny the social and economic differences that existed among urban Chinese under Mao. Yet, the danwei residential pattern made it difficult for people with similar economic statuses to come to live together and cultivate a shared lifestyle, habitus, and a sense of common identification in terms other than as danwei comrades.

4. My analysis is largely inspired by Jean Baudrillard's study of the power of advertising and signs in consumer society (1998).

5. It is important to note a major difference between China and North America in terms of inner-city/suburb dynamics. Suburbanization in China has not led to the decline and hollowing out of the inner city; rather, the development of the suburb and the inner city take place side by side simultaneously. The ideal situation for an upper-middle-class family is to own one luxury condo within the central city and one villa in the suburb.

6. Gating itself is not new to China as it was also used by danwei under socialism, but it has assumed a new meaning given a free market housing context (see Wu 2005).

7. The lower-income neighborhoods include mostly privatized danwei housing compounds and some newly developed, state-subsidized *xiaoqu* for qualified working-class families and those forced out of the core urban districts due to recent city renewal projects.

8. The differentiation of communities is certainly not limited to three kinds; local people make more subtle distinctions. The three levels I focus on illustrate the major distinctions, however.

9. The price of housing, especially the luxury type, had been increasing steadily in all Chinese cities until the recent global financial downturn. It is estimated that in some cities the housing price plummeted about 20% within six months in 2008.

10. Most new commercially developed communities are run by property management agencies and protected by private security guards; thus, they have little contact with the residents' committees (*juweihui*) and the local police (see Read 2000, 2003).

11. This is called *yinxing shouru* ("invisible income"), which often exceeds one's salary. Yet, it is nearly impossible to gauge such incomes because they tend to fluctuate greatly and people are unwilling to talk about invisible incomes.

12. There are countless websites especially created for and by pet lovers nationwide, which indicates that pets are becoming a distinctive part of the new Chinese middle-class culture.

13. Pow observes a similar process in Shanghai's gated communities and provides a detailed account of what he calls "the moral geographies of exclusion" (2007). Elsewhere, I have also written extensively about why and how migrants in China are criminalized in the cities (2001).

14. The "master"/"servant" divide is most centrally expressed in the context of domestic work, which has been explored in depth by Yan Hairong (2008).

15. See arguments made by Anita Chan (2002), C. K. Lee (2000), and Pun Ngai (2005) on the importance of the shared shop floor in workers' mobilization.

16. It is not my intention to debate whether consumption ultimately leads to emancipation or exploitation (Davis 2005; Pun 2003). Rather, I want to emphasize the active role of consumption in shaping class subjects and the contradictory experiences it generates.

5. Accumulation by Displacement

1. This shift has been widely noted and analyzed by China scholars in different contexts (see, for example, Dickson 2003; Liu 2002; Pearson 1997; Unger 1996; Wank 1999; Zhang 2001).

2. T. H. Marshall (1964) clearly identified the development of various rights as central to citizenship. More specifically, property rights are regarded by scholars (such as Bruszt 2001) as a key step in the extension of citizenship rights in postcommunist countries.

3. There are multiple and specific forms of citizenship struggle across different social groups in China even though the term "citizenship" may not be used explicitly by some people (see Goldman and Perry 2002). Lee (2004) and Read (2003) both reject the notion of class struggle or citizen rights in characterizing the nature of the emerging forms of grassroots civic activism among workers and new middle-class homeowners. Elsewhere (Zhang 2002), I have shown that the struggle over citizenship among rural migrants in Chinese cities is centered on the notion of space (not property) and the right to work and live in the city even if they are denied permanent urban *hukou* status (see also Solinger 1999).

4. The regime of property rights in reform China is a highly complicated one marked by regional variations. It is also characterized by multiple forms of "fuzzy ownership" (see Oi and Walder 1999). My analysis here focuses on a particular form of property—urban housing, which has been privatized and commercialized over the past decade. For the processes and effects of the urban housing reform, see Wang and Murie (1999a, 1999b) and Zhang (1998).

5. I have interviewed members of the Fong family extensively several times and thus have gained a deep understanding of their family history and struggle.

6. Compensations only involve the loss of structures, not land, which belongs to the state. In order to obtain land-use rights, developers must negotiate with local governments or work units that hold the original use rights.

7. Nicolas Blomley has noted that in the case of Canada's real estate development, "the logic of highest and best use now becomes the means by which the rightful occupants are to be 'cleansed' from the neighborhood" (2002, 575).

8. The case presented here is based on a newspaper report (Zhao 2003).

9. See "Woman Defies Chinese Developers," BBC News, http://news.bbc.uk/go/pr/fr/-/2/hi/asia-pacific/6483997.stm.

10. Another similar tragedy took place during a forced eviction in Shanghai. A man who refused to relocate protested his eviction by drenching himself in gasoline. When the policemen approached his home, he set himself on fire, shouting that he would rather die than be forced out.

11. Compare Farrar's (2002) discussion of the eviction of alley residents in Washington, D.C., at the turn of the nineteenth century and the notion of the "abject" in the politics of the social body.

12. The Han-Hui relationship has long been a sensitive issue in Chinese ethnic politics. For extensive analysis of this complicated dynamic, see Gladney (1991) and Gillette (2000).

13. Being able to move back is called *huiqian*, the most preferred form of compensation by Chinese residents. But it is usually not offered, as it tends to reduce the profit margin of the developers. The cash compensation rate was about four thousand yuan per square meter for the demolished house, but the retail price for the new housing was eight thousand to nine thousand yuan per square meter.

14. The main charge was that Zhou obtained part of the land in Jingan for free by using his *guanxi* connections with the government without going through a required public land auction. For more accounts of this case, see McGregor (2003) and Kynge (2003).

15. The enactment of the property law took some people by surprise. Mao Shoulong, professor of public policy at the People's University, had predicted that it would take a long time when he commented in 2006 that "our government only moves forward when it feels there is a strong consensus. Right now, the consensus is eroding" (Kahn 2006).

16. Scholars working in other cultural contexts have recently called for a multidimensional understanding of the complex relationship between property rights and development (see Meijl and Benda-Beckmann 1999).

6. Recasting Self-Worth

1. Barlow describes this notion of personhood in Qing China: "Male and female, Confucian subjects always appeared as part of something else, defined not by essence but by context, marked by interdependency and reciprocal obligation rather than by autonomy and contradiction" (1989, 10).

2. This NPR series, "China, a Nation of Individuals," was reported by Rob Gifford from July 25 to July 29, 2007. See also Yunxiang Yan's account of the increased individualism among rural youth and its social consequences (2003).

3. Deborah Davis and Hanlong Lu show that property disputes centered on home ownership have become a widespread and contentious issue in not only conjugal relationships but also in instances of inheritance since the 1990s (2003).

4. Elisabeth Engebretsen's recent study (2009) shows that the seemingly oppressive institution of the "traditional marriage" continues to shape same-sex life aspirations and the family and social relationships in which Chinese lesbians are embedded.

5. Derek Hird's dissertation (2008) provides a rich account of how manliness is constructed among Chinese white collar men in post-Mao times. In particular, the suit, he suggests, has become a marker of respectability, success, integrity, and cleanliness, and thus an embodiment of the new middle-class masculinities.

6. "Raise one's back up" is a Chinese saying, which means to feel confident and rightful.

7. See Rubie Watson's discussion on the importance of property in marital exchange in pre-1949 China (1991).

8. Farrer and Sun (2003) show that extramarital affairs are increasing rapidly in urban China and that there are competing moral discourses on this phenomenon.

9. According to the current PRC Marriage Law, "at the time of divorce, the disposition of the property in the joint possession of husband and wife is subject to agreement between the two parties. In cases where an agreement cannot be reached, the people's court shall make a judgment in consideration of the actual circumstance of the property and on the principle of caring for the rights and interests of the wife and the child or children" (Chapter IV, Article 39). Most people prefer private negotiations between the two parties in order to diminish the likelihood of losing "face" in public court battles.

10. This practice is not unusual in China, where many families, for the sake of convenience, only use one person's name (usually the male head of the household) for the deposits.

11. See Huang's analysis of masculinity in late imperial China (2006) and Farquhar's account of the increased concern over impotency among Chinese men in a postsocialist market order (1999).

12. There is a cultural expectation for a child in Chinese society.

13. The content of this marital exchange is different from what Gayle Rubin has described as the "exchange of women" in kinship systems, in which men are "givers" and women are "gifts." She argues that the traffic in women is a root of female subordination (1975).

14. The objectification I describe here differs from what Hershatter (1991) and Watson (1991) have recounted of women bought and sold as property in early twentieth-century China. This is a conscious strategy by some women to capitalize on their body and appearance in exchange for material control and consolidation of their position.

7. Privatizing Community Governing and Its Limits

1. Although the strategies of privatization shared a great deal of commonality between the so-called advanced liberal capitalist societies and formerly socialist societies, it is important to point out that their starting bases were quite different. In the former case, there already existed a predominant private sector with a firmly established private ownership system; the privatization usually involved public services that had been in the hands of the welfare state. In the latter case, the entire economy was largely dominated by public ownership in all facets of social and economic life. As a result, the processes, meanings, and consequences of privatization are not the same.

2. Aihwa Ong's notion of "graduated sovereignty" is relevant here in rethinking governmentality in the era of globalization. She rightly points out that "even as the state maintains control over its territory, it is also willing in some cases to let corporate entities set the terms for constituting and regulating some domains" (1999, 217).

3. We should not forget that even though the Chinese state is not directly orchestrating community life in the new housing regime, it nevertheless provides the conditions for "the exercise of rule by many other institutions and agents that operate by inciting and stimulating the active choices of enterprising individuals" (Purvis and Hunt 1999, 469). Further, in post-Mao rural China, some anthropologists have argued that state power has actually grown more intimate and spectral in some areas (Friedman 2005; Mueggler 2001).

4. There are more than 120,000 urban residents' committees in China today, each comprising three to seven members of the governing body and the wider membership varies greatly. For a more detailed account of the function and nature of *juweihui* and recent changes in them, see Read (2000).

5. Pan's study on Shanghai neighborhoods suggests that there is a shift of focus in the operation of residents' committees from bureaucratic control to community management, from serving as a tool of state control to acting as social service providers (2001).

6. Benjamin Read's (2003) research indicates that in some new residential communities, the local government has established a branch office, but its function is rather limited. Most residents still do not have direct interactions with such agencies.

7. See Mike Davis's insightful account of the politics of homeowner movements in the United States (1992). Calling them a form of "separatist struggles," Davis is extremely critical of such movements because they promote class and racial segregation by excluding the poor in the name of protecting middle-class lifestyles.

8. Benjamin Read's (2003) research in Beijing and Guangzhou suggests a more optimistic situation. Homeowners in these two cities seem to be better informed and organized; they are able to assert their collective power to advance their agenda.

9. Housing has long been a crucial site for contesting citizenship, as some researchers have clearly demonstrated elsewhere (Caldeira 2000; Holston 1989; Holston and Appadurai 1999).

10. The website, http://www.yiyitong.com, lasted for a year and five months, and was removed after the developer abandoned the new construction plan.

11. In postsocialist Russia, where central state power is relatively weakened by free market forces, it is Mafia-like entities rather than civil society that have sprung up to control much of the economy and social life (Humphrey 1991; Ries 1997; Verdery 1996).

Epilogue

1. See "Global Viewpoint," March 7, 2005, in *New Perspectives Quarterly* 24, no. 3.

2. Some researchers suggest that the neoliberal/New Left divide has grown beyond academia, and even members of the PRC Congress can be divided along this line in terms of their thinking. Matthew Erie, for example, described two camps among the Congress with regard to the draft of the Property Law: "The former claim that private property rights are vital to provide legal guarantees and incentives for marketization.... The latter counter that the draft will not increase social mobility but rather legitimize social stratification and exacerbate inequality" (2007).

3. *New York Times* reporter Howard French (2007) shows that the harmony ideology has had a profound effect on Chinese popular music. Music must now reflect the goal of harmony by becoming blandly homogeneous in the form of gentle love songs and uplifting ballads. He quotes a musician: "Because China emphasizes stability and harmony, the greatest utility of these pop songs is that they aren't dangerous to the system. If people could hear underground music, it would make them feel the problems in their lives and want to change things."

4. Although active support for the party is not required, patriotism is still viewed as a necessary quality of a responsible citizen (see Hoffman 2006).

References

Anagnost, Ann. 1997. *National Past-Times: Narrative, Representation, and Power in Modern China*. Durham: Duke University Press.

——. 2008. "From 'Class' to 'Social Strata': Grasping the Social Totality in Reform-Era China." *Third World Quarterly* 29, no. 3: 497–519.

——. Forthcoming. *Embodiments of Value: The Politics of Quality in China's Reform*. Durham: Duke University Press.

Armijo-Hussein, Jacqueline Misty. 1997. "Sayyid 'Ajall Shams al-Din: A Muslim from Central Asia, Serving the Mongols in China, and Bringing 'Civilization' to Yunnan." PhD dissertation, Inner Asian and Altaic Studies, Harvard University.

Arrighi, Giovanni. 2007. *Adam Smith in Beijing: Lineages of the 21st Century*. London: Verso.

Barker, Adele Marie. 1999. *Consuming Russia: Popular Culture, Sex, and Society since Gorbachev*. Durham: Duke University Press.

Barlow, Tani E. 1989. Introduction to *I Myself Am a Woman: Selected Writings of Ding Ling*, edited by Tani Barlow and Gary Bjorge. Boston: Beacon Press.

Barry, Andrew, Thomas Osborne, and Nikolas Rose. 1996. Introduction to *Foucault and Political Reason: Liberalism, Neo-liberalism, and Rationalities of Government*, edited by Andrew Barry, Thomas Osborne, and Nikolas Rose, 1–17. Chicago: University of Chicago Press.

Bater, James H. 1980. *The Soviet City: Ideal and Reality*. Sage Publications.

Baudrillard, Jean. 1998. *The Consumer Society*. London: Sage.

Blakely, Edward, and Mary Gail Snyder. 1997. *Fortress America: Gated Communities in the United States*. Washington, D.C.: Brookings Institution.

Blomley, Nicholas. 2002. "Mud for the Land." *Public Culture* 14, no. 3: 557–82.

Bourdieu, Pierre. 1977. *Outline of a Theory of Practice*. Cambridge: Cambridge University Press.

——. 1984. *Distinction*. Cambridge: Harvard University Press.

——. 1990. "The Kabyle House or the World Reversed." In *The Logic of Practice*, trans. by Richard Nice, 271–83. Stanford: Stanford University Press.

227

——. 1991. "Social Space and the Genesis of 'Classes'." In *Language and Symbolic Power*, 229–51. Cambridge: Harvard University Press.

——. 2005. *The Social Structures of the Economy.* Cambridge: Polity Press.

Bray, David. 2005. *Social Space and Governance in Urban China: The Danwei System from Origins to Reform.* Stanford: Stanford University Press.

——. 2006. "Building 'Community': New Strategies of Governance in Urban China." *Economy and Society* 35, no. 4: 530–49.

——. 2008. "Designing to Govern: Space and Power in Two Wuhan Communities." *Built Environment* 34, no. 3.

Brown, Wendy. 2003. "Neo-liberalism and the End of Liberal Democracy." *Theory and Event* 7, no. 1.

Brownell, Susan, and Jeffery Wasserstrom, eds. 2002. "Introduction: Theorizing Femininities and Masculinities." In *Chinese Femininities, Chinese Masculinities: A Reader*, 1–41. Berkeley: University of California Press.

Brumann, Christoph. N.d. "Invention and Its Limits: The Social Life of Urban Traditions in Kyoto." Unpublished manuscript.

Bruszt, Laszlo. 2001. "Heterarchies and Developmental Traps." *Brazilian Journal of Political Economy* 1: 37–57.

Buchli, Victor. 1999. *An Archaeology of Socialism.* Oxford: Berg.

Burchell, Graham. 1996. "Liberal Government and Techniques of the Self." In *Foucault and Political Reason: Liberalism, Neo-liberalism, and Rationalities of Government*, edited by Andrew Barry, Thomas Osborne, and Nikolas Rose, 19–36. Chicago: University of Chicago Press.

Butler, Judith. 1993. "Poststructuralism and Postmarxism." *Diacritics* 23, no. 4: 3–11.

Buttiner, Richard J., Anthony Y. X. Gu, and Tyler T. Yang. 2004. "The Chinese Housing Provident Fund." *International Real Estate Review* 7, no. 1: 1–30.

Cai, Jane. 2003. "Lawyers Team Up to Fight Property Rows in Shanghai." *South China Morning Post*, September 23, 2003.

Cai, Yongshun. 2003. "Collective Ownership or Cadres' Ownership? The Non-agricultural Use of Farmland in China." *China Quarterly* 175: 662–80.

Caldeira, Teresa. 2000. *City of Walls: Crime, Segregation, and Citizenship in Sao Paulo.* Berkeley: University of California Press.

Caldwell, Melissa. 2004. *Not By Bread Alone: Social Support in the New Russia.* Berkeley: University of California Press.

Castells, Manuel. 1984. *The City and the Grassroots: A Cross-Cultural Theory of Urban Social Movements.* Berkeley: University of California Press.

Chan, Anita. 2002. "The Culture of Survival: Lives of Migrant Workers through the Prism of Private Letters." In *Popular China: Unofficial Culture in a Globalizing Society*, edited by Perry Link, Richard Madsen, and Paul Pickowicz, 163–88. Lanham, Md.: Rowman and Littlefield.

Chen, Feng. 2006. "Privatization and Its Discontents in Chinese Factories." *China Quarterly* no. 185 (March): 42–60.

Chen, Jiu. 2006. "The Age of 'I' Is Coming." *Xin ZhouKan* (Neweekly), June 7.

Chen, Nancy. 2002. "Embodying Qi and Masculinities in Post-Mao China." In *Chinese Femininities/Chinese Masculinities: A Reader*, edited by Susan Brownell and Jeffrey N. Wasserstrom, 315–29. Berkeley: University of California Press.

Cheng Fang and Zhang Honghe. 2004. "How Big Is the Black Hole Caused by the Loss of Land-Lease Fees?" *People's Daily,* August 11.

Cheng, Tiejun, and Mark Selden. 1994. "The Origins and Social Consequences of China's Hukou System." *China Quarterly* 139: 644–68.

Ch'ien Chiang-hung, Chang Chie, Yang Shanhua, and Chang Jun. 1988. "Marriage-Related Consumption by Young People in China's Large and Medium Cities." *Social Sciences in China* 1: 208–28.

Cho, Mun Yong. N.d. *The Specter of "The People": Managing Urban Poverty in Northeast China.* PhD dissertation, Department of Anthropology, Stanford University.

Chua, Beng-Huat, ed. 2000. *Consumption in Asia: Lifestyles and Identities.* London: Routledge.

Clarke, John. 2004. *Changing Welfare, Changing States: New Directions in Social Policy.* London: Sage.

Collier, Robert. 2007. "China's New Middle Class in Love with Cars—Big Cars." *San Francisco Chronicle,* February 25, A-1.

Collier, Stephen J., and Andrew Lakoff. 2005. "On Regimes of Living." In *Global Assemblages: Technology, Politics, and Ethics as Anthropological Problems,* edited by Aihwa Ong and Stephen J. Collier, 22–39. Malden, Mass.: Blackwell.

Collier, Stephen J., and Aihwa Ong. 2005. "Global Assemblages, Anthropological Problems." In *Global Assemblages: Technology, Politics, and Ethics as Anthropological Problems,* edited by Aihwa Ong and Stephen J. Collier, 1–21. Malden, Mass.: Blackwell.

Cunningham, Hilary. 2000. "The Ethnography of Transnational Social Activism: Understanding the Global as Local Practice." *American Ethnology* 26, no. 3: 583–604.

Davila, Arlene. 2004. *Barrio Dreams: Puerto Ricans, Latinos, and the Neoliberal City.* Berkeley: University of California Press.

Davis, Deborah. 2002. "When a House Becomes His Home." In *Popular China: Unofficial Culture in a Globalizing Society,* edited by Perry Link, Richard Madsen, and Paul Pickowicz, 231–50. Lanham, Md.: Rowman and Littlefield.

——. 2005. "Urban Consumer Culture." *China Quarterly* 183: 692–709.

——, ed. 2000. *The Consumer Revolution in Urban China.* Berkeley: University of California Press.

Davis, Deborah, and Hanlong Lu. 2003. "Property in Transition: Conflicts over Ownership in Post-Socialist Shanghai." *European Journal of Sociology* 44, no. 1: 77–99.

Davis, Mike. 1992. *City of Quartz: Excavating the Future in Los Angeles.* New York: Vintage Books.

De Certeau, Michel. 1984. *The Practice of Everyday Life.* Berkeley: University of California Press.

Derbes, Max J. 1981. "Highest and Best Use—What Is It?" In *Readings in Highest and Best Use,* edited by American Institute of Real Estate Appraisers, 3–15. Chicago.

Dickie, Mure, and Richard McGregor. 2003. "Chinese Warned of Property Bubble." *Financial Times,* September 19.

Dickson, Bruce J. 2003. *Red Capitalists in China: The Party, Private Entrepreneurs, and Prospects for Political Change.* Cambridge: Cambridge University Press.

Duda, Mark, Xiulan Zhang, and Mingzhu Dong. 2005. "China's Homeownership-Oriented Housing Policy: An Examination of Two Programs Using Survey Data from Beijing." Cambridge: Joint Center for Housing Studies, Harvard University.

Dunn, Elizabeth C. 2004. *Privatizing Poland: Baby Food, Big Business, and the Remaking of Labor.* Ithaca: Cornell University Press.

Dutton, Michael. 1998. *Streetlife China.* Cambridge: Cambridge University Press.

Ehrenreich, Barbara. 1989. *Fear of Falling: The Inner Life of the Middle Class.* New York: Pantheon Books.

Engebretsen, Elisabeth Lund. Forthcoming. "Intimate Practices, Conjugal Ideals: Affective Ties and Relationship Strategies among Lala ('Lesbian') Women in Contemporary Beijing." *Sexuality Research and Social Policy.*

Erie, Matthew. 2007. "Land Grab Here and Real Estate Market There." *Anthropology News* (May): 36.

Farquhar, Judith. 1999. "Techologies of Everyday Life: The Economy of Impotence in Reform China." *Cultural Anthropology* 14, no. 2: 155–79.

———. 2002. *Appetites: Food and Sex in Postsocialist China.* Durham: Duke University Press.

Farrar, Margaret E. 2002. "Making the City Beautiful: Aesthetic Reform and the (Dis)placement of Bodies." In *Embodied Utopias: Gender, Social Change, and the Modern Metropolis,* edited by Amy Bingaman, Lise Sanders, and Rebecca Zorach, 37–54. New York: Routledge.

Farrer, J., and Z. Sun. 2003. "Extramarital Love in Shanghai." *China Journal* 50: 1–36.

Fehervary, Krisztina. 2002. "American Kitchens, Luxury Bathrooms, and the Search for a 'Normal' Life in Postsocialist Hungary." *Ethnos* 67, no. 3: 369–400.

Feng, Jian, Fulong Wu, and John Logan. 2008. "From Homogenous to Heterogeneous: The Transformation of Beijing's Socio-Spatial Structure." *Built Environment* 34, no. 4: 482–98.

Ferguson, James, and Akhil Gupta. 2002. "Spatializing States: Toward an Ethnography of Neoliberal Governmentality." *American Ethnologist* 29, no. 4: 981–1002.

Fernandes, Leela. 2006. *India's New Middle Class: Democratic Politics in an Era of Economic Reform.* Minneapolis: University of Minnesota Press.

Fleischer, Friederike. 2007. "To Choose a House Means to Choose a Lifestyle: The Consumption of Housing and Class-Structuration in Urban China." *City & Society* 19, no. 2: 287–311.

Fong, Vanessa. 2004. *Only Hope: Coming of Age under China's One-Child Policy.* Stanford: Stanford University Press.

Foucault, Michel. 1991. "Governmentality." In *The Foucault Effect: Studies in Governmentality,* edited by Graham Burchell, Colin Gordon, and Peter Miller, 87–104. London: Harvester/Wheatsheaf.

Fraser, Davis. 2000. "Inventing Oasis: Luxury Housing Advertisements in Reconfiguring Domestic Space in Shanghai." In *The Consumer Revolution in Urban China,* edited by Deborah Davis, 25–53. Berkeley: University of California Press.

Free, Anthony. 1996. "The Anthropology of Pierre Bourdieu: A Reconsideration." *Critique of Anthropology* 16, no. 4: 395–416.

Freeman, Carla. 2000. *High Tech and High Heels in the Global Economy: Women, Work, and Pink-Collar Identities in the Caribbean.* Durham: Duke University Press.

French, Howard. 2006. "Chinese Children Learn Class, Minus the Struggle." *New York Times,* September 22.

———. 2007. "The Sound, Not of Music, but of Control." *New York Times,* October 25.

Friedman, Edward, Paul G. Pickowicz, and Mark Selden. 2007. *Revolution, Resistance, and Reform in Village China.* New Haven: Yale University Press.

Friedman, Sara. 2005. "The Intimacy of State Power: Marriage, Liberation, and Socialist Subjects in Southeastern China." *American Ethnologist* 32, no. 2: 312–27.

Gaetano, Arianne M. 2004. "Migrant Domestic Workers in Post-Mao Beijing." In *On the Move: Women in Rural-to-Urban Migration in Contemporary China,* edited by Arianne M. Gaetano and Tamara Jacka. New York: Columbia University Press.

Gal, Susan, and Gail Kligman. 2000. *The Politics of Gender after Socialism.* Princeton: Princeton University Press.

Garnaut, Ross, Ligang Song, and Yang Yao. 2006. "Impact and Significance of State-Owned Enterprise Restructuring in China." *China Journal* no. 55: 35–66.

Giddens, Anthony. 1981. *The Class Structure of the Advanced Societies.* London: Hutchinson and Company.

Gillette, Maris Boyd. 2000. *Between Mecca and Beijing: Modernization and Consumption among Urban Chinese Muslims.* Stanford: Stanford University Press.

Gilmartin, Christina K., Gail Hershatter, Lisal Rofel, and Tyrene White. 1994. Introduction to *Engendering China: Women, Culture, and the State,* edited by Christina K. Gilmartin, Gail Hershatter, Lisal Rofel, and Tyrene White. Cambridge: Harvard University Press.

Gladney, Dru. 1991. *Muslim Chinese: Ethnic Nationalism in the People's Republic.* Cambridge: Harvard University Press.

Glosser, Susan L. 2002. "'The Truths I Have Learned': Nationalism, Family Reform, and Male Identity in China's New Culture Movement, 1915–1923." In *Chinese Femininities/Chinese Masculinities: A Reader,* edited by Susan Brownell and Jeffrey N. Wasserstrom, 120–44. Berkeley: University of California Press.

Goldman, Merle, and Elizabeth Perry, eds. 2002. *Changing Meanings of Citizenship in Modern China.* Cambridge: Harvard University Press.

Goodman, David. 1999. "The New Middle Class." In *The Paradox of China's Post-Mao Reforms,* edited by Merle Goldman and Roderick MacFarquhar, 241–61. Cambridge: Harvard University Press.

———, ed. 2008. *The New Rich in China: Future Rulers, Present Lives.* London: Routledge.

Goodman, David, and Xiaowei Zang. 2008. "The New Rich in China: The Dimensions of Social Change." In *The New Rich in China: Future Rulers, Present Lives,* edited by David Goodman, 1–20. London: Routledge.

Goodman, Peter. 2003. "In China, Building Worries as Housing Keeps Going Up, Some Fear the Bubble Will Burst." *Washington Post,* March 5, E01.

Gordon, Colin. 1991. "Governmental Rationality: An Introduction." In *The Foucault Effect: Studies in Governmentality,* edited by Graham Burchell, Colin Gordon, and Peter Miller, 1–51. London: Harvester/Wheatsheaf.

Gupta, Akhil. 1998. *Postcolonial Development: Agriculture in the Making of Modern India.* Durham: Duke University Press.

Hanser, Amy. 2008. *Service Encounters: Class, Gender, and the Market for Social Distinction in Urban China.* Stanford: Stanford University Press.

Hardt, Michael, and Antonio Negri. 2000. *Empire.* Cambridge: Harvard University Press.

Harvey, David. 1973. *Social Justice and the City.* London: Edward Arnold.

——. 2003. *The New Imperialism.* Oxford: Oxford University Press.

——. 2005. *A Brief History of Neoliberalism.* Oxford: Oxford University Press.

Hassard, John, and S. Hassard. 2007. *China's State Enterprise Reform: From Marx to the Market.* London: Routledge.

Hasson, Shlomo, and David Ley. 1994. *Neighborhood Organizations and the Welfare State.* Toronto: University of Toronto Press.

He Qinglian. 1998. *Xiandaihua de Xianjing* (The Trap of Modernization). Beijing: Jinri Zhongguo Chubanshe (Contemporary China Publisher).

He Xueliang, Albert Lo, and Wang Zirun. 1999. *Zhongguo Wuye Guanli* (Chinese Property Management). Shanghai: Wenhui Publisher.

Hershatter, Gail. 1991. "Prostitution and the Market in Women in Early Twentieth-Century Shanghai." In *Marriage and Inequality in Chinese Society,* edited by Rubie S. Watson and Patricia B. Ebrey, 256–85. Berkeley: University of California Press.

Herzfeld, Michael. 2003. "Pom Mahakan: Humanity and Order in the Historic Center of Bangkok." *Thailand Human Rights Journal* 1: 101–119.

——. 2009. *Evicted from Eternity: The Restructuring of Modern Rome.* Chicago: University of Chicago Press.

Hird, Derek. 2008. *White-Collar Men and Masculinity in Contemporary Urban China.* PhD dissertation, Department of Politics and International Relations, University of Westminster.

Hoffman, Lisa. 2006. "Autonomous Choices and Patriotic Professionalism: On Governmentality in Late-Socialist China." *Economy and Society* 35, no. 4: 550–70.

Holston, James. 1989. *The Modernist City: An Anthropological Critique of Brasilia.* Chicago: University of Chicago Press.

Holston, James, and Arjun Appadurai. 1999. Introduction to *Cities and Citizenship,* edited by James Holston, 1–18. Durham: Duke University Press.

Honig, Emily. 2000. "Iron Girls Revisited: Gender and the Politics of Work in the Cultural Revolution, 1966–76." In *Re-Drawing Boundaries: Work, Households, and Gender in China,* edited by Barbara Entwisle and Gail Henderson, 97–110. Berkeley: University of California Press.

Hsing, You-tien. 2006. "Land and Territorial Politics in Urban China." *China Quarterly* 187 (September): 1–18.

——. 2009a. "Urban Housing Mobilizations." In *Reclaiming Chinese Society: The New Social Activism,* edited by You-tien Hsing and Ching Kwan Lee. London: Routledge.

——. 2009b. *The Great Urban Transformation: Politics and Property in China*. Oxford: Oxford University Press.

Hsu, Carolyn L. 2007. *Creating Market Socialism: How Ordinary People Are Shaping Class and Status in China*. Durham: Duke University Press.

Huang, Marin. 2006. *Negotiating Masculinities in Late Imperial China*. Honolulu: University of Hawaii Press.

Hu Bin. 2001. *Zhidu Bianqian zhong de Zhongguo Fangdi Chanye* (China's Real Estate Industry in the Era of Systematic Transformations). Shanghai: Shanghai Finance and Trade University Press.

Humphrey, Caroline. 1991. "'Icebergs,' Barter, and the Mafia in Provincial Russia." *Anthropology Today* no. 7: 8–13.

——. 2002. *The Unmaking of Soviet Life: Everyday Economics after Socialism*. Ithaca: Cornell University Press.

Huters, Theodore. 2005. *Bringing the World Home: Appropriating the West in Late Qing and Early Republican China*. Honolulu: University of Hawaii Press.

Hwang, Kathleen. 2004. "Beijing Ejects Families, Destroys Homes." *United Press International*, March 25.

Hyde, Sandra. 2007. *Eating Spring Rice: The Cultural Politics of AIDS in Southwest China*. Berkeley: University of California Press.

Jefferson, Gary H., and Inderjit Singh, eds. 1999. *Enterprise Reform in China: Ownership, Transition and Performance*. Oxford: Oxford University Press.

Kahn, Joseph. 2003. "Shanghai Lawyer Sentenced in Land Fight." *New York Times*, October 29.

——. 2006. "A Sharp Debate Erupts in China over Ideologies." *New York Times*, March 12.

Kingfisher, Catherine, and Jeff Maskovsky. 2008. "Introduction: The Limits of Neoliberalism." *Critique of Anthropology* 28 no. 2: 115–26.

Kipnis, Andrew. 2007. "Neoliberalism Reified: Suzhi Discourse and Tropes of Neoliberalism in the PRC." *Journal of the Royal Anthropological Institute* 13: 383–99.

Kleinman, Authur, and Joan Kleinman. 1991. "Suffering and Its Professional Transformation: Toward an Ethnography of Interpersonal Experience." *Culture, Medicine and Psychiatry* 15, no. 3: 275–301.

Ko, Dorothy. 2001. *Every Step a Lotus: Shoes for Bound Feet*. Berkeley: University of California Press.

Ku, Agnes, and Ngai Pun. 2004. *Remaking Citizenship in Hong Kong: Community, Nation and the Global City*. London: Routledge.

Kynge, James. 2003. "Tycoon Linked to Top Chinese Officials Arrested." *Financial Times*, September 5.

Lee, Ching Kwan. 2000. "Pathways of Labor Insurgency." In *Chinese Society: Change, Conflict and Resistance*, edited by Elizabeth Perry and Mark Selden, 41–61. London: Routledge.

——. 2002. "From the Specter of Mao to the Spirit of the Law: Labor Insurgency in China." *Theory and Society* 31 (April): 189–228.

——. 2003. "The Subject of Labor Unrest in Reform China." Paper presented at the UC Berkeley conference on "Theoretical Issues in Rural and Small Town China," November 16.

——. 2007. *Against the Law: Labor Protests in China's Rustbelt and Sunbelt.* Berkeley: University of California Press.

Lee, Don. 2004. "Chinese Tycoon Sentenced to 3 Years." *Los Angeles Times,* June 2.

Lefebvre, Henri. 1991. *The Production of Space.* Oxford: Blackwell.

Lett, Denise Potrzeba. 1998. *In Pursuit of Status: The Making of South Korea's "New" Urban Middle Class.* Cambridge: Harvard University Asia Center.

Ley, David. 1996. *The New Middle Class and the Remaking of the Central City.* New York: Oxford University Press.

Li Dezhao. 1999. "Shishi Zongti Guihua, Baohi he Fazhan Lishi Wenhua Mingcheng" (Implementing the Master Plan, Protecting and Developing Renowned Historical-Cultural Cities). *Yunnan Chengshi Guihua (City Planning in Yunnan)* no. 4: 26–28.

Liechty, Mark. 2003. *Suitably Modern: Making Middle-Class Culture in a New Consumer Society.* Princeton: Princeton University Press.

Li Liang. 2006. "2004–2006 Zhongguo Disanci Gaige Zhenglun Shimo" (The Beginning and End of the Debate on China's Third Reform 2004–2006). *Nanfang Zhoumo* (Southern Weekend), March 17.

Li Yuxiang, Chen Foude, and Wang Cuilan. 2000. *Lao Fangzi: Yunnan Minju* (Old Houses: Yunnan Residential Homes). Nanjing Jiangsu Art Publishing House.

Lim, Louisa. 2006. "China Gets Its Own Slice of English Countryside." National Public Radio, December 12.

——. 2009. *The Mirage of China: Anti-Humanism, Narcissism, and Corporeality of the Contemporary World.* Oxford: Berghahn Books.

Litzinger, Ralph A. 2001. "Government from Below: The State, the Popular, and the Problem of Autonomy." *Positions: East Asia Cultures Critique* 9, no. 1 (Spring).

——. 2004. "Damming the Angry River." *China Review* 30 (Autumn): 30–34.

Liu, Xin. 2002. *The Otherness of Self: A Genealogy of the Self in Contemporary China.* Ann Arbor: University of Michigan Press.

Logan, John R., and Harvey L. Molotch. 1988. *Urban Fortunes: The Political Economy of Place.* Berkeley: University of California Press.

Louie, Kam, and Louise Edwards. 1994. "Chinese Masculinity: Theorizing *Wen* and *Wu.*" *East Asian History* 8: 135–48.

Low, Setha M. 2001. "The Edge and the Center: Gated Communities and the Discourse of Urban Fear." *American Anthropologist* 103, no. 1: 45–58.

——. 2004. *Behind the Gates: Life, Security, and the Pursuit of Happiness in Fortress America.* London: Routledge.

Lu, Duanfang. 2006. *Remaking Chinese Urban Form: Modernity, Scarcity and Space, 1949–2005.* London: Routledge.

Lu, Xiaobo, and Elizabeth J. Perry, eds. 1997. *Danwei: The Changing Chinese Workplace in Historical and Comparative Perspective.* Armonk, N.Y.: M. E. Sharpe.

Lu Xueyi, ed. 2002. *Dangdai Zhongguo Shehui Jieceng Yanjiu Paogao* (A Research Report on Contemporary Chinese Social Strata). Beijing: Social Sciences Documentary Publishing House.

Mandel, Ruth, and Caroline Humphrey, eds. 2002. *Markets and Moralities: Ethnographies of Post-socialism.* Oxford: Berg.

Marcuse, Peter. 1996. "Privatization and Its Discontents: Property Rights in Land and Housing in the Transition in Eastern Europe." In *Cities after Socialism: Urban and Regional Change and Conflict in Post-Socialist Societies,* edited by Gregory Andrusz, Michael Harloe, and Iván Szelényi, 119–91. Oxford: Blackwell.

Marris, Peter. 1974. *Loss and Change.* New York: Pantheon Books.

Marshall, T. H. 1964. "Citizenship and Social Class." In *Class, Citizenship, and Social Development,* 65–122. Garden City, N.Y.: Doubleday and Company.

Marx, Karl. 1976. *Capital: Volume One.* New York: Vintage Books.

Marx, Karl, and Frederick Engels. 1998. *The German Ideology.* New York: International Publishers.

Maskovsky, Jeff, and Catherine Kingfisher. 2001. Introduction to special issue on "Global Capitalism, Neoliberal Policy and Poverty." *Urban Anthropology and Studies of Cultural Systems and World Economic Development* 30, nos. 2–3: 105–21.

Mattias, Burell. 2006. "China's Housing Provident Fund: Its Success and Limitations." *Housing Finance International* (March).

Mazzarella, William. 2003. *Shoveling Smoke: Advertising and Globalization in Contemporary India.* Durham: Duke University Press.

McGregor, Richard. 2003. "Pressure Eases in Shanghai Property Corruption Probe." *Financial Times,* July 5.

McKenzie, Evan. 1994. *Privatopia: Homeowner Associations and the Rise of Residential Private Government.* New Haven: Yale University Press.

Meijl, Toon van, and Franz von Benda-Beckmann. 1999. *Property Rights and Economic Development: Land and Natural Resources in Southeast Asia and Oceania.* London: Kegan Paul International.

Meisner, Maurice. 1986. *Mao's China and After: A History of the People's Republic.* New York: Free Press.

Miller, Daniel. 1987. *Material Culture and Mass Consumption.* Oxford: Basil Blackwell.

——. 1994. *Modernity, an Ethnographic Approach: Dualism and Mass Consumption in Trinidad.* Oxford: Berg.

——. 1995. "Consumption and Commodities." *Annual Review of Anthropology* 24: 141–61.

Mills, C. Wright. 1951. *White Collar: The American Middle Classes.* Oxford University Press.

Mills, Mary Beth. 1999. *Thai Women in the Global Labor Force: Consuming Desires, Contested Selves.* New Brunswick, N.J.: Rutgers University Press.

Mollenkopf, John H. 1983. *The Contested City.* Princeton: Princeton University Press.

Mueggler, Erik. 2001 *The Age of Wild Ghosts: Memory, Violence, and Place in Southwest China.* Berkeley: University of California Press.

Nader, Laura. 1990. *Harmony Ideology: Justice and Control in a Zapotec Mountain Village.* Stanford: Stanford University Press.

Naim, Moises. 2008. "Can the World Afford a Middle Class?" *Foreign Policy* (March–April).

Newman, Katherine S. 1999. *Falling from Grace: Downward Mobility in the Age of Affluence.* Berkeley: University of California Press.

O'Brien, Kevin, and Lianjiang Li. 2006. *Rightful Resistance in Rural China.* Cambridge: Cambridge University Press.

Ocko, Jonathan K. 1991. "Women, Property, and Law in the People's Republic of China." In *Marriage and Inequality in Chinese Society,* edited by Rubie S. Watson and Patricia B. Ebrey, 313–46. Berkeley: University of California Press.

O'Driscoll, Gerald, Jr., and Lee Hoskins. 2003. "Property Rights—the Key to Economic Development." *Policy Analysis* no. 482 (August 7).

Oi, Jean, and Andrew G. Walder, eds. 1999. *Property Rights and Economic Reform in China.* Stanford: Stanford University Press.

Ong, Aihwa. 1999. *Flexible Citizenship: The Cultural Logics of Transnationality.* Durham: Duke University Press.

——. 2006. *Neoliberalism as Exception: Mutations in Citizenship and Sovereignty.* Durham: Duke University Press.

Ong, Aihwa, and Li Zhang. 2008. "Introduction: Privatizing China: Powers of the Self, Socialism from Afar." In *Privatizing China, Socialism from Afar,* edited by Li Zhang and Aihwa Ong, 1–19. Ithaca: Cornell University Press.

Palen, John, and Bruce London, eds. 1984. *Gentrification, Displacement, and Neighborhood Revitalization.* Albany: State University of New York Press.

Pan, Tianshu. 2001. "The Professionalization of Neighborhood Organizations in Five Mile Bridge." Paper presented at the Annual Meeting of the Association of Asian Studies, Chicago, March.

——. 2002. "Neighborhood Shanghai: Community Building in Five Mile Bridge." PhD dissertation, Department of Anthropology, Harvard University.

Pearson, Margaret. 1997. *China's New Business Elite: The Political Consequences of Economic Reform.* Berkeley: University of California Press.

Pellow, Deborah. 1996. "Intimate Boundaries: A Chinese Puzzle." In *Setting Boundaries: the Anthropology of Spatial and Social Organization,* edited by Deborah Pellow, 111–36. Westport, Conn.: Bergin and Garvey.

Perry, Elizabeth J. 1989. "State and Society in Contemporary China." *World Politics* 4 (July): 579–91.

——. 1994. "Trends in the Study of Chinese Politics: State-Society Relations." *China Quarterly* 139: 704–13.

Pieke, Frank N. 1995. "Bureaucracy, Friends, and Money: The Growth of Capital Socialism in China." *Comparative Study of Society and History* 37, no. 3: 494–518.

Polanyi, Karl. 1944. *The Great Transformation: The Political and Economic Origins of Our Time.* Boston: Beacon Press.

Pomfret, John. 2003. "Chinese Fight a New Kind of Land War." *Washington Post,* September 14.

Pow, Choon-Piew. 2006. "Gated Communities, Territoriality and the Politics of the Good Life in (Post-)Socialist Shanghai." PhD dissertation, Department of Geography, University of California at Los Angeles.

——. 2007. "Securing the 'Civilized' Enclaves: Gated Communities and the Moral Geographies of Exclusion in (Post-)Socialist Shanghai." *Urban Studies* 44, no. 8: 1539–58.

Pun, Ngai. 2005. *Made in China: Women Factory Workers in a Global Workplace.* Durham: Duke University Press.

——. 2003. "Subsumption or Consumption?" *Cultural Anthropology* 18, no. 4: 469 92.

Purvis, T., and A. Hunt. 1999. "Identity versus Citizenship: Transformations in the Discourses and Practices of Citizenship." *Social and Legal Studies* 8, no. 4: 457–82.

Putnam, Robert D. 2000. *Bowling Alone: The Collapse and Revival of American Community.* New York: Simon and Schuster.

Read, Benjamin L. 2000. "Revitalizing the State's Urban 'Nerve Tips'." *China Quarterly* 163:806–20.

——. 2003. "Democratizing the Neighborhood? New Private Housing and Home-Owner Self-Organization in Urban China." *China Journal* no. 49: 1–29.

——. 2008. "Homeowners' Protests in Shanghai." *China Beat* blog (February 26).

Ren, Hai. Forthcoming. "The Middle-Class as a Social Norm: Consumer Citizenship in China's Reform." In *Global Futures in East Asia,* edited by Ann Anagnost, Andrea Arai, and Hai Ren.

Ren, Xuefei. 2008. "Architecture as Branding: Mega Project Developments in Beijing." *Built Environment* 34, no. 4: 517–31.

Ries, Nancy. 1997. *Russian Talk.* Ithaca: Cornell University Press.

Rivkin-Fish, Michele. 2009. "Tracing Landscapes of the Past in Class Subjectivity: Practices of Memory and Distinction in Marketizing Russia." *American Ethnologist* 36, no. 1: 79–95.

Robi, Richard, ed. 1996. *The New Rich in Asia: Mobile Phones, McDonalds and Middle-class Revolution.* London: Routledge.

Rofel, Lisa. 1999. *Other Modernities: Gendered Yearnings in China after Socialism.* Berkeley: University of California Press.

——. 2007. *Desiring China: Experiments in Neoliberalism, Sexuality, and Public Culture.* Durham: Duke University Press.

Rose, Nikolas. 1996. "Governing 'Advanced' Liberal Democracies." In *Foucault and Political Reason: Liberalism, Neo-liberalism, and Rationalities of Government,* edited by Andrew Barry, Thomas Osborne, and Nikolas Rose, 37–64. Chicago: University of Chicago Press.

——. 1999. *Powers of Freedom: Reframing Political Thought.* Cambridge: Cambridge University Press.

Roy, Arundhati. 2001. *Power Politics.* Cambridge, Mass.: South End Press.

Rubin, Gayle. 1975. "The Traffic in Women: Notes on the 'Political Economy' of Sex." In *Toward an Anthropology of Women,* edited by Rayna R. Reiter, 157–210. New York: Monthly Review Press.

Sassen, Saskia. 1996. *Losing Control? Sovereignty in an Age of Globalization.* New York: Columbia University Press.

Savadove, Bill. 2004. "Shanghai Crackdown Aims to Silence Property Protesters." *South China Morning Post,* March 3.

Schein, Louisa. 2002. "Market Mentalities, Iron Satellite Dishes, and Contested Cultural Developmentalism." *Provincial China* 7, no. 1: 57–72.

Scott, James C. 1985. *Weapons of the Weak: Everyday Forms of Peasant Resistance.* New Haven: Yale University Press.

Shan Xiaohai. 2001. *"Xin Zhuzhai Yundong Shanghai Xuanyan"* (The Shanghai Manifesto of the "New Housing Movement"). In *Marching towards the New Housing* (Zouxiang Xin Zhuzhai), edited by Shan Xiaohai and He Chengjun, 1–3. Beijing: Chinese Construction Industry Press.

Shan Zhenping. 2001. "Shui de Zhufang, Xin zai Hechu?" (Whose Housing, What Is New?). In *Marching towards the New Housing* (*Zouxiang Xin Zhuzhai*), edited by Shan Xiaohai and He Chengjun, 249–54. Beijing: Chinese Construction Industry Press.

Shao, Qin. N.d. "Waving the Red Flag: Cultural Memory and Grassroots Protest in Housing Disputes in Shanghai." Unpublished manuscript.

Shen Hui. 2005. "Zhongchan Jieceng de Rentong jiqi Goujian" (Middle Class Identity and Structure). In *Zhongguo Zhongchan Jieceng Diaocha* (Survey of the Chinese Middle Classes), edited by Zhou Xiaohong, 20–61. Beijing: Social Sciences Academic Press.

Shue, Vivienne. 1988. *The Reach of the State: Sketches of the Chinese Body Politic.* Stanford: Stanford University Press.

Sieber, R. Tomithy. 1987. "Urban Gentrification: Ideology and Practice in Middle-Class Civic Activity." *City & Society* 1, no. 1: 52–63.

Sillanp, Sami. 2004. "Rebellion Swelling in China: New Activist Movement First since Tiananmen." *Helsingin Sanomat*, January 27.

Siu, Helen. 2005. "The Cultural Landscape of Luxury Housing in South China." In *Locating China: Space, Place and Popular Culture*, edited by Jing Wang, 72–93. London: Routledge.

——. 2007. "Grounding Displacement: Uncivil Urban Spaces in South China." *American Ethnologist* 34, no. 2: 329–50.

Skinner, G. William. 1977. "Cities and the Hierarchy of Local Systems." In *The City in Late Imperial China,* edited by G. William Skinner, 275–351. Stanford: Stanford University Press.

Smart, Alan. 1998. "Economic Transformation in China: Property Regimes and Social Relations." In *Theorising Transition: The Political Economy of Post-Communist Transformations,* edited by John Pickles and Adrian Smith, 428–49. London: Routledge.

Smith, David M. 1996. "The Socialist City." In *Cities after Socialism: Urban and Regional Change and Conflict in Post-Socialist Societies,* edited by Gregory Andrusz, Michael Harloe, and Iván Szelényi, 70–99. Oxford: Blackwell.

Smith, Neil. 1996. *The New Urban Frontier: Gentrification and the Revanchist City.* London: Routledge.

Solinger, Dorothy. 1995. "China's Urban Transients in the Transition from Socialism and the Collapse of the Communist 'Urban Public Goods Regime.'" *Comparative Politics* (January): 127–46.

——. 1999. *Contesting Citizenship in Urban China: Peasant Migrants, the State, and the Logic of the Market.* Berkeley: University of California Press.

Stewart, Kathleen. 2007. *Ordinary Affects.* Durham: Duke University Press.

Stiglitz, Joseph. 2002. *Globalization and Its Discontents.* New York: W. W. Norton.

Struyk, Raymond J. 1996. "Housing Privatization in the Former Soviet Bloc to 1995." In *Cities after Socialism: Urban and Regional Change and Conflict in*

Post-Socialist Societies, edited by Gregory Andrusz, Michael Harloe, and Iván Szelényi, 192–213. Oxford: Blackwell.

Sun, Hao. 2002. "Behind the Land Auction Craze." June 23. http://news.xinhuanet. com.

Sun, Wanning. 2009. *Maid in China: Media, Morality, and the Cultural Politics of Boundaries.* London: Routledge.

Szelényi, Iván. 1996. "Cities under Socialism—and After." In *Cities after Socialism: Urban and Regional Change and Conflict in Post-Socialist Societies,* edited by Gregory Andrusz, Michael Harloe, and Iván Szelényi, 286–317. Oxford: Blackwell.

Szelényi, Iván, and Christy M. Glass. 2003. "Winners of the Reforms: The New Economic and Political Elite." In *Inequality and Social Structure during the Transition,* edited by V. Mikhalev. New York: Macmillan.

Thompson, E. P. 1964. *The Making of the English Working Class.* New York: Pantheon Books.

Tolley, George S. 1991. *Urban Housing Reform in China: An Economic Analysis.* Washington, D.C.: World Bank.

Tomba, Luigi. 2004. "Creating an Urban Middle Class: Social Engineering in Beijing." *China Journal* no. 51: 1–26.

———. 2005. "Residential Space and Collective Interest Formation in Beijing's Housing Disputes." *China Quarterly* no. 184.

Tsai, Kellee S. 2002. *Back-Alley Banking: Private Entrepreneurs in China.* Ithaca: Cornell University Press.

———. 2007. *Capitalism without Democracy: The Private Sector in Contemporary China.* Ithaca: Cornell University Press.

Tucker, Robert C. 1978. *The Marx-Engels Reader.* New York: W. W. Norton.

Unger, Jonathan. 1996. "'Bridges': Private Business, the Chinese Government and the Rise of New Associations." *China Quarterly* no. 147 (September): 795–819.

Verdery, Katherine. 1996. *What Was Socialism, and What Comes Next?* Princeton: Princeton University Press.

———. 2004. *The Vanishing Hectare: Property and Value in Postsocialist Transylvania.* Ithaca: Cornell University Press.

Verhovek, Sam Howe. 2003. "Rebellion of the Displaced." *Los Angeles Times,* September 5.

Vogel, Ezra F. 1963. *Japan's New Middle Class: The Salary Man and His Family in a Tokyo Suburb.* Berkeley: University of California Press.

Walder, Andrew. 1986. *Communist Neo-Traditionalism: Work and Authority in Chinese Industry.* Berkeley: University of California Press.

Wang, Hui. 2003. *The 1989 Social Movement and the Historical Roots of China's Neoliberalism.* Edited and translated by Theodore Huters. Cambridge: Harvard University Press.

Wang, Jing. 2005. "Bourgeois Bohemians in China? Neo-Tribes and the Urban Imaginary." *China Quarterly* no. 183 (September): 532–48.

Wang WeiXiang, and Zhou Lang. 2004. "Behind the Amazing 'Land Enclosure' Craze—Investigation into and Reflection of Local Government's Land Violation." *People's Daily,* April 23.

Wang, Ya Ping. 2001. "Urban Housing Reform and Finance in China: A Case Study of Beijing." *Urban Affairs Review* 36, no. 5: 620–45.

Wang, Ya Ping, and Alan Murie. 1999a. "Commercial Housing Development in Urban China." *Urban Studies* 36, no. 9: 1475–94.

———. 1999b. *Housing Policy and Practice in China.* New York: St. Martin's Press.

Wang Zhigang. 2001. *Dapan Shidai Zhongguo Fan Dichan Geming* (The Chinese Pan Real Estate Revolution in the Age of Grand Competition). Chengdu: Sichuan People's Publishing House.

Wank, David L. 1999. *Commodifying Communism: Markets, Trust, and Politics in a South China City.* Cambridge: Cambridge University Press.

Watson, Rubie. 1991. "Afterword: Marriage and Gender Inequality." In *Marriage and Inequality in Chinese Society,* edited by Rubie S. Watson and Patricia B. Ebrey, 347–68. Berkeley: University of California Press.

Weber, Max. 1981. *From Max Weber: Essays in Sociology.* Edited and translated by H. H. Gerth and C. Wright Mills. New York: Oxford University Press.

Whyte, Martin King, and William L. Parish. 1984. *Urban Life in Contemporary China.* Chicago: University of Chicago Press.

Willis, Paul. 1977. *Learning To Labor—How Working Class Kids Get Working Class Jobs.* New York: Columbia University Press.

Wu, Fulong. 2002. "China's Changing Urban Governance in the Transition towards a More Market-Oriented Economy." *Urban Studies* 39, no. 7: 1071–93.

———. 2004. "Transplanting Cityscapes: The Use of Imagined Globalization in Housing Commodification in Beijing." *Area* 36, no. 3: 227–34.

———. 2005. "Rediscovering the 'Gate' under Market Transition: From Work-Unit Compounds to Commodity Housing Enclaves." *Housing Studies* 20, no. 2: 235–54.

———. 2008a. "From Suburbia to Post-Suburbia in China? Aspects of the Transformation of the Beijing and Shanghai Global City Regions." *Built Environment* 34, no. 4: 464–81.

———. 2008b. "Tenure-Based Residential Segregation in Post-Reform Chinese Cities: A Case Study of Shanghai." *Transactions of the Institute of British Geographers* 33: 404–19.

Yan, Hairong. 2003. "Neoliberal Governmentality and Neohumanism: Organizing Suzhi/Value Flow through Labor Recruitment Networks." *Cultural Anthropology* 18, no. 4: 439–523.

———. 2008. *New Masters, New Servants: Migration, Development, and Women Workers in China.* Durham: Duke University Press.

Yan, Yunxiang. 1996. *The Flow of Gifts: Reciprocity and Social Networks in a Chinese Village.* Stanford: Stanford University Press.

———. 2003. *Private Life under Socialism: Love, Intimacy, and Family Change in a Chinese Village, 1949–1999.* Stanford: Stanford University Press.

Yang, Guobin. 2005. "Environmental NGOs and Institutional Dynamics in China." *China Quarterly* no. 181 (March): 46–66.

Yang, Mayfair Mei-hui. 1994. *Gifts, Favors, and Banquets: The Art of Social Relationships in China.* Ithaca: Cornell University Press.

———. 1999. "From Gender Erasure to Gender Difference: State Feminism, Consumer Sexuality, and Women's Public Sphere in China." In *Spaces of Their Own: Women's Public Sphere in Transnational China,* edited by Mayfair Mei-hui Yang. Minneapolis: University of Minnesota Press.

Yao Jianping. 2006. *Xiaofei Rentong* (Consuming and Identification). Beijing: Social Sciences Academic Press.

Yun Zi. 2005. "Hexie Shequ de Lixiang yu Xianshi" (The Ideal and Reality of Harmonious Community). *Wuye Guanli* (Property Management) no. 4: 10–13.

Yunnan Statistical Yearbook. 2005. China Statistics Press.

Yurchak, Alexei. 2006. *Everything Was Forever, until It Was No More: The Last Soviet Generation.* Princeton: Princeton University Press.

Zhang Changhong, Long Jianmin, Zhou Baochang, and Yang Min. 2000. "*Saman Yangguang de Difang*" (A Place Covered by Sunshine). *Yunnan Daily* (August 28–September 1).

Zhang, Li. 2001. *Strangers in the City: Reconfigurations of Space, Power, and Social Networks within China's Floating Population.* Stanford: Stanford University Press.

———. 2002. "Spatiality and Urban Citizenship in Late Socialist China." *Public Culture* 14, no. 2 (Spring): 311–34.

———. 2006. "Contesting Spatial Modernity in Late Socialist China." *Current Anthropology* 47, no. 3: 461–84.

Zhang, Xing Quan. 1998. *Privatization: A Study of Housing Policy in Urban China.* New York: Nova Science Publishers.

Zhang, Zhen. 2000. "Mediating Time: The 'Rice Bowl of Youth' in Fin de Siècle Urban China." *Public Culture* 12, no. 1: 93–113.

———. 2005. *An Amorous History of the Silver Screen: Shanghai Cinema, 1896–1937.* Chicago: University of Chicago Press.

Zhao Lin. 2003. "Chaiqian Shinian Beixiju" (Ten Years of Demolition and Relocation Drama). *Nanfang Zhoumo* (South China Weekend), September 4.

Zheng, Tiantian. 2009. *Red Lights: The Lives of Sex Workers in Postsocialist China.* Minneapolis: University of Minnesota Press.

Zhou Xiaohong. 2005. "Daoyan: Zhongguo Zhongchan Jieceng de Lishi yu Xianzhuang" (Introduction: The History and Current Condition of the Chinese Middle Classes). In *Zhongguo Zhongchan Jieceng Diaocha* (Survey of the Chinese Middle Classes), edited by Zhou Xiaohong, 1–28. Beijing: Social Sciences Academic Press.

Zhufang Zhidu Gaige Fagui Wenjian Xuanbian (The Selected Collection of Law and Rulings regarding Housing Reform). 1998. Beijing: Chinese Construction Industry Press (Zhongguo Jianzhu Gongye Chubanshe).

Zhu Yong. 2005. "Kunming: Zuihou de Shuncheng Jie" (Kunming: The Last Shuncheng Jie). *Renmin Gongan* (People's Public Security), January.

Index